The
Financial
Services
Fact Book
2012

INSURANCE
INFORMATION
INSTITUTE

THE FINANCIAL
SERVICES
ROUNDTABLE

TO THE READER:

The financial services industry's role as a catalyst for economic growth and a provider of essential products and services were especially crucial in 2011, as the nation confronted continued fiscal and economic challenges and an exceptional string of natural disasters impacting millions of American families and businesses.

Since its inception in 2002, the Financial Services Fact Book, a partnership between The Financial Services Roundtable and the Insurance Information Institute, has provided information to help reporters, businesses and researchers understand the trends and statistics shaping the financial services industry.

This year, we present you with new material such as:

- An update on the Dodd Frank Wall Street Reform and Consumer Protection Act enacted in 2010
- A new section on cyber security
- A glossary of financial services designations
- Expanded data on loans to businesses
- Expanded information on Government Supported Enterprises
- The Financial Services Roundtable and I.I.I. resources

As always, this year's book provides a wealth of tables and charts on the workings of the insurance, banking and securities sectors, including data on mergers, employment, financial results and leading companies, as well as data on national savings and debt, the U.S. housing market, and banks' insurance activities and other examples of convergence.

Many organizations, consultants and others who collect industry data have generously given permission to use their data in this book. However, the bulk of the work involved in collecting, integrating and interpreting the material was done by the Insurance Information Institute, which accepts editorial responsibility for the book.

We actively seek your advice, comments and suggestions for next year's edition. Please contact either of us, steve@fsround.org or bobh@iii.org.

Robert P. Hartwig
President
Insurance Information Institute

Steve Bartlett
President and Chief Executive Officer
The Financial Services Roundtable

Contents

- The assets of the financial services sector rose 0.1 percent to $60.8 trillion in 2010, following a 2.3 percent increase the previous year.

- The financial services industry's gross domestic product (GDP), excluding the real estate sector, reached $1.17 trilllon in 2009, accounting for 8.3 percent of the national GDP.

- Financial services employed 5.7 million workers in 2010, down from 5.8 million in 2009. Financial services employment accounted for 5.3 percent of total U.S. employment in private industry in 2010.

- Financial assets of the personal sector grew 6.3 percent to $44.3 trillion in 2010, following a 10.2 percent increase the previous year. The personal sector includes households, nonfarm noncorporate business and farm business.

- Financial services mergers were valued at $106.2 billion in 2010, up 40 percent from $75.9 billion in 2009.

- Retirement assets rose by $1.5 trillion to $17.5 trillion in 2010, after rising $2.1 trillion in 2009.

- Household debt fell 1.9 percent in 2010, following a 1.7 percent decline the previous year. Business debt rose 0.3 percent in 2010, after falling by 2.7 percent in 2009.

- Insurance fee income reported by bank holding companies (BHCs) rose by $500 million to $47.7 billion in 2010, following a $4.7 billion increase in 2009. BHC investment fee income rose by $2.2 billion to $91.96 billion in 2010, after rising by $33.5 billion the previous year.

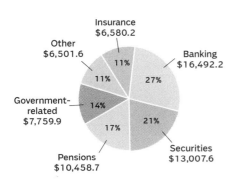

ASSETS OF FINANCIAL SERVICES SECTORS, 2010
($ billions)

- Insurance $6,580.2
- Other $6,501.6
- Banking $16,492.2
- Government-related $7,759.9
- Securities $13,007.6
- Pensions $10,458.7

Source: Board of Governors of the Federal Reserve System.

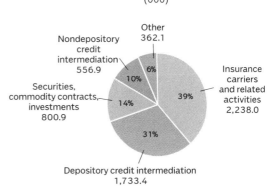

FINANCIAL SERVICES EMPLOYMENT BY INDUSTRY, 2010
(000)

- Other 362.1
- Nondepository credit intermediation 556.9
- Insurance carriers and related activities 2,238.0
- Securities, commodity contracts, investments 800.9
- Depository credit intermediation 1,733.4

Source: U.S. Department of Labor, Bureau of Labor Statistics.

Regulatory Timeline

1916 National Bank Act limiting bank insurance sales except in small
      towns

1933 Glass-Steagall Act prohibiting commercial banks and securities
      firms from engaging in each other's business

1956 Bank Holding Company Act restricting bank holding company
      activities

1995 VALIC U.S. Supreme Court decision allowing banks to sell annuities

1996 Barnett Bank U.S. Supreme Court decision allowing banks to sell
      insurance nationwide

1999 Gramm-Leach-Bliley Act allowing banks, insurance companies and
      securities firms to affiliate and sell each other's products

2008 The Emergency Economic Stabilization Act, a $700 billion rescue
      plan for the U.S. financial services industry

2009 The Financial Stability Plan was implemented by the U.S. Treasury
      to promote economic recovery

2010 New federal rules providing consumer protections related to credit
      cards

2010 Congress enacts the Dodd-Frank Wall Street Reform and
      Consumer Protection Act, a massive overhaul of financial services
      regulation

2011 in Review: Regulatory Reform

July 2011 marked the one-year anniversary of the passage of the Dodd-Frank Wall Street Reform and Consumer Protection Act, a sweeping overhaul of how financial services are regulated in the United States. A year after its passage, there continued to be uncertainty about how and when the law's provisions would be implemented. As of July 2011 regulators had completed 51, or 13 percent, of the 400 rulemaking requirements in the law, according to a report by Davis Polk. (See page 213 for a detailed summary of the law).

- The act established a Financial Stability Oversight Council (FSOC) to provide comprehensive monitoring of financial institutions to ensure the stability of the nation's financial system. The Council is charged with identifying threats to the financial stability of the United States; promoting market discipline; and responding to emerging risks to the stability of the United States financial system. The Council consists of 10 voting members and five nonvoting members and brings together federal financial regulators, state regulators, and an insurance expert appointed by the President. It is chaired by the Secretary of the Treasury. A list of the members is on page 213.

- The law also creates a separate Consumer Financial Protection Bureau (CFPB) to address some of the practices that are believed to have contributed to the crisis. The agency has the authority to write new consumers protection rules and to enforce a number of rules already in place. In July 2011 the President nominated Richard Cordray, former Ohio attorney general, to head the CFPB, a move that requires confirmation by Congress.

- The law does not dismantle state regulation of insurance, but establishes a Federal Insurance Office (FIO) within the U.S. Treasury Department to report to Congress and the President on the insurance industry and serve as a nonvoting member of the FSOC. In March 2011 Treasury Secretary Timothy Geithner named Michael McRaith, former Illinois insurance commissioner, to head the FIO. FSOC also includes a voting member with insurance exper-tise who is appointed by the President and confirmed by the Senate for a six-year term.

- The law reduced the amount that the government could inject into the Troubled Asset Relief Program (TARP), the federal program set up in 2008 as a rescue program for ailing financial institutions, from $700 billion to $475 billion and stipulated that no new TARP programs could be established.

- As of July 2011 taxpayers had recovered approximately $255 billion from TARP's bank programs through repayments, dividends, interest and other income. This exceeds the original financial support provided by TARP of $245 billion by approximately $10 billion. The Treasury expects that TARP will ultimately provide a positive return of approximately $20 billion to taxpayers.

ASSETS OF FINANCIAL SERVICES SECTORS 2006
($ billions)

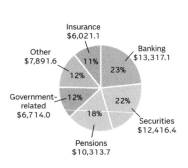

Insurance $6,021.1
Other $7,891.6
Banking $13,317.1
Government-related $6,714.0
Securities $12,416.4
Pensions $10,313.7

Banking 23%
Securities 22%
Pensions 18%
Government-related 12%
Other 12%
Insurance 11%

2010
($ billions)

Insurance $6,580.2
Other $6,501.6
Banking $16,492.2
Government-related $7,759.9
Securities $13,007.6
Pensions $10,458.7

Banking 27%
Securities 21%
Pensions 17%
Government-related 13%
Other 11%
Insurance 11%

Source: Board of Governors of the Federal Reserve System, June 9, 2011.

ASSETS OF FINANCIAL SERVICES SECTORS BY INDUSTRY, 2009-2010
($ billions, end of year)

Sector	2009	2010
Banking		
Commercial banking[1]	$14,288.2	$14,336.1
Savings institutions[2]	1,253.7	1,244.1
Credit unions	882.7	912.0
Total	**$16,424.6**	**$16,492.2**
Insurance		
Life insurance companies	4,823.9	5,176.3
All other insurers	1,387.6	1,403.9
Total	**$6,211.5**	**$6,580.2**
Securities		
Mutual and closed-end funds	10,447.5	10,932.5
Securities broker/dealers[3]	2,084.2	2,075.1
Total	**$12,531.7**	**$13,007.6**
Pensions		
Private pension funds[4]	5,471.0	6,111.8
State and local govt retirement funds	2,673.7	2,931.5
Federal govt retirement funds	1,324.4	1,415.4
Total	**$9,469.1**	**$10,458.7**
Government-related[5]	**$8,390.5**	**$7,759.9**
Other		
Finance companies[6]	1,662.5	1,590.0
Real estate investment trusts	255.5	295.2
Asset-backed securities issuers	3,347.4	2,351.3
Funding corporations	2,420.7	2,265.1
Total	**$7,686.1**	**$6,501.6**
Total all sectors	**$60,713.5**	**$60,800.2**

[1]Includes U.S.-chartered commercial banks, foreign banking offices in the U.S., bank holding companies and banks in U.S.-affiliated areas. [2]Includes savings and loan associations, mutual savings banks and federal savings banks. [3]Includes investment banks. [4]Includes defined benefit and defined contribution plans (including 401(k)s) and the Federal Employees Retirement Thrift Savings Plan. [5]Includes government-sponsored enterprises (GSEs) and agency- and GSE-backed mortgage pools. [6]Includes retail captive finance companies and mortgage companies.

Source: Board of Governors of the Federal Reserve System, June 9, 2011.

NUMBER AND VALUE OF ANNOUNCED FINANCIAL SERVICES MERGERS AND ACQUISITIONS BY SECTOR, 2006-2010[1]

($ billions)

	2006		2007		2008		2009		2010	
	Deals	Value	Deals	Value	Deals	Value	Deals	Value	Deals	Value
Securities[2]	196	$47.9	216	$48.0	205	$66.2	206	$39.0	188	$10.9
Specialty finance[3]	210	33.0	202	21.1	148	63.0	156	23.0	188	48.5
Banks	249	77.7	249	67.9	119	28.3	103	1.0	155	10.3
Thrifts	47	31.1	39	4.2	24	7.3	17	0.3	18	1.9
Insurance	380	16.1	398	34.1	440	30.0	326	12.6	375	34.6
Life/health	40	6.7	36	6.3	35	3.7	33	1.3	36	22.3
Property/casualty	74	6.4	74	14.3	84	18.8	77	9.6	89	9.6
Brokers and agents	243	1.8	270	7.3	308	5.9	203	0.8	235	0.6
Managed care	23	1.3	18	6.3	13	1.5	13	1.0	15	2.1
Total	**1,082**	**$205.8**	**1,104**	**$175.2**	**936**	**$194.8**	**808**	**$75.9**	**924**	**$106.2**

[1]All industry segments include whole and asset deals, except for banks and thrifts, which only include whole deals. Terminated deals are not included.
[2]Includes securities and investment companies, broker/dealers, and asset managers.
[3]Specialty finance firms range from small finance companies to major credit card operations.
Source: SNL Financial LC.

NUMBER OF ANNOUNCED FINANCIAL SERVICES MERGERS AND ACQUISITIONS, 2006-2010

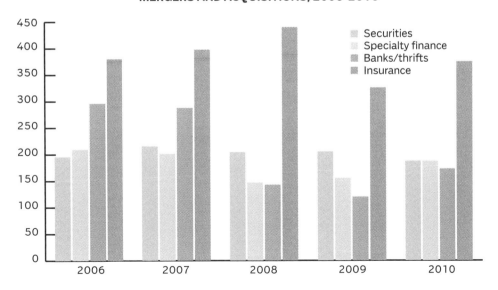

Source: SNL Financial LC.

**TOP TEN CROSS-INDUSTRY FINANCIAL SERVICES ACQUISITIONS
ANNOUNCED IN THE UNITED STATES, 2010[1]**

($ millions)

Rank	Buyer	Buyer industry	Buyer country	Target	Target industry	Seller	Deal value[2]
1	Undisclosed buyer	Not classified	NA	Fixed-income securities assets	Specialty lender	National Credit Union Administration	$9,500.0
2	Toronto-Dominion Bank	Bank	Canada	Chrysler Financial Corp.	Specialty lender	Cerberus Capital Management, L.P.	6,300.0
3	Banco Santander, S.A.	Bank	Spain	Auto loan portfolio	Specialty lender	HSBC Holdings plc	3,560.0
4	General Motors Corporation	Not classified	U.S.	AmeriCredit Corp.	Specialty lender	AmeriCredit Corp.	3,325.4
5	Banco Santander, S.A.	Bank	Spain	Auto loan portfolio	Specialty lender	Citigroup Inc.	3,168.0
6	Macquarie Group Limited	Bank	Australia	Aircraft operating lease portfolio	Specialty lender	International Lease Finance Corporation	1,987.0
7	AXA	Insurance underwriter	France	Portfolio of private equity funds	Asset manager	Bank of America Corporation	1,900.0
8	Investor group	Not classified	U.S.	Residential mortgage backed securities portfolio	Specialty lender	Federal Deposit Insurance Corp.	1,810.0
9	JPMorgan Chase & Co.	Bank	U.S.	RBS Sempra Commodities' global metals, oil and European energy businesses	Broker/dealer	Royal Bank of Scotland Group Plc/Sempra Energy	1,710.0
10	First Niagara Financial Group, Inc.	Bank	U.S.	NewAlliance Bancshares, Inc.	Savings bank/thrift	NewAlliance Bancshares, Inc.	1,498.0

[1]Target is US domiciled. If target country is not available seller country is used. List does not include terminated deals. Buyer and target industry must be different. Only includes deals where buyer or target are financial institutions (excluding financial technology).
[2]At announcement.
NA=Data not available.

Source: SNL Financial LC.

Employment and Compensation

From 2006 to 2010 employment in the financial services industry averaged 5.3 percent of total U.S. employment in private industry. Financial services employment fell by 7.5 percent from 2006 to 2010.

EMPLOYMENT IN THE FINANCIAL SERVICES INDUSTRY, 2006-2010
(000)

Year	Monetary authorities	Depository credit inter-mediation	Non-depository credit inter-mediation	Activities related to credit inter-mediation	Securities, commodity contracts, investments	Insurance carriers and related activities	Funds/ trusts	Total
2006	21.2	1,802.0	776.3	346.6	818.3	2,303.7	87.9	6,156.0
2007	21.6	1,823.5	715.9	327.0	848.6	2,306.8	88.7	6,132.1
2008	22.4	1,815.2	632.7	284.8	864.2	2,305.2	90.5	6,015.0
2009	21.0	1,753.8	571.5	264.8	811.3	2,264.1	88.4	5,774.9
2010	20.8	1,733.4	556.9	254.4	800.9	2,238.0	86.9	5,691.3

Source: U.S. Department of Labor, Bureau of Labor Statistics.

FINANCIAL SERVICES EMPLOYMENT BY INDUSTRY, 2010
(000)

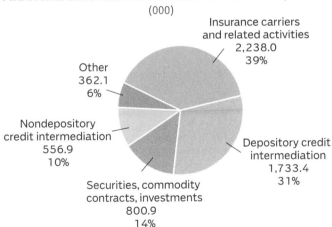

Insurance carriers and related activities
2,238.0
39%

Other
362.1
6%

Nondepository credit intermediation
556.9
10%

Securities, commodity contracts, investments
800.9
14%

Depository credit intermediation
1,733.4
31%

■ Total employment in private industry fell from 114.1 million in 2006 to 107.3 million in 2010.

Source: U.S. Department of Labor, Bureau of Labor Statistics.

FINANCIAL SERVICES EMPLOYMENT BY STATE, 2010[1]

State	Number of employees (000)	Rank	State	Number of employees (000)	Rank
Alabama	69.7	26	Montana	16.0	47
Alaska	8.9	50	Nebraska	59.5	29
Arizona	118.1	17	Nevada	30.8	38
Arkansas	35.2	35	New Hampshire	28.8	39
California	511.9	1	New Jersey	198.8	8
Colorado	101.2	20	New Mexico[2]	32.9	37
Connecticut	115.9	18	New York	489.6	2
D.C.	16.5	46	North Carolina	151.6	10
Delaware	37.1	34	North Dakota	16.8	45
Florida	319.4	4	Ohio	216.1	7
Georgia	148.2	11	Oklahoma	58.3	30
Hawaii	15.6	48	Oregon	55.7	32
Idaho	22.0	43	Pennsylvania	252.9	6
Illinois	288.4	5	Rhode Island	24.9	41
Indiana	98.4	22	South Carolina	71.7	25
Iowa	88.7	24	South Dakota[2]	28.7	40
Kansas	56.8	31	Tennessee	105.9	19
Kentucky	67.8	27	Texas	452.1	3
Louisiana	62.4	28	Utah	51.7	33
Maine	24.8	42	Vermont	9.3	49
Maryland	100.5	21	Virginia	126.1	16
Massachusetts	167.8	9	Washington	89.7	23
Michigan	138.7	12	West Virginia	21.3	44
Minnesota	135.7	13	Wisconsin	132.8	14
Mississippi	33.6	36	Wyoming	6.9	51
Missouri	127.3	15	**United States**	**5,691.3**	

[1]Includes banks, securities firms, insurance carriers and related activities and funds/trusts.
[2]Includes real estate and rental and leasing.

Source: U.S. Department of Labor, Bureau of Labor Statistics.

FINANCIAL SERVICES COMPENSATION BY STATE, 2010[1]

($ millions)

State	Compensation[2]	Rank	State	Compensation[2]	Rank
Alabama	$19,206	25	Montana	$3,729	48
Alaska	2,990	49	Nebraska	14,366	32
Arizona	36,011	19	Nevada	8,890	38
Arkansas	9,075	37	New Hampshire	10,303	35
California	243,164	2	New Jersey	94,096	6
Colorado	35,871	20	New Mexico	5,612	43
Connecticut	81,434	9	New York	441,571	1
Delaware	14,275	33	North Carolina	53,208	11
D.C.	9,431	36	North Dakota	3,761	47
Florida	107,658	5	Ohio	64,907	10
Georgia	52,730	12	Oklahoma	13,724	34
Hawaii	4,439	45	Oregon	17,289	28
Idaho	4,860	44	Pennsylvania	93,072	8
Illinois	124,437	4	Rhode Island	8,888	39
Indiana	26,181	23	South Carolina	18,070	27
Iowa	26,020	24	South Dakota	5,660	42
Kansas	15,990	29	Tennessee	33,974	21
Kentucky	18,713	26	Texas	151,861	3
Louisiana	15,659	30	Utah	14,451	31
Maine	6,893	41	Vermont	2,781	50
Maryland	38,826	16	Virginia	45,238	14
Massachusetts	94,088	7	Washington	32,258	22
Michigan	40,572	15	West Virginia	4,170	46
Minnesota	51,637	13	Wisconsin	37,329	17
Mississippi	7,853	40	Wyoming	1,686	51
Missouri	36,472	18	**United States**	**$2,305,381**	

[1]Does not include real estate.
[2]Includes wage and salary disbursements, bonuses, commissions, pay-in-kind, incentive payments, tips and employer contributions for employee pensions, insurance funds and government social insurance.

Source: U.S. Department of Commerce, Bureau of Economic Analysis.

The Financial Services Industry

Gross Domestic Product

Financial Services Contribution to Gross Domestic Product

Gross domestic product (GDP) is the total value of all final goods and services produced in the economy. The GDP growth rate is the primary indicator of the state of the economy.

GROSS DOMESTIC PRODUCT OF FINANCIAL SERVICES, SHARES BY COMPONENT, INCLUDING REAL ESTATE, 2009

- When real estate transactions (e.g., leasing, renting, management and sales services) are included, financial services accounted for 21.5 percent of the GDP in 2009, compared with 20.7 percent in 2008.

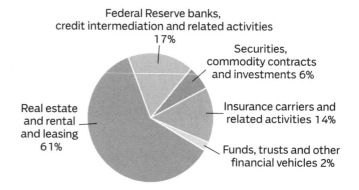

Federal Reserve banks, credit intermediation and related activities 17%

Securities, commodity contracts and investments 6%

Insurance carriers and related activities 14%

Funds, trusts and other financial vehicles 2%

Real estate and rental and leasing 61%

Source: U.S. Department of Commerce, Bureau of Economic Analysis.

GROSS DOMESTIC PRODUCT OF FINANCIAL SERVICES, SHARES BY COMPONENT, EXCLUDING REAL ESTATE, 2009

- With real estate excluded, the remaining financial services industries accounted for 8.3 percent of the GDP in 2009, compared with 7.7 percent in 2008.

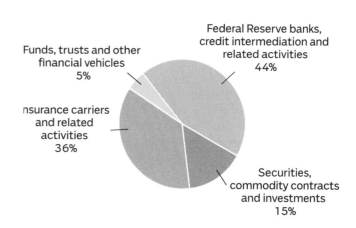

Funds, trusts and other financial vehicles 5%

Federal Reserve banks, credit intermediation and related activities 44%

Insurance carriers and related activities 36%

Securities, commodity contracts and investments 15%

Source: U.S. Department of Commerce, Bureau of Economic Analysis.

GROSS DOMESTIC PRODUCT OF THE FINANCIAL SERVICES INDUSTRY, 2005-2009[1]
($ billions)

	2005	2006	2007	2008	2009
Total GDP	**$12,638.4**	**$13,398.9**	**$14,061.8**	**$14,369.1**	**$14,119.0**
Total financial services industry	**$2,606.5**	**$2,777.6**	**$2,891.3**	**$2,974.9**	**$3,040.3**
Industry percent of total GDP	20.6%	20.7%	20.6%	20.7%	21.5%
Finance and insurance	$1,028.5	$1,105.5	$1,110.4	$1,100.4	$1,171.6
Federal Reserve banks, credit intermediation and related activities	470.7	483.5	476.9	514.3	514.0
Insurance carriers and related activities	337.5	367.4	392.4	350.9	424.5
Securities, commodity contracts and investments	183.0	214.5	199.7	188.9	175.2
Funds, trusts and other financial vehicles	37.3	40.2	41.5	46.3	57.8
Real estate and rental and leasing	$1,577.9	$1,672.1	$1,780.8	$1,874.5	$1,868.7
Real estate	1,424.9	1,488.6	1,595.1	1,688.9	1,686.5
Rental and leasing services and lessors of intangible assets	153.1	183.4	185.7	185.5	182.1

[1]Includes real estate and rental and leasing.
Source: U.S. Department of Commerce, Bureau of Economic Analysis.

FINANCIAL SERVICES SECTOR'S SHARE OF GROSS DOMESTIC PRODUCT, 2005-2009[1]

	Percent of total gross domestic product				
	2005	2006	2007	2008	2009
Total financial services industry	**20.6%**	**20.7%**	**20.6%**	**20.7%**	**21.5%**
Finance and insurance	8.1	8.3	7.9	7.7	8.3
Federal Reserve banks, credit intermediation and related activities	3.7	3.6	3.4	3.6	3.6
Insurance carriers and related activities	2.7	2.7	2.8	2.4	3.0
Securities, commodity contracts and investments	1.4	1.6	1.4	1.3	1.2
Funds, trusts and other financial vehicles	0.3	0.3	0.3	0.3	0.4
Real estate and rental and leasing	12.5	12.5	12.7	13.0	13.2

[1]Includes real estate and rental and leasing.
Source: U.S. Department of Commerce, Bureau of Economic Analysis.

FINANCIAL SERVICES VS. TOTAL U.S. GROSS DOMESTIC PRODUCT GROWTH, 2005-2009
($ billions)

Year	Total U.S. gross domestic product	Percent change from prior year	Finance, insurance, real estate and rental and leasing	Percent change from prior year	Finance and insurance	Percent change from prior year
2005	$12,638.4	6.5%	$2,606.5	8.2%	$1,028.5	10.7%
2006	13,398.9	6.0	2,777.6	6.6	1,105.5	7.5
2007	14,061.8	4.9	2,891.3	4.1	1,110.4	0.4
2008	14,369.1	2.2	2,974.9	2.9	1,100.4	-0.9
2009	14,119.0	-1.7	3,040.3	2.2	1,171.6	6.5

Source: U.S. Department of Commerce, Bureau of Economic Analysis.

FINANCIAL SERVICES PERCENTAGE SHARE OF GROSS STATE PRODUCT, 2010[1]

State	Percent	State	Percent	State	Percent
Alabama	5.4%	Louisiana	3.8%	Oklahoma	4.8%
Alaska	3.7	Maine	7.4	Oregon	5.0
Arizona	7.9	Maryland	5.7	Pennsylvania	8.9
Arkansas	4.7	Massachusetts	10.7	Rhode Island	13.0
California	5.6	Michigan	7.3	South Carolina	5.2
Colorado	6.8	Minnesota	10.0	South Dakota	19.6
Connecticut	19.4	Mississippi	4.6	Tennessee	6.7
Delaware	36.9	Missouri	6.6	Texas	6.7
D.C.	5.5	Montana	5.3	Utah	9.4
Florida	7.6	Nebraska	10.1	Vermont	6.5
Georgia	6.0	Nevada	11.2	Virginia	7.5
Hawaii	4.2	New Hampshire	9.2	Washington	4.7
Idaho	5.7	New Jersey	8.6	West Virginia	4.4
Illinois	10.6	New Mexico	3.7	Wisconsin	9.5
Indiana	6.9	New York	17.2	Wyoming	2.2
Iowa	13.8	North Carolina	11.5	**United States**	**8.5%[2]**
Kansas	6.4	North Dakota	6.4		
Kentucky	5.1	Ohio	9.0		

[1]Excludes real estate.
[2]Differs from data shown elsewhere for United States due to rounding.

Source: U.S. Department of Commerce, Bureau of Economic Analysis.

TOP TEN U.S. FINANCIAL SERVICES FIRMS BY REVENUES, 2010[1]

($ millions)

Rank	Company	Revenues	Profits	Industry
1	Fannie Mae	$153,825	-$14,014	Diversified financial
2	General Electric	151,628	11,644	Diversified financial
3	Berkshire Hathaway	136,185	12,967	Insurance
4	Bank of America Corp.	134,194	-2,238	Banking
5	J.P. Morgan Chase & Co.	115,475	17,370	Banking
6	Citigroup	111,055	10,602	Banking
7	American International Group	104,417	7,786	Insurance
8	Freddie Mac	98,368	-14,025	Diversified financial
9	Wells Fargo	93,249	12,362	Banking
10	State Farm Insurance Cos.	63,177	1,763	Insurance

[1]Based on an analysis of companies in the Fortune 500.
Source: Fortune.

Financial Literacy

The financial services industry has long been active in promoting and assessing financial literacy. To this end, each year the National Foundation for Credit Counseling conducts a survey of the financial behavior of U.S. adults. The latest survey found that 42 percent of Americans reported spending more or the same in 2010, compared with the past two years during the financial crisis, when at least half of U.S. adults reported spending less than in previous years. Other key findings include:

- More than one in three U.S. adults (36 percent) said they are saving less than the previous year. One-third said they do not have any non-retirement savings.
- Nearly three in four adults (73 percent) expressed concern about their finances, primarily about insufficient savings for retirement (48 percent) or emergencies (45 percent).
- One in three U.S. adults (32 percent) said they do not save any portion of their household's income for retirement.
- Most adults have not reviewed their credit score (63 percent) or credit report (65 percent) in the past 12 months. Forty percent carry credit card debt from month to month.
- Forty-one percent of adults would give themselves a grade of C, D or F on their knowledge of personal finance, a significant rise from 2009, when just about one in three rated their financial knowledge so poorly.

Corporate Social Responsibility

Financial services firms are major contributors to charitable causes. In 2009, 15 of the top 50 corporate foundations based on total giving were financial services firms, according to data from the Foundation Center. The 15 firms, which included banks, a diversified financial company, an asset management company and insurers, accounted for $847 million in contributions, or about one-third of the $2.5 billion contributed by the top 50. The financial crisis took a toll on the reputation of the financial services industry, but public confidence is beginning to rebound. Twenty-two percent of respondents gave financial services firms a positive rating in 2011, up from 16 percent in 2010, according to the latest Reputation Quotient Poll from Harris Interactive.

TOP 15 FINANCIAL SERVICES CORPORATE FOUNDATIONS BY TOTAL GIVING[1]

Financial services rank	All industry rank	Foundation (state)	Industry[2]	Amount
1	3	The Bank of America Charitable Foundation, Inc. (NC)	Commercial banking	$190,668,042
2	5	GE Foundation (CT)	Diversified financial	103,573,293
3	6	The Wachovia Wells Fargo Foundation, Inc. (NC)	Commercial banking	99,435,085
4	7	The JPMorgan Chase Foundation (NY)	Commercial banking	81,422,595
5	9	Wells Fargo Foundation (CA)	Commercial banking	68,367,615
6	10	Citi Foundation (NY)	Commercial banking	66,507,524
7	16	MetLife Foundation (NY)	Life insurance	39,465,498
8	20	The Goldman Sachs Foundation (NY)	Commercial banking	36,029,944
9	26	The PNC Foundation (PA)	Commercial banking	29,694,921
10	27	Nationwide Foundation (OH)	Property/casualty insurance	27,990,598
11	33	The Capital Group Companies Charitable Foundation (CA)	Asset management	22,095,559
12	34	The Prudential Foundation (NJ)	Life insurance	21,914,868
13	35	State Farm Companies Foundation (IL)	Property/casualty insurance	21,565,275
14	42	U.S. Bancorp Foundation, Inc. (MN)	Commercial banking	19,968,742
15	48	The Allstate Foundation (IL)	Property/casualty insurance	18,344,750

[1]As of December 2009. Based on financial services companies on the Foundation Center's "50 Largest Corporate Foundations by Total Giving" list published in April 2011.
[2]Based on Fortune Magazine designations.
Source: Foundation Center.

Savings, Investment and Debt Ownership

Individuals and businesses seek to increase their assets through savings and investments. They also borrow to purchase assets or finance business opportunities. The financial services industry exists to manage these activities by bringing savers, investors and borrowers together, a process known as financial intermediation. The banking industry acts as an intermediary by taking deposits and lending funds to those who need credit. The securities industry acts as an intermediary by facilitating the process of buying and selling corporate debt and equity to investors. Finance companies provide credit to both individuals and businesses, funded in large part by issuing bonds, asset-backed securities and commercial paper. The insurance industry safeguards the assets of its policyholders, investing the premiums it collects in corporate and government securities.

National Savings

Gross national savings is the excess of production over cost, or earnings over spending. Spurred largely by increased saving on the part of federal, state and local governments, gross national savings grew in the late 1990s and early 2000s, peaking in 2006. By 2009 gross national savings had fallen to $1.5 trillion, the lowest level since 1997, but grew in 2010, rising to $1.7 trillion. The $164 billion increase in 2010 was fueled by corporate savings, which rose by $161.3 billion that year, following an increase of $118.9 billion in 2009 and a $86.6 billion drop in 2008. In both 2009 and 2010 all levels of government spent $1.3 trillion more than they received, compared with $664 billion in 2008. Personal saving—the excess of personal disposable income over spending—climbed from $447.9 billion in 2008 to $655.3 billion in 2009, the highest level on record and virtually unchanged in 2010.

GROSS NATIONAL SAVINGS, 1940-2010
($ billions)

[1]Includes individuals (including proprietors and partnerships), nonprofit institutions primarily serving individuals, life insurance carriers and miscellaneous entities.

Source: U.S. Department of Commerce, Bureau of Economic Analysis.

Ownership of Equities and Corporate and Municipal Bonds

Equity and debt markets offer individuals and institutional investors the opportunity to participate in the development and expansion of publicly traded companies and municipalities. Equity investments provide an ownership interest in a company through stocks. Debt securities, generally bonds, represent money a corporation or municipality has borrowed from investors and must repay at a specific time and usually at a specific interest rate. Municipal bonds may be tax-exempt.

HOLDINGS OF U.S. CORPORATE EQUITIES, 2006-2010[1]
($ billions, market value, end of year)

	2006	2007	2008	2009	2010	Percent change 2006-2010
Total	**$24,339.3**	**$25,576.0**	**$15,638.1**	**$20,101.4**	**$22,961.6**	**-5.7%**
Household sector	9,643.7	9,627.0	5,738.8	7,429.3	8,239.9	-14.6
State and local governments	106.0	111.6	86.2	122.3	115.1	8.6
Federal government	0.0	0.0	188.7	67.3	41.3	NA
Rest of the world[2]	2,448.1	2,812.2	1,806.7	2,427.9	3,071.3	25.5
Monetary authority	0.0	0.0	0.0	25.1	26.4	NA
Commercial banking	35.3	41.5	6.7	30.3	38.2	8.2
Savings institutions	24.9	25.3	22.7	22.2	19.7	-20.9
Property/casualty insurance companies	227.0	236.2	193.3	219.8	219.2	-3.4
Life insurance companies	1,364.8	1,464.6	1,001.7	1,208.5	1,402.6	2.8
Private pension funds	2,724.8	2,673.3	1,599.7	1,835.7	2,012.3	-26.1
State and local govt retirement funds	1,926.1	2,013.7	1,237.9	1,549.8	1,782.5	-7.5
Federal govt retirement funds	138.1	149.1	85.6	119.4	133.8	-3.1
Mutual funds	4,989.6	5,476.9	3,014.1	4,136.2	4,762.7	-4.5
Closed-end funds	122.5	146.2	72.7	88.4	99.2	-19.0
Exchange-traded funds	402.0	573.7	473.9	669.9	853.9	112.4
Brokers and dealers	186.4	224.8	109.2	124.2	117.2	-37.1
Funding corporations	0.0	0.0	0.0	25.1	26.4	NA

[1]Excludes open-end mutual fund shares.
[2]Holdings of U.S. issues by foreign residents.
NA=Not applicable.

Source: Board of Governors of the Federal Reserve System, June 9, 2011.

HOLDINGS OF U.S. CORPORATE EQUITIES, 2010[1]

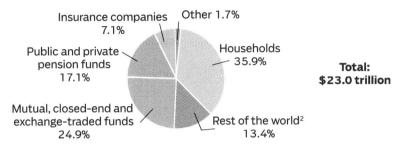

Insurance companies 7.1%

Other 1.7%

Public and private pension funds 17.1%

Households 35.9%

Mutual, closed-end and exchange-traded funds 24.9%

Rest of the world[2] 13.4%

Total: $23.0 trillion

[1]Market value, end of year; excludes open-end mutual fund shares. [2]Holdings of U.S. issues by foreign residents.
Source: Board of Governors of the Federal Reserve System, June 9, 2011.

HOLDINGS OF U.S. CORPORATE AND FOREIGN BONDS, 2006-2010
($ billions, end of year)

	2006	2007	2008	2009	2010	Percent change, 2006-2010
Total	**$9,981.8**	**$11,435.0**	**$11,016.5**	**$11,434.4**	**$11,332.2**	**13.5%**
Household sector	1,552.8	2,017.1	1,956.3	2,067.5	1,763.1	13.5
State and local governments	139.4	145.3	142.9	150.9	161.1	15.6
Federal government	0.0	0.0	0.0	0.6	0.9	NA
Rest of the world[1]	2,320.5	2,719.1	2,354.0	2,489.3	2,446.7	5.4
Commercial banking	780.3	978.2	979.9	861.8	747.2	-4.2
Savings institutions	92.7	142.2	108.5	84.5	73.9	-20.3
Credit unions	30.6	34.6	25.7	18.6	0.0	-100.0
Property/casualty insurance companies	277.0	282.9	267.5	298.3	322.6	16.5
Life insurance companies	1,819.5	1,862.6	1,817.0	1,914.7	2,027.1	11.4
Private pension funds	317.6	357.4	400.1	442.9	483.5	52.2
State and local govt retirement funds	283.4	297.0	312.9	308.6	312.4	10.2
Federal govt retirement funds	2.9	3.0	2.9	3.0	3.2	10.3
Money market mutual funds	368.3	376.8	228.0	169.9	154.2	-58.1
Mutual funds	767.0	889.9	959.9	1,106.1	1,264.5	64.9
Closed-end funds	75.1	74.0	48.7	54.0	58.1	-22.6
Exchange-traded funds	7.6	13.8	27.7	55.3	74.0	873.7

(table continues)

HOLDINGS OF U.S. CORPORATE AND FOREIGN BONDS, 2006-2010 (Cont'd)
($ billions, end of year)

	2006	2007	2008	2009	2010	Percent change, 2006-2010
Government-sponsored enterprises	481.7	464.4	386.6	310.8	293.9	-39.0
Finance companies	184.8	189.4	192.4	198.6	179.0	-3.1
Real Estate Investment Trusts	64.6	34.4	14.4	17.6	22.4	-65.3
Brokers and dealers	355.5	382.8	123.8	171.3	184.3	-48.2
Funding corporations	60.4	170.0	667.3	710.2	760.1	1,158.4

[1]Holdings of U.S. issues by foreign residents. NA=Not applicable.
Source: Board of Governors of the Federal Reserve System, June 9, 2011.

HOLDINGS OF U.S. MUNICIPAL SECURITIES AND LOANS, 2006-2010
($ billions, end of year)

	2006	2007	2008	2009	2010	Percent change, 2006-2010
Total	**$2,403.2**	**$2,618.8**	**$2,680.2**	**$2,808.9**	**$2,925.3**	**21.7%**
Household sector	872.0	896.0	903.8	1,009.6	1,083.8	24.3
Nonfinancial corporate business	28.1	29.2	26.2	27.3	23.7	-15.7
Nonfarm noncorporate business	5.8	5.3	4.9	4.5	4.3	-25.9
State and local governments	5.5	5.7	5.6	5.9	6.3	14.5
Rest of the world	34.4	45.1	50.5	57.0	73.0	112.2
Commercial banking	180.2	192.9	216.7	218.6	246.1	36.6
Savings institutions	11.2	11.0	7.8	9.2	11.1	-0.9
Property/casualty insurance companies	335.2	371.3	381.9	369.4	348.4	3.9
Life insurance companies	36.6	41.4	47.1	73.1	113.3	209.6
State and local govt retirement funds	3.3	2.4	1.4	1.5	1.6	-51.5
Money market mutual funds	370.3	471.0	494.6	401.3	334.4	-9.7
Mutual funds	344.4	372.2	389.6	480.2	526.6	52.9
Closed-end funds	89.4	91.3	77.9	80.9	80.3	-10.2
Exchange-traded funds	0.0	0.6	2.3	5.9	7.6	NA
Government-sponsored enterprises	36.1	33.3	31.3	29.1	24.9	-31.0
Brokers and dealers	50.9	50.1	38.7	35.4	40.0	-21.4

NA=Not applicable. Source: Board of Governors of the Federal Reserve System, June 9, 2011.

Mutual Fund Investments

Mutual fund assets reached a record $7.9 trillion at the end of 2010, up from $7.0 trillion at the end of 2009, according to the Federal Reserve. The household sector holds the largest share of mutual funds, with 60 percent of the industry's assets. In 2010, 51.6 million U.S. households owned mutual funds, accounting for 44 percent of all households, according to the Investment Company Institute. Households headed by 35- to 64-year olds accounted for about two-thirds (67 percent) of mutual-fund owning households in 2010. Households headed by 45- to 54-year olds were the most likely to own mutual funds. In 2010 more than one-quarter (27 percent) of households holding mutual funds were in this group, compared with 20 percent each for 35- to 44-year olds and 55- to 64-year olds. (See page 157 for further information on the mutual fund sector.)

MUTUAL FUNDS BY HOLDER, 2006 AND 2010[1]
(\$ billions, market value, end of year)

	2006		2010	
	Amount	Percent of total	Amount	Percent of total
Household sector	$4,188.1	59.3%	$4,717.2	59.5%
Private pension funds	1,880.4	26.6	2,126.6	26.8
State and local govt retirement funds	287.5	4.1	260.8	3.3
Nonfinancial corporate business	180.7	2.6	222.9	2.8
Life insurance companies	148.8	2.1	155.7	2.0
Commercial banking	24.5	0.3	45.0	0.6
State and local governments	32.5	0.5	32.5	0.4
Property/casualty insurance companies	6.9	0.1	5.7	0.1
Credit unions	2.1	[2]	1.5	[2]
Rest of the world	316.8	4.5	366.6	4.6
Total	**$7,068.3**	**100.0%**	**$7,934.5**	**100.0%**

[1]Open-end investment companies. Excludes money market mutual funds, exchange-traded funds and variable annuity funding vehicles.
[2]Less than 0.1 percent.

Source: Board of Governors of the Federal Reserve System, June 9, 2011.

Ownership of Federal Government Debt

The buying and selling of government securities is a crucial component of each of the financial sectors. Debt is issued and sold based on the changing needs of the federal government. The average daily trading volume in U.S. Treasury securities was $586.3 billion in June 2011, up from $508.0 billion a year earlier, according to the Securities Industry and Financial Markets Association.

ESTIMATED OWNERSHIP OF U.S. PUBLIC DEBT SECURITIES, 2001-2010
($ billions, end of year)

Year	Total	Individuals	Mutual funds/ trusts[1]	Banking institutions[2]	Insurance companies	Pension funds[3]	U.S. monetary authorities	State and local govern- ments	Foreign and inter- national	Other[4]
2001	$3,352.7	12.9%	7.8%	5.7%	3.4%	9.0%	16.5%	9.8%	32.7%	2.2%
2002	3,609.8	7.3	7.8	6.1	4.5	8.7	17.4	9.8	35.6	2.8
2003	4,008.2	10.2	7.1	4.8	4.2	8.0	16.6	9.1	37.8	2.4
2004	4,370.7	11.3	5.9	1.8	4.3	7.4	16.4	8.9	41.5	2.4
2005	4,678.0	9.9	5.6	1.1	4.3	7.2	15.9	10.3	42.4	3.2
2006	4,861.7	7.9	5.4	1.0	4.1	7.5	16.0	10.8	43.7	3.5
2007	5,099.2	5.0	7.5	1.4	2.8	7.8	14.5	10.5	46.6	3.9
2008	6,338.2	3.9	12.6	4.7	2.7	7.0	7.5	7.7	51.3	2.7
2009	7,781.9	10.0	9.1	4.2	2.9	7.8	10.0	6.5	47.5	2.1
2010	9,361.5	11.9	7.4	4.5	2.6	8.6	10.9	5.5	46.8	1.9

[1]Includes mutual funds, money market funds, closed-end funds and exchange-traded funds.
[2]Includes commercial banks, savings institutions, credit unions and brokers and dealers.
[3]Includes state and local government, federal government and private pension funds.
[4]Includes nonfinancial corporate institutions, nonfarm noncorporate institutions, government-sponsored enterprises and asset-backed securities issuers.

Source: Board of Governors of the Federal Reserve System, June 9, 2011.

Household Assets

Where people save their money and how much they save reflect many factors, including their personal finances, their appetite for risk, the investment products and savings incentives available to them, and the state of the economy. Financial assets of the personal sector increased 6.3 percent from 2009 to 2010 to total $44.3 trillion in 2010. Personal sector assets increased 10.2 percent in 2009 after falling 16.8 percent in 2008. This sector includes households, nonfarm noncorporate business and farm business.

ASSETS AND LIABILITIES OF THE PERSONAL SECTOR, 1990-2010[1]
($ billions, end of year)

	Value			Percent of total		
	1990	2000	2010	1990	2000	2010
Total financial assets	**$11,953.1**	**$29,951.6**	**$44,304.0**	**100.0%**	**100.0%**	**100.0%**
Foreign deposits	13.4	48.3	51.3	0.1	0.2	0.1
Checkable deposits and currency	516.0	516.1	732.5	4.3	1.7	1.7
Time and savings deposits	2,540.6	3,280.5	6,772.0	21.3	11.0	15.3
Money market fund shares	396.1	1,009.2	1,217.3	3.3	3.4	2.7
Securities	4,085.7	13,246.9	17,140.3	34.2	44.2	38.7
Open market paper	93.7	97.3	63.4	0.8	0.3	0.1
U.S. savings bonds	126.2	184.8	187.9	1.1	0.6	0.4
Other Treasury securities	390.3	434.5	971.9	3.3	1.5	2.2
Agency- and GSE[2]-backed securities	117.3	594.0	108.7	1.0	2.0	0.2
Municipal securities	647.7	533.7	1,088.1	5.4	1.8	2.5
Corporate and foreign bonds	237.6	551.2	1,763.1	2.0	1.8	4.0
Corporate equities[3]	1,961.4	8,147.3	8,239.9	16.4	27.2	18.6
Mutual fund shares	511.5	2,704.2	4,717.2	4.3	9.0	10.6
Private life insurance reserves	368.1	782.7	1,229.9	3.1	2.6	2.8
Private insured pension reserves	569.8	1,526.3	2,504.7	4.8	5.1	5.7
Private noninsured pension reserves	1,658.5	4,508.1	6,148.3	13.9	15.1	13.9
Govt insurance and pension reserves	1,105.7	3,173.3	4,487.8	9.3	10.6	10.1
Miscellaneous and other assets	699.2	1,860.2	4,020.0	5.8	6.2	9.1

(table continues)

ASSETS AND LIABILITIES OF THE PERSONAL SECTOR, 1990-2010[1] (Cont'd)
($ billions, end of year)

	Value			Percent of total		
	1990	2000	2010	1990	2000	2010
Total liabilities	**$5,181.4**	**$10,201.2**	**$19,410.9**	**100.0%**	**100.0%**	**100.0%**
Mortgage debt on nonfarm homes	2,595.7	5,092.5	10,517.6	50.1	49.9	54.2
Other mortgage debt[4]	900.7	1,213.4	2,412.8	17.4	11.9	12.4
Consumer credit	824.4	1,741.3	2,434.7	15.9	17.1	12.5
Policy loans	62.5	102.8	124.5	1.2	1.0	0.6
Security credit	38.8	235.1	278.2	0.7	2.3	1.4
Other liabilities[4]	759.3	1,816.2	3,643.1	14.7	17.8	18.8

[1]Combined statement for households and nonprofit organizations, nonfarm nonfinancial noncorporate business and noncorporate farm business.
[2]Government-sponsored enterprise.
[3]Only those directly held and those in closed-end and exhange-traded funds. Other equities are included in mutual funds, life insurance and pension reserves.
[4]Includes corporate farms.

Source: Board of Governors of the Federal Reserve System, June 9, 2011.

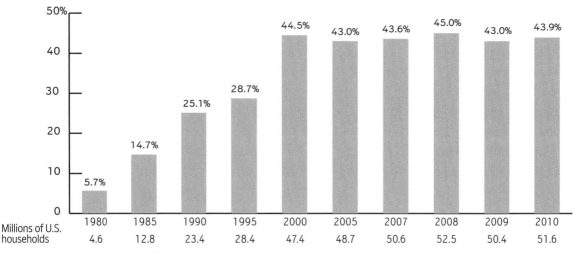

U.S. HOUSEHOLD OWNERSHIP OF MUTUAL FUNDS, 1980-2010
(Percent of all U.S. households)

	1980	1985	1990	1995	2000	2005	2007	2008	2009	2010
Percent	5.7%	14.7%	25.1%	28.7%	44.5%	43.0%	43.6%	45.0%	43.0%	43.9%
Millions of U.S. households	4.6	12.8	23.4	28.4	47.4	48.7	50.6	52.5	50.4	51.6

Source: Investment Company Institute, U.S. Bureau of the Census.

NONFINANCIAL ASSETS HELD BY FAMILIES BY TYPE OF ASSET, 1998-2007

Percent of families owning asset[1]	Vehicles	Primary residence	Other residential property	Equity in non-residential property	Business equity	Other	Any non-financial asset	Any asset
1998	82.8%	66.2%	12.8%	8.6%	11.5%	8.5%	89.9%	96.8%
2001	84.8	67.7	11.3	8.2	11.9	7.5	90.7	96.7
2004	86.3	69.1	12.5	8.3	11.5	7.8	92.5	97.9
2007	87.0	68.6	13.7	8.1	12.0	7.2	92.0	97.7
By age of family head, 2007								
Under 35	85.4	40.7	5.6	3.2	6.8	5.9	88.2	97.1
35 to 44	87.5	66.1	12.0	7.5	16.0	5.5	91.3	96.9
45 to 54	90.3	77.3	15.7	9.5	15.2	8.7	95.0	97.6
55 to 64	92.2	81.0	20.9	11.5	16.3	8.5	95.6	99.1
65 to 74	90.6	85.5	18.9	12.3	10.1	9.1	94.5	98.4
75 and over	71.5	77.0	13.4	6.8	3.8	5.8	87.3	98.1
Percentiles of income, 2007[2]								
Less than 20	64.4	41.4	5.4	2.5	3.0	3.9	73.4	89.8
20 to 39.9	85.9	55.2	6.5	3.9	4.5	5.7	91.2	98.9
40 to 59.9	94.3	69.3	9.9	7.4	9.2	7.4	97.2	100.0
60 to 79.9	95.4	83.9	15.4	9.4	15.9	7.2	98.5	100.0
80 to 89.9	95.6	92.6	21.0	13.6	17.0	9.0	99.6	100.0
90 to 100	94.8	94.3	42.2	21.0	37.5	14.1	99.7	100.0

[1]Families include one-person units.

[2]Ranges represent percentiles rather than income levels. A percentile is a statistical ranking point. The 50th percentile represents the midpoint of all values. For example, at the 50th percentile, half of the families in the ranking fall above this income level and half fall below.

Note: Latest data available. Based on surveys conducted every three years.

Source: Survey of Consumer Finances, Board of Governors of the Federal Reserve System.

FINANCIAL ASSETS HELD BY FAMILIES BY TYPE OF ASSET, 1998-2007

Percentage of families owning asset[1]	Trans-action accounts[2]	Certifi-cates of deposit	Savings bonds	Bonds[3]	Stocks[3]	Mutual funds[4]	Retire-ment accounts[5]	Life insurance[6]	Other assets[7]	Any financial asset[8]
1998	90.5%	15.3%	19.3%	3.0%	19.2%	16.5%	48.9%	29.6%	15.3%	92.9%
2001	91.4	15.7	16.7	3.0	21.3	17.7	52.2	28.0	16.0	93.4
2004	91.3	12.7	17.6	1.8	20.7	15.0	49.7	24.2	17.3	93.8
2007	92.1	16.1	14.9	1.6	17.9	11.4	52.6	23.0	15.1	93.9
By age of family head, 2007										
Under 35	87.3	6.7	13.7	[9]	13.7	5.3	41.6	11.4	10.0	89.2
35 to 44	91.2	9.0	16.8	0.7	17.0	11.6	57.5	17.5	11.8	93.1
45 to 54	91.7	14.3	19.0	1.1	18.6	12.6	64.7	22.3	15.6	93.3
55 to 64	96.4	20.5	16.2	2.1	21.3	14.3	60.9	35.2	16.9	97.8
65 to 74	94.6	24.2	10.3	4.2	19.1	14.6	51.7	34.4	22.6	96.1
75 and over	95.3	37.0	7.9	3.5	20.2	13.2	30.0	27.6	19.3	97.4
Percentiles of income, 2007[10]										
Less than 20	74.9	9.4	3.6	[9]	5.5	3.4	10.7	12.8	9.3	79.1
20 to 39.9	90.1	12.7	8.5	[9]	7.8	4.6	35.6	16.4	13.5	93.2
40 to 59.9	96.4	15.4	15.2	[9]	14.0	7.1	55.2	21.6	15.5	97.2
60 to 79.9	99.3	19.3	20.9	1.4	23.2	14.6	73.3	29.4	14.1	99.7
80 to 89.9	100.0	19.9	26.2	1.8	30.5	18.9	86.7	30.6	17.4	100.0
90 to 100	100.0	27.7	26.1	8.9	47.5	35.5	89.6	38.9	28.9	100.0
Percent distribution of amount of financial assets of all families										
1998	11.4	4.3	0.7	4.3	22.7	12.4	27.6	6.4	10.3	100.0
2001	11.5	3.1	0.7	4.6	21.7	12.2	28.4	5.3	12.6	100.0
2004	13.2	3.7	0.5	5.3	17.6	14.7	32.0	3.0	10.1	100.0
2007	11.0	4.1	0.4	4.2	17.9	15.9	34.6	3.2	8.6	100.0

[1]Families include one-person units. [2]Includes checking, savings and money market deposit accounts; money market mutual funds; and call accounts at brokerages. [3]Covers only those stocks and bonds that are directly held by families outside mutual funds, retirement accounts and other managed assets. [4]Excludes money market mutual funds and funds held through retirement accounts or other managed assets. [5]Covers IRAs, Keogh accounts and employer-provided pension plans. Employer-sponsored accounts are those from current jobs (restricted to those in which loans or withdrawals can be made, such as 401(k) accounts) held by the family head and that person's spouse or partner as well as those from past jobs held by either or both of them. Accounts from past jobs are restricted to those from which the family expects to receive the account balance in the future. [6]Cash value. [7]Includes personal annuities and trusts with an equity interest, managed investment accounts and miscellaneous assets. [8]Includes other types of financial assets, not shown separately. [9]Ten or fewer observations. [10]Ranges represent percentiles rather than income levels. A percentile is a statistical ranking point. The 50th percentile represents the midpoint of all values. For example, at the 50th percentile half of the families in the ranking fall above this income level, and half fall below.

Note: Latest data available. Based on surveys conducted every three years.

Source: Survey of Consumer Finances, Board of Governors of the Federal Reserve System.

529 Educational Savings Plans and Student Loans

To encourage households to save for college education, states have developed the Section 529 college savings plan, named after a part of the Internal Revenue tax code that allows earnings to accumulate free of federal income tax and to be withdrawn tax-free to pay for college costs. Slow to gain acceptance, by the end of 2002, all states had such plans in operation. There are two types of plans: savings and prepaid tuition. Plan assets are managed either by the state's treasurer or an outside investment company. Most offer a range of investment options.

■ The value of dollars invested in 529 plan accounts grew to $157 billion in 2010, an increase of 18 percent from the previous year.

NUMBER OF AND DOLLARS INVESTED IN 529 PLAN ACCOUNTS, 2006-2010[1]

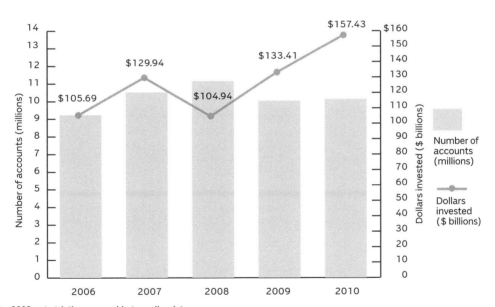

[1]Data prior to 2009 not strictly comparable to earlier data.

Source: National Association of State Treasurers.

TOP TEN 529 SAVINGS PLAN PROVIDERS BY ASSETS, 2010

($ billions, end of year)

- The top 10 providers of 529 savings plans held $113.2 billion in assets at the end of 2010, compared with $99.3 billion at the end of 2009.

Rank	Provider	Assets
1	American Funds	$29.6
2	Vanguard	28.4
3	Fidelity	17.6
4	Alliance	7.7
5	TIAA-CREF	7.2
6	T. Rowe Price	6.2
7	Merrill Lynch	5.6
8	Oppenheimer	5.2
9	Wells Fargo	3.0
10	Franklin Templeton	2.7
	Top 10 Providers	**$113.2**

Source: National Association of State Treasurers.

TOP TEN STATES FOR 529 PLANS BY ASSETS UNDER MANAGEMENT, 2010

($ billions, end of year)

Rank	State	Assets under management
1	Virginia	$33.3
2	New York	11.0
3	New Hampshire	9.6
4	Florida	8.4
5	Rhode Island	7.7
6	Ohio	6.2
7	Maine	5.6
8	Nevada	7.3
9	California	4.1
10	Alaska	4.0

Source: National Association of State Treasurers.

Federal Student Loans

The Health Care and Education Reconciliation Act, the massive healthcare law enacted in 2010, prohibits private entities from originating federal student loans after July 2010. This eliminates an arrangement, begun in 1965, in which private lenders that made student loans were granted federal subsidies and guarantees. Federal student loans are now originated by the federal government.

TOP 20 PRIVATE HOLDERS OF FEDERAL STUDENT LOANS, 2009-2010[1]

($ millions)

Rank	Loan holder[2]	Amount outstanding	
		Fiscal year 2009	Fiscal year 2010
1	SLM Corporation (Sallie Mae)	$154,141.9	$143,821.9
2	Citibank, Student Loan Corp.	32,474.1	27,911.8
3	National Ed Loan Network (NELNET)	25,256.2	24,514.3
4	Wells Fargo Bank N.A.	14,595.4	20,722.4
5	Brazos Group	13,048.3	12,080.4
6	JPMorgan Chase Bank	11,099.7	9,616.5
7	Pennsylvania Higher Education Assistance Agency (PHEAA)	11,126.0	9,575.1
8	College Loan Corp.	9,658.8	8,669.4
9	Student Loan Xpress	9,629.2	8,317.3
10	Pittsburgh National Corp. (PNC)	5,298.7	7,549.0
11	Goal Financial	7,197.8	6,881.4
12	Access Group	6,644.8	5,737.8
13	GCO Education Loan Funding	5,729.9	5,228.9
14	Northstar	5,164.7	4,903.4
15	Bank of America	10,066.5	4,777.0
16	U.S. Bank	4,385.6	4,768.7
17	Edsouth	5,481.1	4,244.0
18	Suntrust Bank	3,634.5	4,067.3
19	Missouri Higher Education Loan Authority	3,755.1	3,610.6
20	College Foundation Inc.	3,955.9	3,386.9

[1]Includes Stafford (subsidized and unsubsidized) and Plus Loans; excludes consolidation loans.
[2]Entity that holds a loan promissory note and has the right to collect from the borrower. As many banks sell loans, the initial lender and current holder could be different.
Note: Does not include direct federal loans.

Source: U.S. Department of Education, Federal Student Aid.

Savings, Investment and Debt Ownership

Consumer and Business Loans and Debt

Lending to businesses and individuals by FDIC-insured banks rose 1.3 percent from $7.3 trillion in 2009 to $7.4 trillion in 2010, reflecting a 66.6 percent increase in credit card loans to individuals. Credit card loans rose from $421 billion in 2009 to $702 billion in 2010. Real estate loans fell 4.4 percent from 2009 to 2010 while commercial and industrial loans fell 2.3 percent. See page 132 for lending by thrift institutions.

PERSONAL AND BUSINESS LENDING BY FDIC-INSURED BANKS, 2008-2010

($ millions, end of year)

	2008	2009	2010
Number of institutions reporting	8,305	8,012	7,658
Loans and leases, gross[1]	**$7,876,382**	**$7,285,567**	**$7,377,757**
All real estate loans	4,705,287	4,461,630	4,266,518
Real estate loans in domestic offices	4,640,876	4,398,648	4,209,337
Construction and land development	591,014	450,759	321,438
Commercial real estate	1,066,221	1,091,206	1,070,659
Multifamily residential real estate	206,477	212,723	214,741
1-4 family residential	2,713,464	2,577,367	2,534,514
Farmland	63,700	66,594	67,985
Real estate loans in foreign offices	64,411	62,982	57,181
Farm loans	59,801	59,578	59,329
Commercial and industrial loans	1,493,953	1,213,990	1,186,467
Loans to individuals	1,088,871	1,057,792	1,317,602
Credit cards	444,692	421,479	702,058
Related plans	61,567	61,549	58,152
Other loans to individuals	582,612	574,765	557,391
Total other loans and leases[2]	528,470	492,577	547,841

[1]Includes loan loss allowance and unearned income.
[2]Other loans and leases category items may not total for savings institutions regulated by the Office of Thrift Supervision due to reporting differences.
Source: Federal Deposit Insurance Corporation.

TWELVE-MONTH LOAN GROWTH RATES AT FDIC-INSURED BANKS, 2001-2010
(Percent)

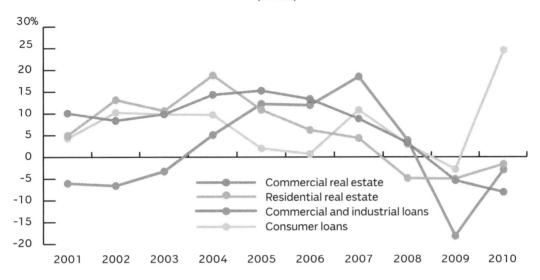

Source: Federal Deposit Insurance Corporation.

DEBT GROWTH BY SECTOR, 2006-2010[1]

	2006	2007	2008	2009	2010
Domestic nonfinancial sectors	**9.0%**	**8.6%**	**6.0%**	**3.0%**	**4.2%**
Households					
Home mortgage	11.1	6.8	-0.5	-1.5	-2.8
Consumer credit	4.1	5.8	1.5	-4.4	-1.8
Total household	**10.0%**	**6.7%**	**0.2%**	**-1.7%**	**-1.9%**
Business					
Corporate	8.6	12.7	3.8	0.1	3.3
Total business	**10.6%**	**13.1%**	**5.5%**	**-2.7%**	**0.3%**
Government					
State and local govt	8.3	9.5	2.3	4.8	4.4
Federal govt	3.9	4.9	24.2	22.7	20.2
Domestic financial sectors	**10.0%**	**12.6%**	**5.6%**	**-10.8%**	**-6.4%**
Foreign	**22.0%**	**9.0%**	**-10.6%**	**11.3%**	**5.0%**

[1]Percent change from prior year on an end-of-year basis.

Source: Board of Governors of the Federal Reserve System, June 9, 2011.

DEBT GROWTH BY SELECTED SECTOR, 2001-2010[1]

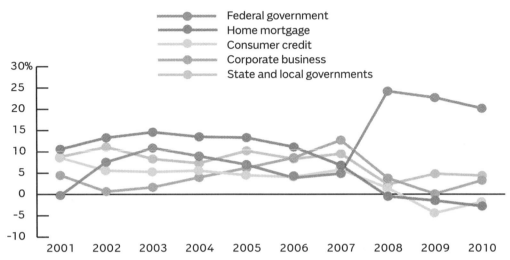

- Federal government
- Home mortgage
- Consumer credit
- Corporate business
- State and local governments

[1]Percent change from prior year on an end-of-year basis.

Source: Board of Governors of the Federal Reserve System, June 9, 2011.

- Household debt fell 1.7 percent from 2008 to 2009, the same rate of decline as from 2009 to 2010, while business debt was virtually unchanged in 2009 and rose 3.1 percent in 2010. Over the 10 years, 2001-2010, household debt rose 74.8 percent, compared with a rise of 48.7 percent for business debt.

CREDIT MARKET DEBT OUTSTANDING, OWED BY HOUSEHOLDS AND BUSINESSES, 2001-2010[1]

($ billions, end of year)

Year	Household sector	Nonfinancial corporate business
2001	$7,657.6	$4,826.7
2002	8,482.4	4,860.5
2003	9,508.9	4,966.1
2004	10,575.9	5,163.1
2005	11,763.7	5,472.3
2006	12,943.2	5,943.4
2007	13,805.6	6,703.0
2008	13,843.8	6,950.6
2009	13,611.2	6,963.9
2010	13,386.2	7,176.3

[1]Selected domestic nonfinancial sectors. Excludes corporate equities and mutual fund shares.

Source: Board of Governors of the Federal Reserve System, June 9, 2011.

Credit and Debit Card Payments

There were 108.9 billion noncash payments with a value of $72.3 trillion in the U.S. in 2009, including those made by check, card or Automated Clearing House (ACH), according to the latest payments study by the Federal Reserve. More than three-quarters of all U.S. noncash payments were made electronically in 2009, a 9.3 percent annual increase since the Fed's last study in 2007. Debit cards were the most widely used noncash payment, based on number of payments (accounting for 35 percent of payments), followed by checks (22 percent), credit cards (20 percent), ACH (18 percent) and prepaid cards (5 percent). The ACH system, a national payments network that includes Social Security benefit payments, payroll direct deposits and ecommerce, among others, accounted for 51.4 percent of payments, based on value, followed by checks (43.7 percent), credit cards (2.7 percent), debit cards (2.0 percent) and prepaid cards (0.2 percent).

NUMBER AND VALUE OF NONCASH PAYMENTS, 2006 AND 2009

	Number (billions)			Value ($trillions)		
	2006	2009	Compound annual growth rate, 2006-2009	2006	2009	Compound annual growth rate, 2006-2009
Checks (paid)	30.5	24.4	-7.2%	$41.60	$31.59	-8.8%
ACH[1]	14.6	19.1	9.3	31.02	37.16	6.2
Credit card	21.7	21.6	-0.2	2.12	1.92	-3.2
Debit card	25.0	37.9	14.8	0.97	1.46	14.4
Prepaid card	3.3	6.0	21.5	0.08	0.14	22.4
Total	**95.2**	**108.9**	**4.6**	**$75.79**	**$72.28**	**-1.6**

[1]Automated Clearing House.

Source: Federal Reserve System.

DISTRIBUTION OF THE NUMBER OF NONCASH PAYMENTS, 2006 AND 2009

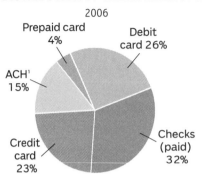

2006

Prepaid card 4%
Debit card 26%
ACH[1] 15%
Credit card 23%
Checks (paid) 32%

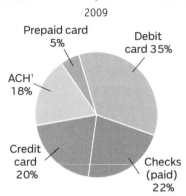

2009

Prepaid card 5%
Debit card 35%
ACH[1] 18%
Credit card 20%
Checks (paid) 22%

[1]Automated Clearing House. Source: Federal Reserve System.

Consumer Debt

DEBT HELD BY FAMILIES BY TYPE OF DEBT, 1998-2007

Percentage of families holding debt[1]	Home-secured	Other residential property	Installment loans	Credit card balances	Other lines of credit	Other	Any debt
1998	43.1%	5.1%	43.7%	44.1%	2.3%	8.8%	74.1%
2001	44.6	4.6	45.2	44.4	1.5	7.2	75.1
2004	47.9	4.0	46.0	46.2	1.6	7.6	76.4
2007	48.7	5.5	46.9	46.1	1.7	6.8	77.0
By age of family head, 2007							
Under 35	37.3	3.3	65.2	48.5	2.1	5.9	83.5
35 to 44	59.5	6.5	56.2	51.7	2.2	7.5	86.2
45 to 54	65.5	8.0	51.9	53.6	1.9	9.8	86.8
55 to 64	55.3	7.8	44.6	49.9	1.2	8.7	81.8
65 to 74	42.9	5.0	26.1	37.0	1.5	4.4	65.5
75 and over	13.9	0.6	7.0	18.8	[2]	1.3	31.4
Percentiles of income, 2007[3]							
Less than 20	14.9	1.1	27.8	25.7	[2]	3.9	51.7
20 to 39.9	29.5	1.9	42.3	39.4	1.8	6.8	70.2
40 to 59.9	50.5	2.6	54.0	54.9	[2]	6.4	83.8
60 to 79.9	69.7	6.8	59.2	62.1	2.1	8.7	90.9
80 to 89.9	80.8	8.5	57.4	55.8	[2]	9.6	89.6
90 to 100	76.4	21.9	45.0	40.6	2.1	7.0	87.6

[1]Families include one-person units. [2]Ten or fewer observations. [3]Ranges represent percentiles rather than income levels. A percentile is a statistical ranking point. The 50th percentile represents the midpoint of all values. For example, at the 50th percentile half of the families in the ranking fall above this income level and half fall below. Note: Latest data available. Based on surveys conducted every three years.

Source: Survey of Consumer Finances, Board of Governors of the Federal Reserve System.

DEBT HELD BY FAMILIES BY TYPE OF DEBT AND LENDING INSTITUTION, 1998-2007

Type of debt	1998	2001	2004	2007
Total	**100.0%**	**100.0%**	**100.0%**	**100.0%**
Home-secured debt	71.4	75.2	75.2	74.7
Installment loans	13.1	12.3	11.0	10.2
Other residential property	7.5	6.2	8.5	10.1
Credit card balances	3.9	3.4	3.0	3.5
Other debt	3.7	2.3	1.6	1.1
Other lines of credit	0.3	0.5	0.7	0.4
Purpose of debt				
Total	**100.0%**	**100.0%**	**100.0%**	**100.0%**
Home purchase	67.9	70.9	70.2	69.5
Other residential property	7.8	6.5	9.5	10.8
Goods and services	6.3	5.8	6.0	6.2
Vehicles	7.6	7.8	6.7	5.5
Education	3.5	3.1	3.0	3.6
Home improvement	2.1	2.0	1.9	2.3
Investment, excluding real estate	3.3	2.8	2.2	1.6
Other	1.5	1.1	0.6	0.5
Type of lending institution				
Total	**100.0%**	**100.0%**	**100.0%**	**100.0%**
Mortgage or real estate lender	35.6	38.0	39.4	41.6
Commercial bank	32.8	34.1	35.1	37.3
Thrift institution[1]	9.7	6.1	7.3	4.2
Credit union	4.3	5.5	3.6	4.2
Credit and store cards	3.9	3.7	3.0	3.6
Finance or loan company	4.1	4.3	4.1	3.4
Other nonfinancial	1.3	1.4	2.0	2.0
Brokerage	3.8	3.1	2.5	1.6
Individual lender	3.3	2.0	1.7	1.4
Government	0.6	1.1	0.7	0.4
Pension account	0.4	0.3	0.3	0.2
Other loans	0.3	0.5	0.2	0.2

[1]Savings and loan association or savings bank.
Note: Latest data available. Based on surveys conducted every three years.
Source: Survey of Consumer Finances, Board of Governors of the Federal Reserve System.

Savings, Investment and Debt Ownership

Consumer and Business Loans and Debt

CONSUMER CREDIT FINANCE RATES BY INSTITUTION AND TYPE OF LOAN, 2001-2010

	2001	2002	2003	2004	2005	2006	2007	2008	2009	2010
Commercial banks										
New automobiles (48 months)	8.50%	7.62%	6.93%	6.60%	7.07%	7.72%	7.77%	7.02%	6.72%	6.21%
Personal (24 months)	13.22	12.54	11.95	11.89	12.06	12.41	12.38	11.37	11.10	10.87
Credit card plans	14.87	13.40	12.30	12.72	12.51	13.21	13.30	12.08	13.40	13.78
Finance companies										
New automobiles	5.65	4.29	3.81	4.92	6.02	4.99	4.87	5.52	3.82	4.26
Used automobiles	12.18	10.74	9.86	8.81	8.81	9.61	9.24	NA	NA	NA

NA=Data not available.

Source: Board of Governors of the Federal Reserve System.

- Delinquency rates for residential real estate loans were 11.34 percent in second-quarter 2010, the highest since record-keeping began in 1991.
- By the first quarter of 2011, residential delinquency rates were 10.23 percent.

DELINQUENCY RATES, RESIDENTIAL REAL ESTATE AND CONSUMER CREDIT CARD LOANS, 2001-2010[1]

Year	Residential real estate[2]	Credit cards	Year	Residential real estate[2]	Credit cards
2001	2.23%	4.69%	2006	1.94%	3.95%
2002	1.97	4.85	2007	3.07	4.60
2003	1.78	4.43	2008	6.60	5.64
2004	1.39	4.03	2009	10.37	6.34
2005	1.63	3.54	2010	10.03	4.15

[1]All figures are for the fourth quarter and are based on loans at commercial banks, measured as a percentage of loans. [2]Residential real estate loans. Includes loans secured by 1 to 4 family properties, including home equity lines of credit.

Source: Board of Governors of the Federal Reserve System.

Credit Cards

Bank cards, credit cards issued by banks, are the most widely held type of credit card, with 96.1 percent of cardholders having such cards in 2007. Balances on bank cards accounted for 87.1 percent of outstanding credit card balances in 2007, up from 84.9 percent in 2004, according to the Federal Reserve's latest Consumer Finance Survey. Store cards were also popular, with 56.7 percent of cardholders having such cards in 2007.

In February 2010 new federal rules for credit card companies went into effect. Along with other consumer protections, the rules require credit card companies to provide consumers with 45-day notice of any major changes to their card's interest rates, fees and other material terms.

FAMILIES WITH CREDIT CARDS, 2004 AND 2007

	2004[1]	2007
All families		
Percent of all families with credit cards	74.9%	73.0%
Percent of all families with credit card balance	46.2	46.1
Median amount of credit card balance ($000)	$2.4	$3.0
Families with credit card balance		
By percentile of income		
Less than 20	28.8%	25.7%
20 to 39.9	42.9	39.4
40 to 59.9	55.1	54.9
60 to 79.9	56.1	62.1
80 to 89.9	57.6	55.8
90 to 100	38.5	40.6
Median amount of credit card balance ($000)		
By percentile of income		
Less than 20	$1.1	$1.0
20 to 39.9	2.0	1.8
40 to 59.9	2.4	2.4
60 to 79.9	3.3	4.0
80 to 89.9	3.0	5.5
90 to 100	4.4	7.5

[1]All 2004 dollars adjusted to 2007 dollars.

Note: Latest data available. Based on surveys conducted every three years.

Source: Survey of Consumer Finances, Board of Governors of the Federal Reserve System.

STUDENTS WITH CREDIT CARDS, BY RACE/ETHNICITY, FAMILY INCOME AND GRADE LEVEL, 2010

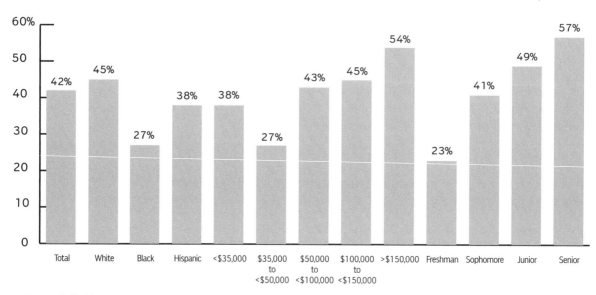

Source: Sallie Mae.

TOP TEN DEPOSITORY INSTITUTIONS BY CREDIT CARD LOANS OUTSTANDING, 2009-2010[1]

($000)

Rank	Institution	2009	2010
1	Bank of America Corporation	$109,192,355	$177,013,566
2	Citigroup Inc.	74,178,000	166,566,000
3	JPMorgan Chase & Co.	70,264,000	130,869,000
4	American Express Company	33,141,361	61,199,650
5	Capital One Financial Corporation	14,698,796	52,765,277
6	Discover Financial Services	48,232,468	46,231,088
7	HSBC North America Holdings Inc.	45,160,595	33,860,830
8	Wells Fargo & Company	31,639,000	29,449,000
9	U.S. Bancorp	20,329,000	20,280,000
10	Barclays Delaware Holdings LLC	NA	10,234,851

[1]The total dollar amount outstanding of credit card loans and other revolving credit plans.
NA=Data not available.

Source: SNL Financial LC.

Small Business Lending

Small businesses, independent businesses with fewer than 500 employees, are an important sector of the U.S. economy, employing about half of all private sector workers in the United States, according to the Small Business Administration. Small business lending rose from $687.8 billion in 2007 to $695.2 billion in 2009, based on data from FDIC-insured banks. However, conditions began to slide in 2010, with small business lending dropping by 6.2 percent to $652.2 billion. Loans fell further to $609.4 billion in the first quarter of 2011, a 6.6 percent drop when compared with first quarter 2010. (See chart page 36.)

BUSINESS LENDING BY LOAN SIZE AND SIZE OF BANK, 2011[1]

Size of loans ($000)	Value of loans ($ millions)	
	Large banks[2]	Small banks
$7.5 to $99	$2,097	$859
$100 to $999	8,340	2,154
$1,000 to $9,999	14,359	2,142
$10,000 and over	16,441	3,513

[1]Based on a sample of 348 domestically chartered commercial banks, May 2-6, 2011. [2]As of March 31, 2011, assets of large banks were at least $4.3 billion.

Source: Board of Governors of the Federal Reserve System.

Savings, Investment and Debt Ownership

Consumer and Business Loans and Debt

LOANS TO SMALL BUSINESSES AT FDIC-INSURED INSTITUTIONS, 2005-2011[1]

($ millions)

	2005	2006	2007	2008	2009	2010	March 31, 2011
Loan balances							
Commercial and industrial (C&I) loans of $1 million or less	$286,358	$296,326	$326,699	$336,404	$323,202	$309,955	$283,540
Nonfarm nonresidential loans of $1 million or less	315,121	337,863	360,061	375,048	372,023	342,292	325,875
Total small business loan balances	$601,480	$634,189	$686,760	$711,453	$695,225	$652,247	$609,416
Percent change from year ago							
Commercial and industrial (C&I) loans of $1 million or less	3.7%	3.5%	10.2%	3.0%	-3.9%	-4.1%	-10.3%
Nonfarm nonresidential loans of $1 million or less	4.7	7.2	6.6	4.2	-0.8	-8.0	-7.2
Total small business loan balances	4.2%	5.4%	8.3%	3.6%	-2.3%	-6.2%	-6.6%
Numbers of loans							
Commercial and industrial (C&I) loans of $1 million or less	19,317,043	19,315,245	22,068,041	25,375,955	21,404,058	20,656,256	19,740,922
Nonfarm nonresidential loans of $1 million or less	1,714,937	1,947,069	2,458,493	1,844,338	1,797,329	1,731,706	1,502,367
Total small business loans	21,031,980	21,262,314	24,526,534	27,220,293	23,201,387	22,387,962	21,243,289

[1]As of June 30 of each year.

Source: Federal Deposit Insurance Corporation.

Community Development Lending

The Federal Community Reinvestment Act (CRA) requires commercial banks and savings institutions with total assets of $1.1 billion to report data regarding their small business, small farm and community development loans. In 2010, 880 of these institutions reported originations or purchases of about 4.3 million small business loans, totaling $180 billion, and about 147,000 small farm loans, totaling $11.8 billion. The mandatory CRA reporting threshold adjusts annually based on changes to the Consumer Price Index; for 2010 it was $1.098 billion. During 2010, commercial banks and savings institutions with assets of $1.098 billion or more originated or purchased 93 percent of the small business loans reported under CRA, based on the dollar value of the loans.

Seventy-four percent of the 880 lenders, or 648 institutions, extended community development loans in 2010, a 5 percent drop from the number making such loans in 2009. When both loan originations and purchases are considered, the dollar volume of community development lending increased by 16 percent from $34.7 billion in 2009 to $40.3 billion in 2010.

COMMUNITY DEVELOPMENT LENDING, 2010[1]

Asset size of lender ($ millions)	CRA loans				CRA reporting institutions			
	Number		Amount ($000)		Total		Community development loans	
	Total	Percent	Total	Percent	Number	Percent	Number extending	Percent extending
Less than $100	264	1.5%	$91,022	0.2%	6	0.7%	4	0.6%
$100 to $249	19	0.1	5,688	(2)	9	1.0	3	0.5
$250 to $1,097	1,614	9.0	1,163,458	2.9	320	36.4	202	31.2
$1,098 or more	16,086	89.5	39,061,519	96.9	545	61.9	439	67.7
Total	**17,983**	**100.0%**	**$40,321,687**	**100.0%**	**880**	**100.0%**	**648**	**100.0%**

[1]As per the Community Reinvestment Act (CRA), enacted in 1977 to encourage banks to help meet the needs of the communities in which they operate, including low and moderate income neighborhoods. The act mandates that the reporting threshold adjusts annually to the Consumer Price Index, bringing the threshold to $1.098 billion in assets in 2010.
[2]Less than 0.1 percent.
Source: Federal Financial Institutions Examination Council.

Savings, Investment and Debt Ownership

Bankruptcy

There are three major types of bankruptcies: Chapter 7 is a liquidation, under which assets are distributed by a court-appointed trustee. If there are no assets, the debt is discharged and creditors receive nothing. Chapter 11 is a reorganization, used mostly by businesses, under which debts are restructured and a payment schedule is worked out. Chapter 13 is a debt repayment plan, under which debts are repaid in part or in full over a period of time, normally three years, under the supervision of a trustee.

The Bankruptcy Abuse Prevention and Consumer Protection Act of 2005 (BAPCA), which was the most comprehensive revision of bankruptcy laws in 25 years, instituted a means test that requires people who earn above their state's median income and can repay at least $6,000 over five years to file for bankruptcy protection under Chapter 13, which mandates a repayment plan. (Under the previous law more debtors were eligible to file under Chapter 7, with its less stringent provisions). There was a precipitous drop in filings in 2006 after the law took effect. However, filings have been rising steadily in recent years, with annual increases of over 30 percent from 2007 to 2009. In 2010 a total of 1.6 million bankruptcy petitions were filed in U.S. courts, the greatest number since the 2.1 million bankrupties recorded in 2005.

BANKRUPTCY PETITIONS FILED BY TYPE, 2006-2010

Year	Business	Percent change	Nonbusiness	Percent change	Total	Percent change
2006	19,695	-49.8%	597,965	-70.7%	617,660	-70.3%
2007	28,322	43.8	822,590	37.6	850,912	37.8
2008	43,546	53.8	1,074,225	30.6	1,117,771	31.4
2009	60,837	39.7	1,412,838	31.5	1,473,675	31.8
2010	56,282	-7.5	1,536,799	8.8	1,593,081	8.1

Source: Administrative Office of the U.S. Courts.

Retirement Funds, IRAs and 401(k)s

In addition to Social Security and private savings, a large number of Americans rely on invest-ments in formal plans to prepare for retirement. A report by the Investment Company Institute (ICI) found that 70 percent of U.S. households (or 82 million households) reported that they had employer-sponsored retirement plans, IRAs, or both in 2010. Retirement market assets rose by $1.5 trillion or 9.1 percent to $17.5 trillion in 2010 from 2009.

U.S. RETIREMENT ASSETS, 2006 AND 2010

($ trillions, year-end)

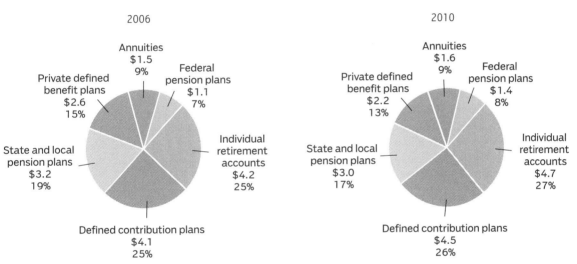

Source: Investment Company Institute.

Retirement Funds

Workplace plans play a major part in retirement savings, with 64 percent of Americans' retirement assets held in private or public employer-sponsored plans in 2010, according to the Investment Company Institute. Almost one-third (26.9 percent) of such assets were in individual retirement accounts and 9.0 percent were in annuities.

Retirement plans are generally administered by a bank, life insurance company, mutual fund, brokerage firm or pension fund manager. Because payouts are relatively predictable, pension funds invest primarily in long-term securities. They are among the largest investors in the stock market. Pension plan assets made up 17.2 percent of total financial services industry assets in 2010.

U.S. RETIREMENT ASSETS, BY TYPE, 2001-2010
($ trillions, end of year)

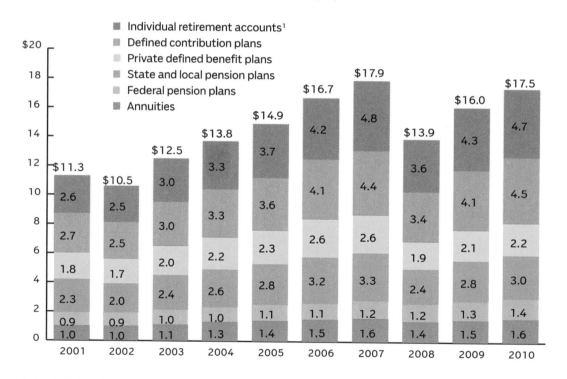

[1]Data for 2003, 2005, 2008, 2009 and 2010 are estimates. Data for 2006 and 2007 are preliminary.
Source: Investment Company Institute.

ASSETS OF PRIVATE PENSION FUNDS BY TYPE OF ASSET, 2006-2010[1]

($ billions, end of year)

	2006	2007	2008	2009	2010
Total financial assets	**$6,082.8**	**$6,410.6**	**$4,552.7**	**$5,471.0**	**$6,111.8**
Checkable deposits and currency	11.2	11.8	12.3	16.4	28.0
Time and savings deposits	63.1	67.7	67.9	72.7	77.1
Money market fund shares	90.1	93.5	95.7	96.4	96.3
Security repurchase agreements[2]	22.4	25.8	33.1	36.2	37.1
Credit market instruments	758.3	860.8	951.4	1,063.0	1,171.0
Open market paper	31.7	26.9	37.2	26.7	15.0
Treasury securities	130.8	169.5	184.9	310.7	486.7
Agency- and GSE[3]-backed securities	268.6	296.8	318.1	269.1	170.9
Corporate and foreign bonds	317.6	357.4	400.1	442.9	483.5
Mortgages	9.5	10.2	11.1	13.6	15.0
Corporate equities	2,724.8	2,673.3	1,599.7	1,835.7	2,012.3
Mutual fund shares	1,880.4	2,110.6	1,366.0	1,817.3	2,126.6
Miscellaneous assets	532.5	567.1	426.5	533.3	563.5
Unallocated insurance contracts [4]	387.9	431.3	317.6	412.8	457.5
Contributions receivable	42.8	47.2	47.9	50.5	49.2
Other	101.8	88.6	61.0	70.0	56.8
Pension fund reserves (liabilities)[5]	6,120.5	6,444.8	4,588.0	5,507.4	6,148.3

[1]Private defined benefit plans and defined contribution plans (including 401(k) type plans).
[2]Short-term agreements to sell and repurchase government securities by a specified date at a set price.
[3]Government-sponsored enterprise.
[4]Assets of private pension plans held at life insurance companies (e.g., variable annuities).
[5]Equal to the value of tangible and financial assets. These liabilities are assets of the household sector.

Source: Board of Governors of the Federal Reserve System, June 9, 2011.

Retirement Funds, IRAs and 401(k)s

ASSETS OF PRIVATE PENSION FUNDS, 1945-2010
($ billions, end of year)

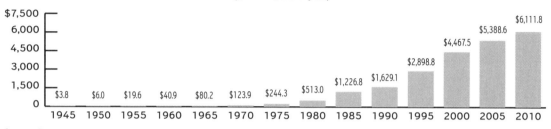

Source: Board of Governors of the Federal Reserve System, June 9, 2011.

ASSETS OF STATE AND LOCAL GOVERNMENT EMPLOYEE RETIREMENT FUNDS BY TYPE OF ASSET, 2006-2010
($ billions, end of year)

	2006	2007	2008	2009	2010
Total financial assets	**$3,089.8**	**$3,198.8**	**$2,324.5**	**$2,673.7**	**$2,931.5**
Checkable deposits and currency	13.1	17.9	17.8	17.7	17.3
Time and savings deposits	0.8	0.7	0.7	0.7	0.7
Money market fund shares	13.8	12.4	14.3	14.3	13.9
Security repurchase agreements[1]	24.1	21.7	23.5	23.5	22.8
Credit market instruments	808.0	820.3	833.5	824.7	816.5
Open market paper	42.8	38.4	25.9	24.0	22.4
U.S. government securities	464.0	472.7	483.9	481.4	470.8
Treasury securities	156.2	141.6	146.4	174.5	185.6
Agency- and GSE[2]-backed securities	307.8	331.1	337.5	306.9	285.2
Municipal securities	3.3	2.4	1.4	1.5	1.6
Corporate and foreign bonds	283.4	297.0	312.9	308.6	312.4
Mortgages	14.4	9.7	9.4	9.3	9.4
Corporate equities	1,926.1	2,013.7	1,237.9	1,549.8	1,782.5
Mutual fund shares	287.5	296.4	181.1	226.7	260.8
Miscellaneous assets	16.3	15.7	15.7	16.2	17.0
Pension fund reserves (liabilities)[3]	3,156.6	3,297.9	2,414.7	2,759.8	3,024.0

[1]Short-term agreements to sell and repurchase government securities by a specified date at a set price.
[2]Government-sponsored enterprise.
[3]Equal to the value of tangible and financial assets. These liabilities are assets of the household sector.

Source: Board of Governors of the Federal Reserve System, June 9, 2011.

Types of Retirement Plans

There are two basic types of pension funds: defined benefit and defined contribution plans. In a defined benefit plan, the income the employee receives in retirement is guaranteed, based on predetermined benefits formulas. Typically, benefits are based on a percentage of the participant's "terminal earnings," i.e., earnings at retirement. In a defined contribution plan, a type of savings plan in which taxes on earnings are deferred until funds are withdrawn, the amount of retirement income depends on the contributions made and the earnings generated by the securities purchased. The employer generally matches the employee contribution up to a certain level and the employee selects investments from among the options the employer's plan offers. 401(k) plans fall into this category, as do 403(b) plans for nonprofit organizations and 457 plans for goverment workers.

Other types of retirement funds include profit sharing plans, in which employers contribute to accounts based on their profits, and Keogh plans for the self-employed and employees of small businesses. Some workers who do not fall into these categories may make limited contributions to an individual retirement account (IRA). IRAs allow individuals to save money without paying taxes until they withdraw it. With the Roth IRA, a plan created in 1998 for individuals earning below specified income levels, individuals pay taxes on the money before it is saved and withdraw funds without paying federal taxes. Beginning in 2010 people with traditional IRAs were able to convert them to Roths. Roth 401(k)s were introduced in 2001 and made permanent by federal law in 2007.

There has been a dramatic shift away from defined benefit plans to defined contribution plans over the past 20 years. As the number of employers offering defined benefit plans shrank, the percent of workers participating in such plans dropped from 35 percent in 1990 to 10 percent in 2010. Defined contribution plan participation rose from 34 percent to 45 percent during the same period.

PARTICIPATION IN DEFINED BENEFIT AND DEFINED CONTRIBUTION PLANS, 1990-2010[1]
(Percent)

Percent of all workers participating	1990-1991	2000	2005	2007	2008	2009	2010
Defined benefit pension plans	35%	19%	21%	20%	20%	20%	10%
Defined contribution plans	34	36	42	43	43	43	45

[1]All private industry.

Source: U.S. Bureau of Labor Statistics.

- In defined benefit plans, the share of investments in bonds rose from 32 percent in 2009 to 38 percent in 2010 and the share of investments in equities rose from 28 percent to 35 percent at the same time.

- In defined contribution plans, the share of the investments in mutual funds rose from 40 percent in 2009 to 47 percent in 2010. However, investments in equities fell from 34 percent in 2009 to 31 percent in 2010, while investments in bonds remained at 8 percent during the same period.

RETIREMENT FUNDS ASSET MIX, 2010
Private Defined Benefit Plans

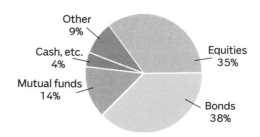

Private Defined Contribution Plans

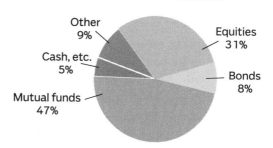

Source: Securities Industry and Financial Markets Association.

DISTRIBUTION OF PRIVATE PENSION FUND ASSETS, 1985-2010

Year	Financial assets ($ billions)	Percent of financial assets	
		Defined benefit	Defined contribution
1985	$1,226	64.9%	35.1%
1990	1,627	55.3	44.7
1995	2,902	50.5	49.5
2000	4,468	44.3	55.7
2005	5,302	43.0	57.0
2006	6,083	41.6	58.4
2007	6,411	40.5	59.5
2008	4,553	40.7	59.3
2009	5,471	38.5	61.5
2010	6,080	36.4	63.6

Source: Securities Industry and Financial Markets Association.

INVESTMENT MIX OF PRIVATE DEFINED BENEFIT PLAN ASSETS, 2006-2010
($ billions)

Year	Equity	Bonds	Mutual funds	Cash items	Other assets	Total assets
2006	$1,521	$497	$296	$59	$156	$2,529
2007	1,424	587	339	56	191	2,596
2008	777	648	228	68	132	1,853
2009	805	767	286	70	177	2,105
2010	781	850	314	78	193	2,215

Source: Securities Industry and Financial Markets Association.

INVESTMENT MIX OF PRIVATE DEFINED CONTRIBUTION PLAN ASSETS, 2006-2010
($ billions)

Year	Equity	Bonds	Mutual funds	Cash items	Other assets	Total assets
2006	$1,204	$229	$1,584	$160	$376	$3,554
2007	1,250	247	1,772	169	376	3,815
2008	823	266	1,138	178	294	2,699
2009	1,031	270	1,531	179	356	3,366
2010	1,202	306	1,818	175	364	3,865

Source: Securities Industry and Financial Markets Association.

Pension Benefit Guaranty Corporation

The Pension Benefit Guaranty Corporation (PBGC), a federal corporation created by the Employee Retirement Income Security Act of 1974, protects the pensions of workers in private defined benefit plans. The PBGC operates two pension programs. The Single-Employer Program, set up by individual companies, covers nearly 34 million workers and retirees in about 28,000 pension plans. The Multiple-Employer program, usually set up by two or more unrelated employers from the same industry, protects 10 million workers and retirees in about 1,500 pension plans. In 2006 Congress passed the Pension Protection Act, landmark pension reform legislation enacted to close shortfalls in employers' funding of defined benefit pension plans. The act gave employers seven years to fully fund their plans but gave some airlines in bankruptcy proceedings an extra 10 years to meet their obligations. The PBGC's Single-Employer Program for pension plans reported a deficit of $21.6 billion in fiscal year 2010, $500 million more than the previous year's $21.1 billion shortfall.

- Overall single employer benefit payments rose to $5.5 billion in 2010 from $4.5 billion in 2009.

- In 2010 the PBGC Single-Employer Program covered 147 newly terminated pension plans and made payments to almost 750,000 people.

NUMBER OF PAYEES, PBGC, SINGLE-EMPLOYER PROGRAM, 1980-2009

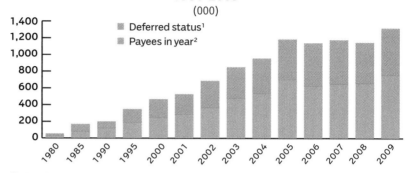

(000)

[1]Deferred status refers to individuals eligible for future payments.
[2]Payees are retired participants or their beneficiaries receiving payments.

Source: Pension Benefit Guaranty Corporation.

Individual Retirement Accounts (IRAs)

An individual retirement arrangement, or IRA, is a personal savings plan that allows individuals to set aside money for retirement, while offering tax advantages. Traditional IRAs are defined as those first allowed under the Employee Retirement Income Security Act of 1974. Amounts in a traditional IRA, including earnings, generally are not taxed until distributed to the holder. Roth IRAs were created by the Taxpayer Relief Act of 1997. Unlike traditional IRAs, Roth IRAs do not allow holders to deduct contributions. However, qualified distributions are tax free. Other variations include Simplified Employee Pensions (SEP), which enable businesses to contribute to traditional IRAs set up for their workers, and Savings Incentive Match Plans for Employees (SIMPLE) plans, a similar arrangement for small businesses.

According to the Investment Company Institute, 49 million households (or 41.4 percent of U.S. households) had IRAs in 2010. Of these, 38.5 million households (32.8 percent) had traditional IRAs, 19.5 million (16.6 percent) had Roth IRAs and 9.4 million (8.0 percent) had SEP or SIMPLE IRAs.

IRAs BY HOLDER, 2006-2010
($ billions, market share, end of year)

Holder	2006	2007	2008	2009	2010
Commercial banking[1]	$202.0	$210.7	$248.1	$275.5	$296.5
Saving institutions[1]	57.6	71.2	77.9	81.2	86.8
Credit unions[1]	53.2	58.2	65.5	74.2	77.2
Life insurance companies	406.0	426.0	381.6	405.5	431.0
Money market mutual funds[2]	176.0	220.0	266.0	226.0	203.0
Mutual funds[2]	1,772.0	1,992.0	1,272.0	1,664.0	1,927.0
Other self-directed accounts	1,540.2	1,805.9	1,273.9	1,524.6	1,688.5
Total	$4,207.0	$4,784.0	$3,585.0	$4,251.0	$4,710.0

[1]Includes Keogh accounts.
[2]Excludes variable annuities.

Source: Board of Governors of the Federal Reserve System, June 9, 2011.

IRA MARKET SHARES BY HOLDER, 2006 AND 2010

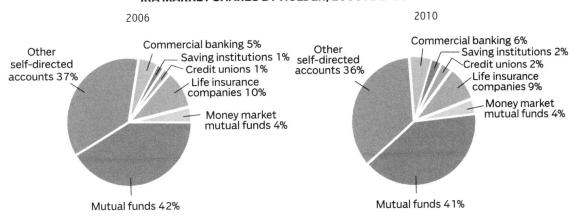

2006

Other self-directed accounts 37%
Commercial banking 5%
Saving institutions 1%
Credit unions 1%
Life insurance companies 10%
Money market mutual funds 4%
Mutual funds 42%

2010

Other self-directed accounts 36%
Commercial banking 6%
Saving institutions 2%
Credit unions 2%
Life insurance companies 9%
Money market mutual funds 4%
Mutual funds 41%

Source: Board of Governors of the Federal Reserve System, June 9, 2011.

401(k) and Other Defined Contribution Plans

Defined contribution plans, retirement savings plans based on contributions from employers and/or employees, accounted for 40 percent of employer-sponsored retirement plan assets in 2010, up from 27 percent in 1985, according to the Investment Company Institute. Assets in these plans grew from $1.7 trillion in 1995 to $4.5 trillion in 2010. 401(k) plans are the most popular type of defined contribution plan, accounting for $3.1 trillion in assets in 2010. Two other plans similar to 401(k)s—403(b) plans for employees of certain educational institutions and nonprofits and 457 plans for employees of state and local governments and some tax-exempt organizations— accounted for another $939 billion in defined contribution assets. The remaining $530 billion in defined contribution assets were held by plans without 401(k) features.

DEFINED CONTRIBUTION PLAN ASSETS BY TYPE OF PLAN, 2001-2010
($ billions, end of year)

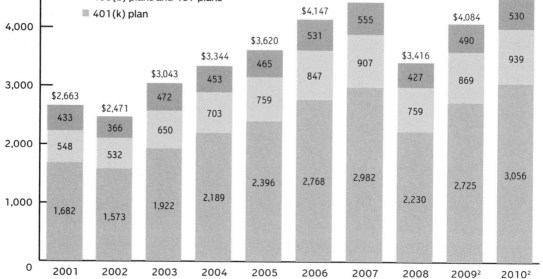

[1]Includes Keoghs and other defined contribution plans, such as profit-sharing plans, without 401(k) features.
[2]Estimated.

Source: Investment Company Institute.

AVERAGE ASSET ALLOCATION FOR ALL 401(K) PLAN BALANCES, 2009[1]

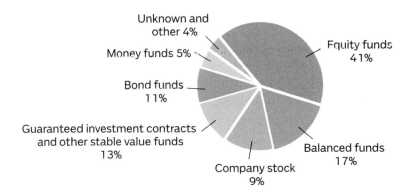

- Unknown and other 4%
- Money funds 5%
- Bond funds 11%
- Guaranteed investment contracts and other stable value funds 13%
- Company stock 9%
- Balanced funds 17%
- Equity funds 41%

[1]Percentages are dollar weighted averages.

Source: Investment Company Institute.

401(k) Plan Participants

Fifty-three percent of people who participate in 401(k) plans are in their thirties or forties, according to an analysis by the Employee Benefits Research Institute and the Investment Company Institute. The median age of participants in 2009 was 45 years. Thirty-eight percent of participants had five or fewer years of tenure in their firms, while 6 percent were at their firms for over 30 years. The median tenure at the current employer was six years in 2009.

401(K) PLAN PARTICIPANTS BY AGE, 2009

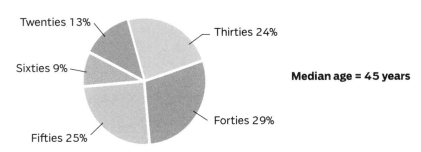

- Twenties 13%
- Thirties 24%
- Sixties 9%
- Fifties 25%
- Forties 29%

Median age = 45 years

Source: Investment Company Institute.

Sales of Fixed and Variable Annuities

There are two major types of annuities: fixed and variable. Fixed annuities guarantee the principal and a minimum rate of interest. Generally, interest credited and payments made from a fixed annuity are based on rates declared by the company, which can change only yearly. Fixed annuities are considered "general account" assets. In contrast, variable annuity account values and payments are based on the performance of a separate investment portfolio, thus their value may fluctuate daily. Variable annuities are considered "separate account" assets.

There are a variety of fixed annuities and variable annuities. One example, the equity indexed annuity, is a hybrid of the features of fixed and variable annuities. It credits a minimum rate of interest, just as other fixed annuities do, but its value is also based on the performance of a specified stock index—usually computed as a fraction of that index's total return. The financial services overhaul enacted into law in July 2010 included language keeping equity indexed annuities under state regulation. Variable annuities are subject to both state insurance regulation and federal securities regulation.

Annuities can be deferred or immediate. Deferred annuities generally accumulate assets over a long period of time, with withdrawals usually as a single sum or as an income payment beginning at retirement. Immediate annuities allow purchasers to convert a lump sum payment into a stream of income that begins right away. Annuities can be written on an individual or group basis. (See the Premiums by Line table, page 107.)

- Individual fixed annuity sales in the U.S. declined by 27 percent in 2010, following 1 percent growth the previous year. Variable annuity sales increased 10 percent, following an 18 percent drop in 2009.

INDIVIDUAL ANNUITY CONSIDERATIONS, 2006-2010[1]
($ billions)

Year	Variable	Fixed	Total	
			Amount	Percent change from prior year
2006	$160.4	$78.3	$238.7	10.3%
2007	184.0	72.8	256.8	7.6
2008	155.7	109.3	265.0	3.2
2009	128.0	110.6	238.6	-10.0
2010	140.5	80.8	221.3	-7.3

[1]Based on LIMRA's estimates of the total annuity sales market. Includes some considerations (i.e., premiums) that though bought in group settings involve individual buying decisions.

Source: LIMRA International.

Annuity Distribution Systems

Insurance agents, including career agents, who sell the products of a single life insurance company, and independent agents, who represent several insurers, accounted for 40 percent of annuity sales in 2010. State and federal regulators require sellers of variable annuities, which are similar to stock market-based investments, to register with NASD and the Securities and Exchange Commission.

SALES OF INDIVIDUAL ANNUITIES BY DISTRIBUTION CHANNELS, 2006 AND 2010[1]

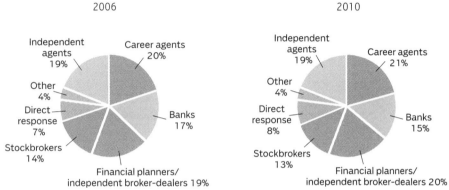

2006

Independent agents 19%
Career agents 20%
Other 4%
Direct response 7%
Banks 17%
Stockbrokers 14%
Financial planners/ independent broker-dealers 19%

2010

Independent agents 19%
Career agents 21%
Other 4%
Direct response 8%
Banks 15%
Stockbrokers 13%
Financial planners/ independent broker-dealers 20%

[1]Preliminary.
Source: LIMRA International.

INDIVIDUAL ANNUITY SALES BY PRODUCT TYPE, 2010
($ billions)

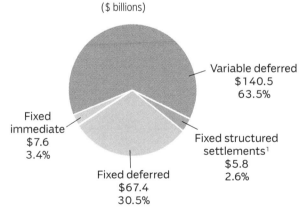

Variable deferred $140.5 63.5%

Fixed immediate $7.6 3.4%

Fixed structured settlements[1] $5.8 2.6%

Fixed deferred $67.4 30.5%

■ Individual annuity sales totaled $221.3 billion in 2010, including $140.5 billion in variable annuities and $80.6 billion in fixed annuities. This is down 7 percent from 2009, when $128 billion in variable annuities and $110.6 billion in fixed annuities were recorded.

[1]Single premium contracts bought by property/casualty insurers to distribute awards in personal injury or wrongful death lawsuits over a period of time, rather than as lump sums.
Source: LIMRA International.

DEFFERED ANNUITY ASSETS, 2001-2010
($ billions, year-end)

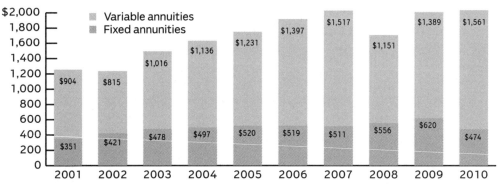

Variable annuities
Fixed annuities

2001: $904, $351
2002: $815, $421
2003: $1,016, $478
2004: $1,136, $497
2005: $1,231, $520
2006: $1,397, $519
2007: $1,517, $511
2008: $1,151, $556
2009: $1,389, $620
2010: $1,561, $474

Source: LIMRA International.

INDIVIDUAL IMMEDIATE ANNUITY SALES, 2006-2010
($ billions)

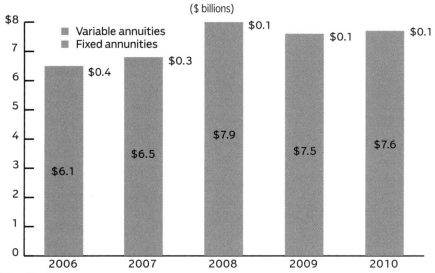

Variable annuities
Fixed annuities

2006: $0.4, $6.1
2007: $0.3, $6.5
2008: $0.1, $7.9
2009: $0.1, $7.5
2010: $0.1, $7.6

Source: LIMRA International.

MUTUAL FUND RETIREMENT ASSETS, 2001-2010
($ billions, end of year)

Year	Employer-sponsored defined contribution accounts[1]	IRAs	Total retirement
2001	$1,227	$1,167	$2,394
2002	1,094	1,037	2,131
2003	1,410	1,317	2,727
2004	1,634	1,509	3,143
2005	1,838	1,688	3,526
2006	2,159	2,015	4,174
2007	2,409	2,288	4,697
2008	1,639	1,585	3,224
2009	2,102	1,953	4,054
2010	2,466	2,222	4,687

[1]Includes 401(k) plans, 403(b) plans, 457 plans, Keoghs and other defined contribution plans without 401(k) features; does not include defined benefit plan mutual fund assets.

Note: Components may not add to totals due to rounding.

Source: Investment Company Institute.

MUTUAL FUND RETIREMENT ASSETS BY TYPE OF PLAN, 2010[1]
($ billions, end of year)

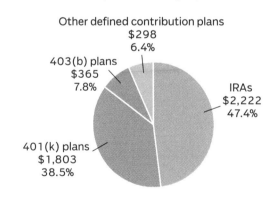

Other defined contribution plans
$298
6.4%

403(b) plans
$365
7.8%

IRAs
$2,222
47.4%

401(k) plans
$1,803
38.5%

- Of the total $4.7 trillion in mutual fund assets held by retirement plans at the end of 2010, 59 percent were invested in equity funds, including 44 percent in domestic funds and 14 percent in foreign funds.

[1]Preliminary data. Does not include defined benefit plans.

Source: Investment Company Institute.

Overview

The Gramm-Leach-Bliley Financial Services Modernization Act of 1999 (GLB) removed many of the Depression-era barriers that restricted affiliations between banks, securities firms and insurance companies. The arrangement that provided the major impetus for the passage of GLB, Citigroup's merger with Travelers Insurance Group, was short lived, with Citigroup selling off its Travelers property/casualty insurance and life insurance units in 2002 and 2005, respectively. However, the convergence of financial products has continued as companies look for innovative ways to tap the market for financial products. This has generally taken place without the mega-mergers envisioned by GLB. Banks have tended to concentrate on distributing insurance products by buying existing agencies and brokers rather than by setting up their own agencies or purchasing insurers. For their part, insurance companies have set up thrift or banking divisions rather than buying existing banks.

The economic downturn and subsequent regulatory changes have prompted some structural changes in the financial services industry. In 2008 securities giants Goldman Sachs and Morgan Stanley converted to bank holding companies and eventually gained financial holding company status (see below). In 2011 MetLife and Allstate announced plans to sell their banking units.

Financial Holding Companies

Gramm-Leach-Bliley permits banks, securities firms and insurance companies to affiliate with each other through the financial holding company (FHC) structure. The first step in electing FHC status is to become a bank holding company (BHC), a company that owns one or more banks. BHCs must meet certain eligibility requirements in terms of capital, management and community investment to become an FHC.

GLB also allows banks owned by BHCs to expand into financial services activities by creating financial subsidiaries. The activities permitted by these subsidiaries are not as broad as those of the FHCs. The Dodd-Frank Wall Street Reform and Consumer Protection Act, passed in July 2010, increases regulation of large bank holding companies and expands the authority of the Federal Reserve to regulate subsidiaries of BHCs.

NUMBER OF FINANCIAL HOLDING COMPANIES, 2006-2010[1]

	2006	2007	2008	2009	2010
Number of domestic FHCs[2]	599	597	557	479	430
Number of foreign FHCs[3]	44	43	45	46	43
Total number of FHCs	**643**	**640**	**602**	**525**	**473**

- In 2010, 34 domestic FHCs had assets over $15 billion.

[1]To avoid double-counting, only the top-tier bank holding company in a multitier organization is included. [2]Bank holding company whose ultimate parent is incorporated in the United States. [3]Bank holding company whose ultimate parent is a foreign bank or other organization chartered outside the United States.

Source: Board of Governors of the Federal Reserve System.

Bank Holding Companies

Each year Michael White Associates benchmarks and ranks the insurance, securities, and mutual fund and annuity fee income programs of banks and bank holding companies (BHCs), based on data reported to the FDIC and the Federal Reserve. The charts on pages 59-64 show data from institutions with insurance and/or investment operations located within BHC subsidiaries. The charts on pages 65-70 show data from banks that have generated insurance and investment income either directly or through bank subsidiaries and report the data at the bank level. See the Overview section of the Banking chapter for additional information on bank holding companies, including ranking of the largest BHCs.

Securities And Insurance Activities of Banks and Bank Holding Companies

The charts on pages 56-73 detail the securities and insurance activities of banks and BHCs. A summary of those activities for banks and BHCs combined in 2010, based on data from Michael White Associates, is below.

- $59.6 billion in investment banking, advisory and underwriting income, $101.8 billion in investment fee income and $39.0 billion in securities brokerage income.
- $26.0 billion in mutual fund and annuity income, and $3.3 billion in annuity commissions.
- $50.8 billion in insurance income, including $16.1 billion in insurance brokerage fee income and $34.7 billion in insurance underwriting income.

BHCs: Securities Activities

BHCs recorded $54.3 billion in investment banking, advisory and underwriting income in 2010.

BANK HOLDING COMPANY INVESTMENT BANKING, ADVISORY AND UNDERWRITING INCOME, 2008-2010

| Year | Reporting investment banking, advisory and underwriting income | | Investment banking, advisory and underwriting income ($ billions) | Mean investment banking, advisory and underwriting income | Median investment banking, advisory and underwriting income |
	Number	Percent			
2008	279	31.6%	$35.64	$127,755,735	$310,000
2009	265	28.9	52.64	198,638,698	237,000
2010	251	27.6	54.28	216,273,092	275,000

Source: Michael White Bank Investment Fee Income Report - 2011.

TOP TEN BANK HOLDING COMPANIES IN INVESTMENT BANKING, ADVISORY AND UNDERWRITING INCOME, 2009-2010
($000)

Rank	Bank holding company	State	Investment banking, advisory and underwriting income				
			2009	2010	Percent change	Percent of noninterest income, 2010	2010 Assets
1	Morgan Stanley	NY	$8,538,000	$9,919,000	16.17%	32.70%	$807,698,000
2	Goldman Sachs Group, Inc.	NY	8,637,000	9,316,000	7.86	27.72	908,580,000
3	JPMorgan Chase & Co.	NY	7,936,000	8,107,000	2.15	16.56	2,115,583,000
4	Citigroup Inc.	NY	8,396,000	6,303,000	-24.93	21.32	1,913,410,000
5	Franklin Resources, Inc.	CA	4,478,999	6,014,583	34.28	97.08	12,290,974
6	Bank of America Corporation	NC	5,565,469	5,520,086	-0.82	10.11	2,261,499,723
7	Wells Fargo & Company	CA	3,945,000	3,443,000	-12.72	8.59	1,258,010,000
8	Taunus Corporation	NY	919,000	1,481,000	61.15	27.72	372,556,000
9	PNC Financial Services Group	PA	422,144	822,270	94.78	14.04	264,414,112
10	RBC USA Holdco Corporation	NY	0	752,991	NA	30.27	99,150,441

NA=Not applicable.
Source: Michael White Bank Investment Fee Income Report - 2011.

BANK HOLDING COMPANY INVESTMENT FEE INCOME, 2006-2010[1]

Year	Reporting investment fee income		Investment fee income ($ billions)	Mean investment fee income	Median investment fee income
	Number	Percent			
2006[2]	629	73.7%	$56.43	$89,717,957	$409,000
2007	632	73.7	62.19	98,402,304	549,500
2008	638	72.3	56.34	88,303,589	501,000
2009	653	71.3	89.75	137,441,992	440,000
2010	634	69.6	91.96	145,041,200	486,000

[1]Income from investment banking, advisory, brokerage and underwriting fees and annuity commissions.
[2]Due to a 2006 redefinition of what constitutes a "small" bank holding company, most BHCs with less than $500 million in consolidated assets were exempt from filing detailed noninterest fee income data. The change reduced the number of BHCs that file the data by 1,300. The lower number of these small BHCs drove national means and medians higher.
Source: Michael White Bank Investment Fee Income Report - 2011.

BHCs: Securities Activities

TOP TEN BANK HOLDING COMPANIES IN INVESTMENT FEE INCOME, 2009-2010
($000)

| Rank | Bank holding company | State | Investment fee income | | | | 2010 Assets |
			2009	2010	Percent change	Percent of noninterest income, 2010	
1	Morgan Stanley	NY	$14,805,000	$17,423,000	17.68%	57.44%	$807,698,000
2	Bank of America Corporation	NC	15,834,181	15,427,405	-2.57	28.25	2,261,499,723
3	Goldman Sachs Group, Inc.	NY	12,630,000	12,923,000	2.32	38.45	908,580,000
4	JPMorgan Chase & Co.	NY	11,168,000	11,170,000	0.02	22.81	2,115,583,000
5	Wells Fargo & Company	CA	8,003,000	9,138,000	14.18	22.81	1,258,010,000
6	Citigroup Inc.	NY	8,458,000	6,415,000	-24.15	21.70	1,913,410,000
7	Franklin Resources, Inc.	CA	4,478,999	6,014,583	34.28	97.08	12,290,974
8	Taunus Corporation	NY	1,869,000	2,432,000	30.12	45.52	372,556,000
9	Bank of New York Mellon Corp.	NY	1,638,000	1,505,000	-8.12	13.71	247,222,000
10	RBC USA Holdco Corporation	NY	0	1,474,235	NA	59.26	99,150,441

NA=Not applicable.
Source: Michael White Bank Investment Fee Income Report - 2011.

BANK HOLDING COMPANY SECURITIES BROKERAGE INCOME, 2008-2010

| Year | Reporting securities brokerage income | | Securities brokerage income ($ billions) | Mean securities brokerage income | Median securities brokerage income |
	Number	Percent			
2008	510	57.8%	$18.09	$35,466,912	$335,500
2009	530	57.9	34.49	65,071,925	265,500
2010	526	57.7	35.10	66,724,935	323,000

Source: Michael White Bank Securities Brokerage Fee Income Report - 2011.

TOP TEN BANK HOLDING COMPANIES IN SECURITIES BROKERAGE INCOME, 2009-2010
($000)

| Rank | Bank holding company | State | Securities brokerage income | | | | 2010 Assets |
			2009	2010	Percent change	Percent of noninterest income, 2010	
1	Bank of America Corporation	NC	$10,016,884	$9,727,936	-2.88%	17.81%	$2,261,499,723
2	Morgan Stanley	NY	6,014,000	7,173,000	19.27	23.65	807,698,000
3	Wells Fargo & Company	CA	3,380,000	4,989,000	47.60	12.45	1,258,010,000
4	Goldman Sachs Group, Inc.	NY	3,981,000	3,592,000	-9.77	10.69	908,580,000
5	JPMorgan Chase & Co.	NY	2,904,000	2,804,000	-3.44	5.73	2,115,583,000
6	Bank of New York Mellon Corp.	NY	1,621,000	1,488,000	-8.20	13.55	247,222,000
7	Taunus Corporation	NY	950,000	951,000	0.11	17.80	372,556,000
8	Stifel Financial Corp.	MO	685,717	789,130	15.08	59.34	4,213,115
9	Regions Financial Corp.	AL	717,868	742,184	3.39	25.24	132,399,290
10	RBC USA Holdco Corporation	NY	0	634,289	NA	25.50	99,150,441

NA=Not available.

Source: Michael White Bank Securities Brokerage Fee Income Report - 2011.

BHCs: Insurance Activities

During 2010, 595 bank holding companies (BHCs) earned some type of insurance-related revenue, down from 609 the previous year. BHCs recorded total insurance revenue of $47.74 billion in 2010, including $13.30 billion in brokerage income (i.e., sales and referrals) and $34.31 billion from underwriting activities (i.e., generated by insurance companies owned by bank holding companies). Insurance income produced at the bank level (as opposed to the BHC level) totaled $3.06 billion in 2010, including $2.76 billion in brokerage income and $302.9 million in insurance income (see page 68). This brings total bank and BHC insurance income to $50.8 billion. Tables on page 62 and page 69 show the leading BHCs and banks with insurance underwriting operations.

**BANK HOLDING COMPANY INSURANCE BROKERAGE, UNDERWRITING AND
TOTAL INSURANCE FEE INCOME, 2006-2010**

Year	Insurance brokerage fee income[1]				
	Reporting insurance brokerage fee income		Insurance brokerage fee income ($ billions)	Mean insurance brokerage fee income	Median insurance brokerage fee income
	Number	Percent			
2006[2]	583	68.3%	$12.12	$20,787,417	$233,000
2007	588	68.5	12.25	20,827,117	166,000
2008	585	66.3	11.80	20,177,880	161,000
2009	606	66.2	12.36	20,396,550	139,000
2010	593	65.1	13.30	22,480,518	132,000

Year	Insurance underwriting fee income[3]				
	Reporting insurance underwriting fee income		Insurance underwriting fee income ($ billions)	Mean insurance underwriting fee income ($ millions)	Median insurance underwriting fee income
	Number	Percent			
2006[2]	77	9.0%	$31.35	$407.1	$720,000
2007	72	8.4	31.42	436.4	$609,500
2008	66	7.5	30.73	465.6	$497,000
2009	69	7.5	34.88	505.5	$509,000
2010	68	7.5	34.41	506.1	$499,500

Year	Total insurance fee income				
	Reporting total insurance fee income		Total insurance fee income ($ billions)	Mean total insurance fee income ($ millions)	Median total insurance fee income
	Number	Percent			
2006[2]	586	68.6%	$43.46	$74.17	$267,500
2007	592	69.0	43.66	73.76	190,500
2008	588	66.7	42.53	72.34	184,500
2009	609	66.5	47.24	77.57	155,000
2010	595	65.3	47.74	80.24	156,000

[1]Income from nonunderwriting activities, mostly from insurance product sales and referrals, service charges and commissions, and fees earned from insurance and annuity sales. [2]Due to a 2006 redefinition of what constitutes a "small" bank holding company, most BHCs with less than $500 million in consolidated assets were exempt from filing detailed noninterest fee income data. The change reduced the number of BHCs that file the data by 1,300. The lower number of these small BHCs drove national means and medians higher, mainly for insurance brokerage fee income. [3]Income from underwriting activities.

Source: Michael White-Prudential Bank Insurance Fee Income Report - 2011.

TOP TEN BANK HOLDING COMPANIES IN INSURANCE BROKERAGE FEE INCOME, 2009-2010[1]

($000)

| Rank | Bank holding company | State | Insurance brokerage fee income | | | | 2010 Assets |
			2009	2010	Percent change	Percent of noninterest income, 2010	
1	MetLife, Inc.	NY	$5,702,106	$6,276,232	10.07%	17.43%	$723,027,733
2	Citigroup Inc.	NY	1,040,000	1,862,000	79.04	6.30	1,913,410,000
3	Wells Fargo & Company	CA	1,725,000	1,780,000	3.19	4.44	1,258,010,000
4	BB&T Corporation	NC	922,489	933,349	1.18	33.05	157,081,396
5	Morgan Stanley	NY	191,000	298,000	56.02	0.98	807,698,000
6	American Express Company	NY	136,016	196,899	44.76	0.94	145,849,493
7	Discover Financial Services	IL	128,796	139,131	8.02	7.75	63,894,877
8	Goldman Sachs Group, Inc.	NY	124,000	131,000	5.65	0.39	908,580,000
9	Ally Financial Inc.	MI	122,000	110,000	-9.84	1.22	172,006,000
10	Regions Financial Corp.	AL	110,721	107,920	-2.53	3.67	132,399,290

[1]Income from nonunderwriting activites, insurance product sales and referrals, service charges and commissions, and fees earned from insurance and annuity sales.

Source: Michael White-Prudential Bank Insurance Fee Income Report - 2011.

TOP TEN BANK HOLDING COMPANIES IN INSURANCE UNDERWRITING NET INCOME, 2010

($000)

Rank	Bank holding company	State	Total insurance underwriting net income	Total net income/loss	Insurance net income as a percent of total net income	Assets
1	MetLife, Inc.	NY	$2,692,678	$2,884,028	93.37%	$723,027,733
2	Bank of America Corporation	NC	794,930	-2,238,025	NA	2,261,499,723
3	Wells Fargo & Company	CA	611,000	12,362,000	4.94	1,258,010,000
4	Ally Financial Inc.	MI	552,000	1,075,000	51.35	172,006,000
5	Citigroup Inc.	NY	524,000	10,602,000	4.94	1,913,410,000
6	Goldman Sachs Group, Inc.	NY	195,000	8,354,000	2.33	908,580,000
7	JPMorgan Chase & Co.	NY	121,000	17,370,000	0.70	2,115,583,000
8	American Express Company	NY	94,138	4,057,174	2.32	145,849,493
9	HSBC North America Holdings Inc.	NY	72,038	-445,916	NA	343,681,793
10	BB&T Corporation	NC	33,384	816,050	4.09	157,081,396

NA=Not applicable.

Source: Michael White-Prudential Bank Insurance Fee Income Report - 2011.

Convergence

BHCs: Insurance Activities/Annuities Activities

**TOP TEN BANK HOLDING COMPANIES IN
TOTAL INSURANCE PREMIUMS UNDERWRITTEN, 2009-2010**
($000)

Rank	Bank holding company	State	Total insurance premiums			2010 Assets
			2009	2010	Percent change	
1	MetLife, Inc.	NY	$26,460,448	$27,393,880	3.53%	$723,027,733
2	Bank of America Corporation	NC	2,296,617	2,206,734	-3.91	2,261,499,723
3	Citigroup Inc.	NY	1,980,000	821,000	-58.54	1,913,410,000
4	Ally Financial Inc.	MI	806,000	816,000	1.24	172,006,000
5	JPMorgan Chase & Co.	NY	325,000	411,000	26.46	2,115,583,000
6	Goldman Sachs Group, Inc.	NY	318,000	356,000	11.95	908,580,000
7	Wells Fargo & Company	CA	392,000	340,000	-13.27	1,258,010,000
8	American Express Company	NY	293,020	255,291	-12.88	145,849,493
9	HSBC North America Holdings Inc.	NY	308,522	245,138	-20.54	343,681,793
10	RBC USA Holdco Corporation	NY	0	177,624	NA	99,150,441

NA=Not applicable.

Source: Michael White-Prudential Bank Insurance Fee Income Report - 2011.

BHCs: Annuities Activities

BANK HOLDING COMPANY MUTUAL FUND AND ANNUITY INCOME, 2006-2010

Year	Reporting mutual fund and annuity income		Mutual fund and annuity income ($ billions)	Mean mutual fund and annuity income	Median mutual fund and annuity income
	Number	Percent			
2006[1]	553	63.6%	$19.32	$34,943,586	$360,000
2007	555	64.7	22.81	41,102,155	432,000
2008	554	62.8	21.97	39,648,787	399,000
2009[2]	336	36.7	20.18	60,069,405	714,000
2010	322	35.4	23.23	72,138,161	863,000

[1]Due to a 2006 redefinition of what constitutes a "small" bank holding company, most BHCs with less than $500 million in consolidated assets were exempt from filing detailed noninterest fee income data. The change reduced the number of BHCs that file the data by 1,300. The lower number of these small BHCs drove national means and medians higher.
[2]Effective 2009, only banks with assets greater than $1 billion are required to report combined mutual fund and annuity fee income. Hence, the large decline in 2009 in banks reporting that form of fee income.

Source: Michael White Bank Mutual Fund and Annuity Fee Income Report - 2011.

TOP TEN BANK HOLDING COMPANIES IN PROPRIETARY
MUTUAL FUND AND ANNUITIES ASSETS UNDER MANAGEMENT, 2009-2010
($000)

| Rank | Bank holding company | State | Proprietary mutual fund and annuities assets under management | | Percent change | 2010 Assets |
			2009	2010		
1	JPMorgan Chase & Co.	NY	$757,815,000	$713,952,000	-5.79%	$2,115,583,000
2	Bank of New York Mellon Corp.	NY	333,106,000	322,367,000	-3.22	247,222,000
3	Wells Fargo & Company	CA	250,825,000	237,606,000	-5.27	1,258,010,000
4	Goldman Sachs Group, Inc.	NY	274,312,000	227,404,000	-17.10	908,580,000
5	State Street Corporation	MA	133,684,912	163,982,022	22.66	158,890,975
6	Taunus Corporation	NY	127,394,000	113,215,000	-11.13	372,556,000
7	Northern Trust Corporation	IL	100,020,930	99,670,267	-0.35	83,843,874
8	U.S. Bancorp	MN	80,282,000	65,296,000	-18.67	307,786,000
9	Bank of America Corporation	NC	211,387,091	61,356,316	-70.97	2,261,499,723
10	RBC USA Holdco Corporation	NY	0	43,722,000	NA	99,150,441

NA=Not applicable.

Source: Michael White Bank Mutual Fund & Annuity Fee Income Report - 2011.

TOP TEN BANK HOLDING COMPANIES IN MUTUAL FUND AND ANNUITY FEE INCOME, 2009-2010
($000)

| Rank | Bank holding company | State | Mutual fund and annuity fee income | | Percent change | Percent of non-interest income, 2010 | 2010 Assets |
			2009	2010			
1	Franklin Resources, Inc.	CA	$4,041,367	$5,508,100	36.29%	88.91%	$12,290,974
2	Wells Fargo & Company	CA	3,144,000	4,847,000	54.17	12.10	1,258,010,000
3	MetLife, Inc.	NY	3,084,002	3,751,522	21.64	10.42	723,027,733
4	JPMorgan Chase & Co.	NY	2,136,000	2,123,000	-0.61	4.34	2,115,583,000
5	Morgan Stanley	NY	1,403,000	1,741,000	24.09	5.74	807,698,000
6	Bank of New York Mellon Corp.	NY	978,000	903,000	-7.67	8.22	247,222,000
7	Goldman Sachs Group, Inc.	NY	815,000	801,000	-1.72	2.38	908,580,000
8	Bank of America Corporation	NC	1,281,401	589,910	-53.96	1.08	2,261,499,723
9	Taunus Corporation	NY	354,000	352,000	-0.56	6.59	372,556,000
10	RBC USA Holdco Corporation	NY	0	243,461	NA	9.79	99,150,441

NA=Not applicable.

Source: Michael White Bank Mutual Fund & Annuity Fee Income Report - 2011.

Convergence

BHCs: Annuities Activities

BANK HOLDING COMPANY ANNUITY COMMISSIONS, 2008-2010

| Year | Reporting annuity commissions | | Annuity commissions ($ billions) | Mean annuity commissions | Median annuity commissions |
	Number	Percent			
2008	385	43.7%	$2.61	$6,768,091	$227,000
2009	392	42.8	2.62	6,689,403	210,000
2010	386	42.4	2.57	6,669,065	199,000

Source: Michael White-ABIA Bank Annuity Fee Income Report - 2011.

TOP TEN BANK HOLDING COMPANIES IN ANNUITY COMMISSIONS, 2009-2010
($000)

| Rank | Bank holding company | State | Annuity commissions | | | | 2010 Assets |
			2009	2010	Percent change	Percent of noninterest income, 2010	
1	Wells Fargo & Company	CA	$678,000	$706,000	4.13%	1.76%	$1,258,010,000
2	Morgan Stanley	NY	253,000	331,000	30.83	1.09	807,698,000
3	JPMorgan Chase & Co.	NY	328,000	259,000	-21.04	0.53	2,115,583,000
4	Bank of America Corporation	NC	251,828	179,383	-28.77	0.33	2,261,499,723
5	Regions Financial Corp.	AL	93,532	102,807	9.92	3.50	132,399,290
6	RBC USA Holdco Corporation	NY	0	86,955	NA	3.50	99,150,441
7	PNC Financial Services Group	PA	121,284	77,013	-36.50	1.31	264,414,112
8	Suntrust Banks, Inc.	GA	80,455	63,267	-21.36	1.84	172,875,298
9	Keycorp	OH	60,725	59,199	-2.51	3.16	90,795,572
10	U.S. Bancorp	MN	66,000	56,000	-15.15	0.67	307,786,000

NA=Not applicable.

Source: Michael White-ABIA Bank Annuity Fee Income Report - 2011.

Banks: Securities, Insurance and Annuities Activities

The preceding charts showed activities at the bank holding company level. Pages 65-74 show activities at the bank level, as tracked by Michael White Associates. The Michael White charts in the following section focus on institutions that have generated such income either directly or through bank subsidiaries and report the data at the bank level, rather than at the bank holding company level. Banks reported $9.86 billion in investment fee income in 2010, down 17.8 percent from the previous year.

BANK INVESTMENT BANKING, ADVISORY AND UNDERWRITING INCOME, 2008-2010

Year	Reporting investment banking, advisory and underwriting income		Investment banking, advisory and underwriting income ($ billions)	Mean investment banking, advisory and underwriting income	Median investment banking, advisory and underwriting income
	Number	Percent			
2008	688	9.2%	$5.27	$7,656,314	$65,000
2009	622	8.6	6.61	10,625,217	57,500
2010	570	8.2	5.30	9,296,068	66,500

Source: Michael White Bank Investment Fee Income Report - 2011.

TOP TEN BANKS IN INVESTMENT BANKING, ADVISORY AND UNDERWRITING INCOME, 2009-2010
($000)

Rank	Bank	State	Investment banking, advisory and underwriting income		Percent change	Percent of noninterest income, 2010	2010 Assets
			2009	2010			
1	JPMorgan Chase Bank, N.A.	OH	$3,959,000	$3,235,000	-18.29%	9.05%	$1,631,621,000
2	Bank of America, N.A.	NC	687,692	298,712	-56.56	1.12	1,482,278,257
3	Deutsche Bank Trust Company Americas	NY	83,000	170,000	104.82	14.81	45,504,000
4	Fifth Third Bank	OH	123,560	139,354	12.78	5.41	108,971,662
5	Goldman Sachs Bank USA	NY	161,000	133,000	-17.39	4.23	89,447,000
6	PNC Bank, N.A.	DE	87,670	124,089	41.54	2.66	256,638,747
7	State Street Bank and Trust Company	MA	114,195	118,288	3.58	2.00	155,528,576
8	KeyBank N.A.	OH	118,241	113,686	-3.85	7.19	88,591,610
9	Wells Fargo Bank, N.A.	SD	10,000	109,000	990.00	0.38	1,102,278,000
10	U.S. Bank N.A.	OH	162,712	108,114	-33.55	1.37	302,259,544

Source: Michael White Bank Investment Fee Income Report - 2011.

Convergence

Banks: Securities Activities

- From 2006 to 2010, banks bought an average of 42 securities firms each year. (See Chapter 7: Mergers and Acquisitions of U.S. Securities Firms.)

BANK INVESTMENT FEE INCOME, 2006-2010[1]

Year	Reporting investment fee income		Investment fee income ($ billions)	Mean investment fee income	Median investment fee income
	Number	Percent			
2006	2,228	28.4%	$11.97	$5,370,943	$85,000
2007	2,216	28.8	14.21	6,412,762	110,000
2008	2,150	28.7	13.28	6,178,356	115,000
2009	2,034	28.1	12.00	5,898,968	95,000
2010	1,905	27.5	9.86	5,178,409	109,000

[1]Income from investment banking, advisory and underwriting, securities brokerage and annuity commissions.

Source: Michael White Bank Investment Fee Income Report - 2011.

TOP TEN BANKS IN INVESTMENT FEE INCOME, 2009-2010[1]
($000)

Rank	Bank	State	Investment fee income		Percent change	Percent of noninterest income, 2010	2010 Assets
			2009	2010			
1	JPMorgan Chase Bank, N.A.	OH	$5,259,000	$4,553,000	-13.42%	12.74%	$1,631,621,000
2	Bank of America, N.A.	NC	2,204,615	1,052,768	-52.25	3.95	1,482,278,257
3	Wells Fargo Bank, N.A.	SD	272,000	472,000	73.53	1.64	1,102,278,000
4	PNC Bank, N.A.	DE	326,970	337,106	3.10	7.22	256,638,747
5	Fifth Third Bank	OH	192,528	208,551	8.32	8.09	108,971,662
6	KeyBank N.A.	OH	193,876	200,818	3.58	12.71	88,591,610
7	State Street Bank and Trust Company	MA	167,904	178,640	6.39	3.01	155,528,576
8	Deutsche Bank Trust Company Americas	NY	83,000	170,000	104.82	14.81	45,504,000
9	Goldman Sachs Bank USA	NY	161,000	133,000	-17.39	4.23	89,447,000
10	Citibank, N.A.	NV	68,000	125,000	83.82	0.76	1,154,293,000

[1]Income from broker-dealer activities such as investment banking, advisory and underwriting; securities brokerage; and annuity commissions.

Source: Michael White Bank Investment Fee Income Report - 2011.

BANK SECURITIES BROKERAGE INCOME, 2008-2010

Year	Reporting securities brokerage income		Securities brokerage income ($ billions)	Mean securities brokerage income	Median securities brokerage income
	Number	Percent			
2008	1,585	21.1%	$7.01	$4,424,686	$87,000
2009	1,525	21.1	4.57	2,993,721	71,000
2010	1,447	20.9	3.85	2,657,839	88,000

Source: Michael White Bank Securities Brokerage Fee Income Report - 2011.

TOP TEN BANKS IN SECURITIES BROKERAGE INCOME, 2009-2010
($000)

Rank	Bank	State	Securities brokerage income		Percent change	Percent of noninterest income, 2010	2010 Assets
			2009	2010			
1	JPMorgan Chase Bank, N.A.	OH	$1,300,000	$1,318,000	1.38%	3.69%	$1,631,621,000
2	Bank of America, N.A.	NC	1,494,211	754,056	-49.53	2.83	1,482,278,257
3	Wells Fargo Bank, N.A.	SD	262,000	362,000	38.17	1.26	1,102,278,000
4	PNC Bank, N.A.	DE	118,021	136,004	15.24	2.91	256,638,747
5	The Bank of New York Mellon	NY	161,000	102,000	-36.65	1.64	181,855,000
6	Chase Bank USA, N.A.	DE	86,184	80,268	-6.86	2.36	131,082,741
7	Citibank, N.A.	NV	43,000	70,000	62.79	0.42	1,154,293,000
8	State Street Bank and Trust Company	MA	53,709	60,352	12.37	1.02	155,528,576
9	RBS Citizens, N.A.	RI	36,014	48,331	34.20	4.90	107,835,697
10	Morgan Stanley Private Bank, N.A.	NY	0	45,556	NA	34.74	7,503,099

NA=Not applicable.

Source: Michael White Bank Securities Brokerage Fee Income Report - 2011.

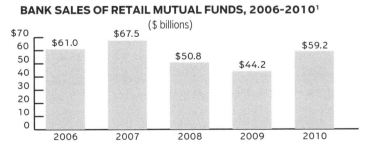

BANK SALES OF RETAIL MUTUAL FUNDS, 2006-2010[1]
($ billions)

- Bank sales of retail mutual funds rose to $59.2 billion in 2010 from $44.2 billion in 2009 but were still below the record $67.5 billion total for 2007.

[1] Estimated.

Source: Kehrer-LIMRA.

Convergence

Banks: Insurance Activities

See pages 59-62 for bank holding companies' insurance activities.

BANK INSURANCE BROKERAGE, UNDERWRITING AND TOTAL INSURANCE FEE INCOME, 2006-2010

Year	Insurance brokerage fee income[1]				
	Reporting insurance brokerage fee income		Insurance brokerage fee income ($ billions)	Mean insurance brokerage fee income	Median insurance brokerage fee income
	Number	Percent			
2006	3,648	46.5%	$4.08	$1,117,370	$20,000
2007	3,519	45.7	4.04	1,149,359	18,000
2008	3,372	45.0	3.51	1,041,330	18,000
2009	3,249	44.8	3.45	1,063,287	15,000
2010	3,080	44.5	2.76	895,653	14,000

Year	Insurance underwriting fee income[2]				
	Reporting insurance underwriting fee income		Insurance underwriting fee income ($ millions)	Mean insurance underwriting fee income	Median insurance underwriting fee income
	Number	Percent			
2006	227	2.9%	$354.8	$1,563,141	$6,000
2007	247	3.2	414.9	1,679,781	8,000
2008	223	3.0	459.3	2,059,534	9,000
2009	209	2.9	431.1	2,062,852	7,000
2010	179	2.7	302.9	1,691,922	5,000

Year	Total insurance fee income				
	Reporting insurance fee income		Total insurance fee income ($ billions)	Mean total insurance fee income	Median total insurance fee income
	Number	Percent			
2006	3,774	48.2%	$4.43	$1,174,085	$19,000
2007	3,625	47.0	4.46	1,230,207	18,000
2008	3,468	46.3	3.97	1,145,210	17,000
2009	3,332	46.0	3.89	1,166,193	15,000
2010	3,156	45.6	3.06	970,046	13,000

[1]Income from non-underwriting activities, mostly from insurance product sales and referrals, service charges and commissions, and fees earned from insurance and annuity sales.
[2]Income from underwriting activities.

Source: Michael White-Prudential Bank Insurance Fee Income Report - 2011.

TOP TEN BANKS IN INSURANCE BROKERAGE FEE INCOME, 2009-2010
($000)

| Rank | Bank | State | Insurance brokerage fee income | | | | 2010 Assets |
			2009	2010	Percent change	Percent of noninterest income, 2010	
1	Branch Banking and Trust Company	NC	$963,126	$930,372	-3.40%	41.96%	$150,828,452
2	Citibank, N.A.	NV	714,000	743,000	4.06	4.50	1,154,293,000
3	Discover Bank	DE	128,796	139,131	8.02	9.69	62,457,738
4	Bank of America, N.A.	NC	172,029	100,377	-41.65	0.38	1,482,278,257
5	BancorpSouth Bank	MS	81,351	82,602	1.54	33.90	13,620,949
6	Eastern Bank	MA	58,627	55,427	-5.46	42.31	6,590,094
7	TD Bank, N.A.	DE	53,717	50,253	-6.45	3.66	168,748,912
8	First Niagara Bank, N.A.	NY	0	50,228	NA	28.30	21,029,999
9	Compass Bank	AL	50,366	42,132	-16.35	5.37	63,311,543
10	Associated Bank, N.A.	WI	41,187	41,662	1.15	13.74	21,598,387

NA=Not applicable.

Source: Michael White Bank Securities Brokerage Fee Income Report - 2011.

TOP TEN BANKS IN INSURANCE UNDERWRITING INCOME, 2010
($000)

| Rank | Bank | State | Insurance underwriting income | | | Assets |
			Amount	Percent of total insurance income	Percent of noninterest income	
1	JPMorgan Chase Bank, N.A.	OH	$84,000	80.77%	0.24%	$1,631,621,000
2	Wells Fargo Bank, N.A.	SD	56,000	57.73	0.19	1,102,278,000
3	SunTrust Bank	GA	38,465	99.36	1.46	162,509,568
4	Bank of America, N.A.	NC	35,960	26.38	0.13	1,482,278,257
5	PNC Bank, N.A.	DE	23,427	47.14	0.50	256,638,747
6	U.S. Bank N.A.	OH	20,221	99.02	0.26	302,259,544
7	HSBC Bank USA, N.A.	VA	9,341	52.48	0.33	181,118,463
8	Fifth Third Bank	OH	7,672	28.82	0.30	108,971,662
9	Branch Banking and Trust Company	NC	3,831	0.41	0.17	150,828,452
10	Manufacturers and Traders Trust Company	NY	3,664	9.32	0.32	67,054,535

Source: Michael White-Prudential Bank Insurance Fee Income Report - 2011.

Banks: Insurance Activities

TOP TEN BANKS IN TOTAL INSURANCE FEE INCOME, 2009-2010
($000)

| Rank | Bank | State | Insurance fee income | | | | 2010 Assets |
			2009	2010	Percent change	Percent of noninterest income, 2010	
1	Branch Banking and Trust Company	NC	$966,438	$934,203	-3.34%	42.13%	$150,828,452
2	Citibank, N.A.	NV	714,000	743,000	4.06	4.50	1,154,293,000
3	Discover Bank	DE	128,796	139,131	8.02	9.69	62,457,738
4	Bank of America, N.A.	NC	220,379	136,337	-38.14	0.51	1,482,278,257
5	JPMorgan Chase Bank, N.A.	OH	112,000	104,000	-7.14	0.29	1,631,621,000
6	Wells Fargo Bank, N.A.	SD	80,000	97,000	21.25	0.34	1,102,278,000
7	BancorpSouth Bank	MS	81,354	82,604	1.54	33.90	13,620,949
8	Eastern Bank	MA	58,627	55,427	-5.46	42.31	6,590,094
9	TD Bank, N.A.	DE	53,717	50,253	-6.45	3.66	168,748,912
10	First Niagara Bank, N.A.	NY	[1]	50,228	NA	28.30	21,029,999

[1] First Niagara Bank was not regulated by the Office of Thrift Supervision in 2009 and therefore was exempt from reporting these data. NA=Not applicable.

Source: Michael White-Prudential Bank Insurance Fee Income Report - 2011.

Banks In Insurance Surveys

The preceding pages show Michael White Associates data on the insurance activities of banks and bank holding companies, based on the firm's analysis of Federal Reserve and FDIC data. The charts on pages 70-71 provide data on banks in insurance, based on research by Kehrer-LIMRA and SNL.

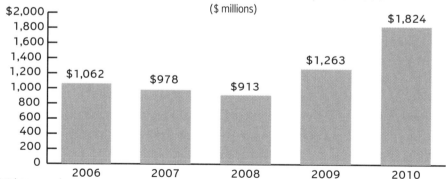

BANK INDIVIDUAL LIFE INSURANCE SALES, 2006-2010[1]
($ millions)

- 2006: $1,062
- 2007: $978
- 2008: $913
- 2009: $1,263
- 2010: $1,824

[1] Based on total new premium.
Source: Kehrer-LIMRA.

WEIGHTED BANK SALES OF INDIVIDUAL LIFE INSURANCE, 2006-2010[1]

Year	Sales ($ millions)	Share of industry annualized premium
2006	$261	2.0%
2007	227	1.6
2008	176	1.3
2009	203	1.8
2010	277	NA

[1]The weighted premium method of calculating annual sales volume emphasizes recurring premiums, i.e., policies with periodic payments. It deducts 90 percent of single premium sales, i.e., policies with one-time payments.
NA=Data not available.

Source: Kehrer-LIMRA.

- Weighted bank sales of individual life insurance rose 36.5 percent in 2010.

BANK PURCHASES OF INSURANCE AGENCIES, 2006-2010[1]

	2006	2007	2008	2009	2010
Number of deals	65	62	56	26	26
Deal value[2] ($ millions)	$45.6	$101.1	$124.0	$25.5	$13.4

[1]Target is an insurance broker and buyer is a bank or thrift. List does not include terminated deals.
[2]At announcement.

Source: SNL Financial LC.

- The value of bank/agency deals dropped by 47.5 percent in 2010, while the number of deals held steady.

BANKS' DISTRIBUTION METHODS FOR MARKETING LIFE INSURANCE

Method	Percent of banks surveyed
Financial consultants	95%
Platform banker[1]	57
Direct response	26
Advanced agents	16
Agents in standalone offices	9
Referrals to outside agencies	5
Retail agents in branches	1

[1]Customer service area in bank lobby.

Source: 2009/2010 Kehrer-LIMRA Bank Life Insurance Sales Study.

BANK MUTUAL FUND AND ANNUITY INCOME, 2006-2010

Year	Reporting mutual fund and annuity income		Mutual fund and annuity income ($ billions)	Mean mutual fund and annuity income	Median mutual fund and annuity income
	Number	Percent			
2006	1,902	24.3%	$5.38	$2,830,081	$97,000
2007	1,841	23.9	5.80	3,152,999	112,000
2008	1,737	23.2	5.14	2,960,917	115,000
2009[1]	338	4.7	4.10	12,140,453	669,500
2010	345	5.0	2.80	8,107,110	718,000

[1]Effective 2009 only banks with assets over $1 billion are required to report combined mutual fund and annuity fee income, causing a large decline in such income.
Source: Michael White Bank Mutual Fund and Annuity Fee Income Report - 2011.

TOP TEN BANKS IN MUTUAL FUND AND ANNUITY INCOME, 2009-2010
($000)

Rank	Bank	State	Mutual fund and annuity commissions				2010 Assets
			2009	2010	Percent change	Percent of noninterest income, 2010	
1	Bank of America, N.A.	NC	$1,043,153	$570,102	-45.35%	2.14%	$1,482,278,257
2	Wells Fargo Bank, N.A.	SD	262,000	353,000	34.73	1.23	1,102,278,000
3	PNC Bank, N.A.	DE	244,972	215,381	-12.08	4.61	256,638,747
4	JPMorgan Chase Bank, N.A.	OH	483,000	176,000	-63.56	0.49	1,631,621,000
5	State Street Bank and Trust Company	MA	131,436	148,827	13.23	2.51	155,528,576
6	U.S. Bank N.A.	OH	162,722	108,187	-33.51	1.37	302,259,544
7	RBS Citizens, N.A.	RI	75,731	82,497	8.93	8.37	107,835,697
8	Fifth Third Bank	OH	87,689	82,479	-5.94	3.20	108,971,662
9	Chase Bank USA, N.A.	DE	85,942	80,268	-6.60	2.36	131,082,741
10	Branch Banking and Trust Company	NC	70,482	72,551	2.94	3.27	150,828,452

Source: Michael White Bank Mutual Fund and Annuity Fee Income Report - 2011.

BANK ANNUITY COMMISSIONS, 2008-2010

Year	Reporting annuity commissions		Annuity commissions ($ millions)	Mean annuity commissions	Median annuity commissions
	Number	Percent			
2008	1,038	13.9%	$1,003.0	$966,083	$65,000
2009	985	13.6	824.2	836,743	63,000
2010	938	13.5	720.2	767,822	59,500

Source: Michael White-ABIA Bank Annuity Fee Income Report - 2011.

TOP TEN BANKS IN ANNUITY COMMISSIONS, 2009-2010

($000)

Rank	Bank	State	Annuity commissions				2010 Assets
			2009	2010	Percent change	Percent of noninterest income, 2010	
1	PNC Bank, N.A.	DE	$121,279	$77,013	-36.50%	1.65%	$256,638,747
2	KeyBank N.A.	OH	60,725	59,199	-2.51	3.75	88,591,610
3	Compass Bank	AL	43,095	50,784	17.84	6.47	63,311,543
4	Branch Banking and Trust Company	NC	46,074	44,090	-4.31	1.99	150,828,452
5	RBS Citizens, N.A.	RI	39,717	34,166	-13.98	3.47	107,835,697
6	Regions Bank	AL	29,364	30,602	4.22	1.70	128,372,729
7	Manufacturers and Traders Trust Co.	NY	39,011	29,740	-23.77	2.60	67,054,535
8	Bank of the West	CA	30,546	29,376	-3.83	7.62	57,652,826
9	Fifth Third Bank	OH	28,232	24,990	-11.48	0.97	108,971,662
10	Citibank, N.A.	NV	19,000	18,000	-5.26	0.11	1,154,293,000

Source: Michael White-ABIA Bank Annuity Fee Income Report - 2011.

TOP TEN BANKS IN PROPRIETARY MUTUAL FUND AND ANNUITIES ASSETS UNDER MANAGEMENT, 2010

($000)

Rank	Bank	State	Proprietary mutual fund and annuities assets under management	Assets
1	The Northern Trust Company	IL	$99,670,267	$70,373,450
2	U.S. Bank N.A.	OH	65,296,031	302,259,544
3	Bank of America, N.A.	NC	61,356,316	1,482,278,257
4	HSBC Bank USA, N.A.	VA	20,411,522	181,118,463
5	PNC Bank, N.A.	DE	16,971,026	256,638,747
6	Bessemer Trust Company, N.A.	NY	15,249,307	1,392,677
7	KeyBank N.A.	OH	12,640,533	88,591,610
8	Fifth Third Bank	OH	9,837,483	108,971,662
9	UMB Bank, N.A.	MO	9,089,117	10,694,374
10	Union Bank, N.A.	CA	8,034,073	78,674,854

Source: Michael White Bank Mutual Funds & Annuity Fee Income Report - 2011.

BANK SHARE OF FIXED AND VARIABLE ANNUITY PREMIUMS, 2001-2010
($ billions)

Year	Fixed annuity premiums			Variable annuity premiums		
	Total market	Banks	Bank share	Total market	Banks	Bank share
2001	$68.3	$27.4	40.1%	$111.0	$10.9	9.8%
2002	97.4	36.4	37.4	116.6	12.5	10.7
2003	89.4	33.1	37.0	129.4	16.2	12.5
2004	87.9	29.7	33.8	132.9	16.9	12.7
2005	79.5	21.8	27.4	136.9	17.9	13.1
2006	78.3	19.2	24.5	160.4	21.7	13.5
2007	72.8	16.9	23.2	184.0	25.5	13.9
2008	109.3	33.3	30.5	155.7	18.7	12.0
2009	110.6	31.4	28.4	128.0	13.1	10.2
2010	81.9	17.3	21.1	140.5	15.6	11.1

Source: Kehrer-LIMRA.

Insurance Industry: Banking Activities

A number of insurance companies have entered the banking arena by establishing thrifts institutions. A small number of insurance companies, including MetLife, have obtained financial holding company status, which allows them to engage in banking activities. Some insurers, such as USAA, own industrial banks.

TEN LARGEST THRIFTS OWNED BY INSURANCE COMPANIES BY ASSETS, 2010
($000, end of year)

Rank	Parent company	Subsidiary	Subsidiary total assets	Subsidiary total deposits
1	ING Groep N.V.	ING Bank FSB	$87,804,525	$77,666,241
2	United Services Automobile Association	USAA Federal Savings Bank	44,720,014	39,887,741
3	MetLife Inc.	MetLife Bank National Association	16,309,974	10,316,666
4	State Farm Mutual Automobile Insurance Co.	State Farm Bank FSB	15,117,941	9,380,612
5	United Services Automobile Association	USAA Savings Bank	14,444,489	703,203
6	Mutual of Omaha Insurance Co.	Mutual of Omaha Bank	4,876,840	3,996,612
7	Nationwide Mutual Group	Nationwide Bank	3,942,789	2,824,101
8	Ameriprise Financial Inc.	Ameriprise Bank FSB	3,862,039	3,547,022
9	Principal Financial Group Inc.	Principal Bank	2,408,485	2,219,338
10	Prudential Financial Inc.	Prudential Bank & Trust FSB	2,035,472	1,757,227

Source: SNL Financial LC.

TOP TEN WRITERS OF FIXED ANNUITIES SOLD THROUGH BANKS, 2010
($ millions)

Rank	Company	Premiums
1	AIG Companies	$4,236
2	New York Life	2,440
3	Symetra Financial	1,639
4	Lincoln Financial Group	1,287
5	Jackson National Life	977
6	Western & Southern Financial Group	906
7	Great American	729
8	Protective Life	719
9	Pacific Life	599
10	Principal Financial Group	543

Source: LIMRA International.

TOP TEN WRITERS OF VARIABLE ANNUITIES SOLD THROUGH BANKS, 2010
($ millions)

Rank	Company	Premiums
1	Prudential Annuities	$3,682
2	Jackson National Life	2,551
3	Nationwide Financial	1,720
4	MetLife	1,315
5	Pacific Life	1,023
6	Lincoln Financial Group	868
7	AEGON USA	645
8	Sun Life Financial	574
9	AXA Equitable	517
10	Hartford Life	491

Source: LIMRA International.

**TOP TEN UNDERWRITERS OF BANK LIFE PREMIUMS
BY TOTAL NEW PREMIUM, 2010**

($ millions)

Rank	Company	Premiums
1	Great West L & A	$379.6
2	Liberty Life of Boston	356.6
3	Transamerica	328.5
4	Hartford	87.5
5	OneAmerica	75.7
6	Protective	31.2
7	American General	24.8
8	CUNA	17.2
9	Vantis Life	4.1
10	SunLife	1.4

Source: Kehrer-LIMRA.

Industrial Banks

Nonbank Ownership of Industrial Banks

Industrial banks, also known as state-chartered industrial loan companies (ILCs), were first formed in the early part of the 20th century to make consumer loans and offer deposit accounts as part of a move to secure credit for low- and moderate-income workers. Their growth was initially spurred by a 1987 federal banking law modification that gave nonbanking companies a way to own FDIC-insured industrial banks. ILCs have broad banking powers and may be owned by banks and other financial services businesses such as finance companies, credit card issuers and securities firms as well as by nonfinancial businesses such as automakers and department stores. Some regulators oppose the access to the financial services industry that ILCs provide to nonbanks. In 2003 California and Colorado passed laws that prohibit nonfinancial firms from owning ILCs. There are about five dozen FDIC-insured ILCs, mostly headquartered in Utah and California. Five other states—Colorado, Minnesota, Indiana, Hawaii and Nevada—permit these charters. In 2010 the top 10 industrial banks had total assets of $123.3 billion.

LARGEST INDUSTRIAL BANKS BY ASSETS, 2010
($000)

Rank	Institution	Parent	Institution Assets
1	UBS Bank USA	UBS AG	$30,852,887
2	American Express Centurion Bank	American Express Company	29,947,154
3	USAA Savings Bank	USAA Insurance Group	14,444,489
4	BMW Bank of North America	BMW of North America, LLC	9,237,367
5	Capmark Bank	KKR Millennium Fund L.P.	8,819,365
6	Sallie Mae Bank	SLM Corporation	7,581,687
7	GE Capital Financial Inc.	General Electric Company	7,545,027
8	Beal Bank Nevada	Beal Financial Corporation	6,225,232
9	CapitalSource Bank	CapitalSource Inc.	6,134,904
10	Woodlands Commercial Bank	Lehman BrothersHoldings Inc.	2,557,493

Source: SNL Financial LC.

- A wide variety of firms own industrial banks. Such diverse firms as American Express (a financial services firm), USAA (an insurer) and BMW (an automaker) are among the owners of the largest institutions.

Overview

The insurance industry safeguards the assets of its policyholders by transferring risk from an individual or business to an insurance company. Insurance companies act as financial intermediaries in that they invest the premiums they collect for providing this service. Insurance company size is usually measured by net premiums written, that is, premium revenues less amounts paid for reinsurance. There are three main insurance sectors: property/casualty (P/C), life/health (L/H) and health insurance. Property/casualty consists mainly of auto, home and commercial insurance. Life/health consists mainly of life insurance and annuity products. Health insurance is offered by private health insurance companies and some P/C and L/H insurers, as well as by government programs such as Medicare.

Regulation

All types of insurance are regulated by the states, with each state having its own set of statutes and rules. State insurance departments oversee insurer solvency, market conduct and, to a greater or lesser degree, review and rule on requests for rate increases for coverage. The National Association of Insurance Commissioners develops model rules and regulations for the industry, many of which must be approved by state legislatures. The McCarran-Ferguson Act, passed by Congress in 1945, refers to continued state regulation of the insurance industry as being in the public interest. Under the 1999 Gramm-Leach-Bliley Financial Services Modernization Act, insurance activities—whether conducted by banks, broker-dealers or insurers—are regulated by the states.

The Dodd-Frank Wall Street Reform and Consumer Protection Act, the sweeping financial services regulatory overhaul enacted in 2010, established a Federal Insurance Office (FIO), an entity that reports to Congress and the President on the insurance industry. Insurance continues to be regulated by the states, but the act includes a narrow preemption of state insurance laws in areas where the FIO determines that the state law is inconsistent with a negotiated international agreement and treats a non-U.S. insurer less favorably than a U.S. insurer. The FIO covers insurers, including reinsurers, but not health insurance. In 2010 Michael McRaith, a former Illinois insurance commissioner, was named as the first director of the FIO. McRaith also has a seat on the Financial Stability Oversight Council (FSOC), another body created by Dodd-Frank. The FSOC is charged with designating financial institutions that present a systemic risk to the economy, making them subject to greater regulation. A summary of the Dodd-Frank Act is on page 213.

Accounting

Insurers are required to use statutory accounting principles (SAP) when filing annual financial reports with state regulators and the Internal Revenue Service. SAP, which evolved to enhance the industry's financial stability, is more conservative than the generally accepted accounting principles (GAAP), established by the independent Financial Accounting Standards Board (FASB). The Securities and Exchange Commission (SEC) requires publicly owned companies to report their financial results using GAAP rules. Insurers outside the United States use standards that differ from SAP and GAAP.

As global markets developed, the need for more uniform accounting standards became clear. In 2001 the International Accounting Standards Board (IASB), an independent international accounting standards setting organization, began work on a set of standards, called International Financial Reporting Standards (IFRS) that it hopes will be used around the world. Since 2001 over 100 countries have required or permitted the use of IFRS.

In 2007 the SEC voted to stop requiring non-U.S. companies that use IFRS to re-issue their financial reports for U.S. investors using GAAP. In 2008 the National Association of Insurance Commissioners began to explore ways to move from statutory accounting principles to IFRS. Also in 2008, the FASB and IASB undertook a joint project to develop a common and improved framework for financial reporting.

All Sectors

Distribution

Property/casualty and life insurance policies were once sold almost exclusively by agents—either by captive agents, representing one insurance company, or by independent agents, representing several companies. Insurance companies selling through captive agents and/or by mail, telephone or via the Internet are called "direct writers." However, the distinctions between direct writers and independent agency companies have been blurring since the 1990s, when insurers began to use multiple channels to reach potential customers. In addition, in the 1980s banks began to explore the possibility of selling insurance through independent agents, usually buying agencies for that purpose. (See Chapter 4: Convergence, page 55.) Other distribution channels include sales through professional organizations and through workplaces.

Mergers and Acquisitions

Global insurance-related mergers and acquisitions (M&A) were up significantly in 2010, following a sharp decline in 2009. In 2010 there were 721 M&A transactions with a reported value of $79.2 billion, compared with 601 transactions and a reported value of $52.4 billion in 2009, according to Conning Research and Consulting. Transactions and their values in 2010 were up 20 percent and 51 percent, respectively, from 2009. In terms of transaction value, distribution sector M&A value rose at the fastest pace, up 194 percent, followed by the life/annuity sector (up 85 percent), the services sector (up 47 percent) and the property/casualty sector (up 11 percent). In contrast, M&A transaction value in the health/managed care sector fell 56 percent. U.S. acquirers accounted for 54 percent of transaction value in 2010, up significantly from 20 percent in 2009. U.S. companies were the acquirers in 57 percent of all transactions in 2010, up from 51 percent in 2009. The number of transactions where a U.S. company was the acquirer and/or the target increased by 36 percent from 320 in 2009 to 436 in 2010, according to Conning, and the reported value increased by 224 percent from $14.4 billion in 2009 to $46.5 billion in 2010.

TOP TEN INSURANCE-RELATED MERGERS AND ACQUISITIONS REPORTED IN 2010[1]

Rank	Buyer	Country	Target	Country	Deal value ($ millions)[2]
1	MetLife, Inc.	U.S.	American Life Insurance Company/ Delaware American Life Insurance Company	U.S.	$15,545.1
2	Prudential Financial, Inc.	U.S.	AIG subsidiaries	U.S.	4,200.0
3	Berkshire Hathaway Inc.	U.S.	Asbestos and environmental pollution liabilities of CNA Financial	U.S.	2,000.0
4	Fairfax Financial Holdings Limited	Canada	Zenith National Insurance Corp.	U.S.	1,318.5
5	CVS Caremark Corporation	U.S.	Universal American Corp.	U.S.	1,250.0
6	ACE Limited	Switzerland	Rain and Hail Insurance Service Incorporated	U.S.	1,100.0
7	Investor group	Canada	Liberty Life Insurance Company	U.S.	628.1
8	QBE Insurance Group Limited	Australia	NAU Holding Company, LLC	U.S.	565.0
9	HealthSpring, Inc.	U.S.	Bravo Health, Inc.	U.S.	545.0
10	ACE Limited	Switzerland	New York Life Insurance subsidiaries	U.S.	425.0

[1] Target is a U.S.-domiciled insurance underwriter. List does not include terminated deals.
[2] At announcement.

Source: SNL Financial LC.

Profitability

ANNUAL RATE OF RETURN, GAAP ACCOUNTING, PROPERTY/CASUALTY, LIFE/HEALTH AND HEALTHCARE INSURANCE, 2006-2010

Year	Property/casualty		Life/health		Healthcare insurance[2]
	Stock	Mutual	Stock	Mutual	
2006	14.0%	9.0%	12.0%	12.0%	19.0%
2007	14.0	9.0	11.0	10.0	19.0
2008	3.0	1.5	9.0	-8.0	11.0
2009	7.0	3.5	7.0	0.0	14.0
2010	9.0	3.5	8.0	5.0	12.0

[1]Based on return on shareholders equity of insurance companies in the Fortune 500.
[2]Healthcare insurance and managed care.

Source: Fortune.

Net Premiums Written, Property/Casualty and Life/Health

PROPERTY/CASUALTY AND LIFE/HEALTH INSURANCE NET PREMIUMS WRITTEN, 2001-2010
($000)

Year	Property/casualty[1]	Life/health[2]	Total
2001	$320,763,542	$458,704,906	$779,468,448
2002	367,545,259	489,038,709	856,583,968
2003	404,214,743	478,033,311	882,248,054
2004	425,059,714	507,613,338	932,673,052
2005	426,794,082	520,607,848	947,401,930
2006	448,930,825	575,663,027	1,024,593,852
2007	446,938,523	610,322,595	1,057,261,118
2008	440,231,323	624,238,629	1,064,469,952
2009	422,917,708	508,923,002	931,840,710
2010	426,207,884	581,185,851	1,007,393,735
Percent change 2001-2010	**32.9%**	**26.7%**	**29.2%**

[1]Net premiums written, excluding state funds.
[2]Premium annuity considerations (fees for annuity contracts) and deposit-type funds for life/health insurance companies.

Source: SNL Financial LC.

GROWTH IN U.S. PREMIUMS, PROPERTY/CASUALTY AND LIFE/HEALTH INSURANCE, 2001-2010
(Percent change from prior year)

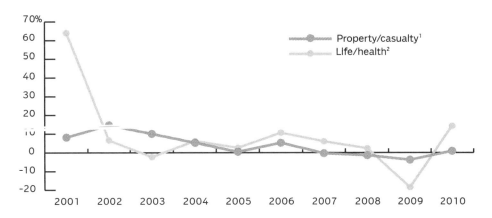

Legend:
- Property/casualty[1]
- Life/health[2]

[1]Net premiums written, excluding state funds.
[2]Premiums and annuity considerations (fees for annuity contracts) for life/health insurance companies. Includes deposit-type funds beginning in 2001.

Source: SNL Financial LC.

U.S. PROPERTY/CASUALTY AND LIFE/HEALTH INSURANCE PREMIUMS, 2010[1]

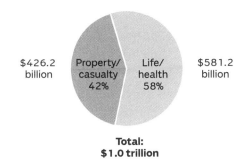

$426.2 billion — Property/casualty 42%

Life/health 58% — $581.2 billion

Total:
$1.0 trillion

[1]Property/casualty: net premiums written, excluding state funds; life/health: premiums, annuity considerations (fees for annuity contracts) and deposit-type funds.

Source: SNL Financial LC.

Insurance

All Sectors

- Over the last 10 years, employment in the insurance industry (all sectors) has averaged 2.0 percent of the total U.S. employment in private industry.

- Insurance industry employment fell by 1.2 percent in 2010. By sector the drop was 3.1 percent for the property/casualty industry, 1.8 percent for agency/brokerage jobs and 1.5 percent for reinsurance. Employment in the life sector grew by 1 percent.

EMPLOYMENT IN INSURANCE, 2001-2010
(000)

Year	Insurance companies[1]		Reinsurers	Insurance agencies, brokerages and related services[2]	Total industry
	Life, health and medical	Property/casualty			
2001	807.7	591.3	31.4	803.2	2,233.7
2002	791.1	590.0	31.7	820.4	2,233.2
2003	789.0	608.6	31.0	837.4	2,266.0
2004	764.4	604.4	29.8	860.1	2,258.6
2005	761.9	595.0	28.8	873.6	2,259.3
2006	787.4	597.4	28.0	890.8	2,303.7
2007	784.0	586.1	27.0	909.8	2,306.8
2008	797.6	571.2	27.9	908.5	2,305.2
2009	799.7	550.2	27.5	886.7	2,264.1
2010	807.3	533.1	27.1	870.5	2,238.0

[1]Described by the Bureau of Labor Statistics as "direct insurers."
[2]Includes claims adjusters, third-party administrators of insurance funds and other service personnel such as advisory and insurance ratemaking services.
Source: U.S. Department of Labor, Bureau of Labor Statistics.

U.S. Insurance Companies

An insurance company is said to be "domiciled" in the state that issued its primary license; it is "domestic" in that state. Once licensed in one state, it may seek licenses in other states as a "foreign" insurer. An insurer incorporated in a foreign country is called an "alien" insurer in the U.S. states in which it is licensed.

According to the National Association of Insurance Commissioners (NAIC), there were 2,689 P/C companies in the United States in 2010, compared with 2,737 in 2009. The L/H insurance industry consisted of 1,061 companies in 2010, compared with 1,106 in 2009, according to the NAIC.

DOMESTIC INSURANCE COMPANIES BY STATE, PROPERTY/CASUALTY AND LIFE/HEALTH INSURANCE, 2010

State	Property/ casualty	Life/ health	State	Property/ casualty	Life/ health
Alabama	20	7	Montana	4	2
Alaska	5	0	Nebraska	30	33
Arizona	51	190	Nevada	13	4
Arkansas	12	30	New Hampshire	46	2
California	117	15	New Jersey	68	9
Colorado	19	10	New Mexico	11	2
Connecticut	71	28	New York	197	81
Delaware	91	30	North Carolina	68	5
D.C.	6	3	North Dakota	17	3
Florida	130	11	Ohio	139	39
Georgia	34	16	Oklahoma	35	26
Hawaii	18	4	Oregon	13	4
Idaho	9	1	Pennsylvania	189	30
Illinois	193	58	Rhode Island	24	4
Indiana	77	31	South Carolina	22	10
Iowa	61	26	South Dakota	17	2
Kansas	27	11	Tennessee	19	13
Kentucky	8	7	Texas	225	136
Louisiana	32	45	Utah	13	16
Maine	18	1	Vermont	15	2
Maryland	37	6	Virginia	18	11
Massachusetts	54	14	Washington	20	10
Michigan	74	25	West Virginia	17	0
Minnesota	41	11	Wisconsin	180	22
Mississippi	15	19	Wyoming	3	0
Missouri	50	29	**United States**[1]	**2,689**	**1,061**

- Many insurance companies are part of larger organizations. According to A.M. Best, in 2010 the P/C insurance industry contained about 1,036 organizations (as opposed over 2,000 companies), including 624 stock (or public) organizations, 338 mutual organizations (firms owned by their policyholders) and 59 reciprocals (a type of self-insurance). The remainder consisted of Lloyd's organizations and state funds.

[1]Includes U.S. territories and possessions.

Source: Insurance Department Resources Report, 2010, published by the National Association of Insurance Commissioners (NAIC). Reprinted with permission. Further reprint or redistribution strictly prohibited without written permission of NAIC.

World Insurance Market

Outside the United States, the insurance industry is divided into life and nonlife or general insurance rather than life/health and property/casualty. World insurance premiums increased from $4.11 trillion in 2009 to $4.34 trillion in 2010, as economic growth helped drive up premiums, according to the latest Swiss Re *sigma* study. The study found that while capital continued to build in the nonlife sector, it remained below pre-crisis levels in the life sector.

- Nonlife premiums accounted for 42 percent of world premiums. Life insurance accounted for 58 percent.

WORLD LIFE AND NONLIFE INSURANCE PREMIUMS, 2008-2010[1]

(Direct premiums written, U.S. $ millions)

Year	Life	Nonlife[2]	Total
2008	$2,438,966	$1,780,013	$4,218,979
2009	2,367,442	1,742,193	4,109,635
2010	2,520,072	1,818,893	4,338,964

[1]Before reinsurance transactions.
[2]Includes accident and health insurance.
Source: Swiss Re, *sigma* database, *sigma* 2/2011.

Property/Casualty Insurance: Financial

Property/casualty insurance covers the property and liability losses of businesses and individuals. These losses range from damage and injuries resulting from car accidents to the cost of lawsuits stemming from faulty products and alleged professional misconduct. In terms of premiums written, private auto insurance is by far the largest single line, nearly three times greater than the next largest line, homeowners multiple peril. Property/casualty insurance companies tend to specialize in commercial or personal insurance, but some sell both, and some companies have expanded into other financial services sectors, including personal banking and mutual funds.

Property/casualty insurers invest largely in high-quality liquid securities, which can be sold quickly to pay for claims resulting from a major hurricane, earthquake or a man-made disaster such as a terrorist attack.

PROPERTY/CASUALTY INSURER FINANCIAL ASSET DISTRIBUTION, 2006-2010
($ billions)

	2006	2007	2008	2009	2010
Total financial assets	**$1,335.8**	**$1,385.8**	**$1,309.4**	**$1,387.6**	**$1,403.9**
Checkable deposits and currency	29.9	42.7	27.9	27.6	32.6
Money market fund shares	13.5	20.7	32.8	29.6	25.6
Security repurchase agreements[1]	1.9	3.6	4.4	4.5	3.8
Credit market instruments	864.1	869.3	853.4	886.7	890.6
Open market paper	16.4	13.3	19.1	9.8	7.9
U.S. government securities	232.0	197.1	179.9	204.7	207.5
Treasury	110.0	71.3	65.6	88.5	91.7
Agency- and GSE[2] backed securities	122.0	125.8	114.3	116.2	115.8
Municipal securities	335.2	371.3	381.9	369.4	348.4
Corporate and foreign bonds	277.0	282.9	267.5	298.3	322.6
Commercial mortgages	3.5	4.8	5.0	4.4	4.1
Corporate equities	227.0	236.2	193.3	219.8	219.2
Mutual fund shares	6.9	6.8	4.4	5.3	5.7
Trade receivables	87.0	85.4	86.7	83.0	83.8
Miscellaneous assets	105.5	121.1	106.6	131.1	142.6

[1]Short-term agreements to sell and repurchase government securities by a specified date at a set price. [2]Government-sponsored enterprise. Source: Board of Governors of the Federal Reserve System, June 9, 2011.

Financial Results

A property/casualty insurer must maintain a certain level of surplus to underwrite risks. This financial cushion is known as "capacity" or policyholders' surplus. When the industry is hit by high losses, such as a major hurricane, capacity is diminished. It can be restored by increases in net income, favorable investment returns, reinsuring more risk and/or raising additional capital. The industry's policyholders' surplus was a record $556.9 billion at year-end 2010, up $45.5 billion, or 8.9 percent, from $511.4 billion at year-end 2009, according to ISO. The 2010 surplus exceeds the previous record set in 2007, before the recession and credit crisis took its toll.

Insurers use various measures to gauge financial performance. The combined ratio after dividends is a measure of underwriting profitability. It reflects the percentage of each premium dollar an insurer spends on claims and expenses. The combined ratio does not take investment income into account. A combined ratio above 100 indicates an underwriting loss. In 2010 the combined ratio was 102.4 after dividends according to ISO, a deterioration from the combined ratio after dividends of 101.0 in 2009.

P/C INSURANCE INDUSTRY INCOME ANALYSIS, 2006-2010[1]

($ billions)

	2006	2007	2008	2009	2010
Net written premiums	$443.5	$440.6	$434.9	$418.4	$422.1
Percent change	4.2%	-0.6%	-1.3%	-3.8%	0.9%
Earned premiums	$435.5	$438.9	$438.3	$422.3	$420.5
Losses incurred	231.3	244.7	286.3	253.8	256.5
Loss adjustment expenses incurred	52.6	52.3	51.7	52.5	52.6
Other underwriting expenses	117.1	120.1	119.6	117.0	119.6
Policyholder dividends	3.4	2.4	2.0	2.0	2.3
Underwriting gain/loss	31.1	19.3	-21.2	-3.0	-10.4
Investment income	52.3	55.1	51.5	47.1	47.2
Miscellaneous income/loss	1.2	-1.0	0.4	0.9	1.0
Operating income/loss	84.6	73.4	30.6	45.0	37.8
Realized capital gains/losses	3.5	8.9	-19.8	-7.9	5.7
Incurred federal income taxes/credit	22.4	19.8	7.8	8.4	8.9
Net income after taxes	65.8	62.5	3.0	28.7	34.7

[1]Data in this chart may not agree with similar data shown elsewhere due to different sources.

Source: ISO.

- The U.S. property/casualty insurance industry posted a $10.4 billion net loss on underwriting in 2010, compared with a $3.0 billion loss in 2009. However, net income after taxes grew $6 billion during the same period, due to the $13.6 billion improvement in realized capital gains, according to ISO.

The ranking below is based on Fortune magazine's annual analysis of the 500 largest U.S. companies, based on revenues. Fortune organizes the 500 companies into broad industry categories. Each company is assigned one category, even though some companies are involved in several industries. For example, some of the leading property/casualty insurance companies also write significant amounts of life insurance.

TOP U.S. PROPERTY/CASUALTY COMPANIES BY REVENUES, 2010
($ millions)

Rank	Group	Revenues	Assets
1	Berkshire Hathaway	$136,185	$372,229
2	American International Group	104,417	683,443
3	State Farm Insurance Cos.	63,177	192,794
4	Liberty Mutual Insurance Group	33,193	112,350
5	Allstate	31,400	130,874
6	Travelers Cos.	25,112	105,181
7	Hartford Financial Services	22,383	318,346
8	Nationwide	20,265	148,702
9	United Services Automobile Association (USAA)	17,946	94,262
10	Progressive	14,963	21,150
11	Loews (CNA)	14,621	76,277
12	Chubb	13,319	50,249
13	Assurant	8,528	26,397
14	American Family Insurance Group	6,492	16,788
15	Fidelity National Financial	5,740	7,888
16	Auto-Owners Insurance	5,396	15,316
17	Erie Insurance Group	4,890	14,344
18	W.R. Berkley	4,724	17,529
19	American Financial Group	4,497	32,454

Source: Fortune.

Distribution Channels

Agency writers, whose products are sold by independent agents or brokers representing several companies; and direct writers, which sell their own products through captive agents by mail, telephone, the Internet and other means, each account for about half of the property/casualty market. There is a degree of overlap as many insurers use multiple channels.

Property/Casualty: Financial

A.M. Best organizes insurance into two main distribution channels: agency writers and direct writers. Its "agency writers" category includes insurers that distribute through independent agencies, brokers, general agents, and managing general agents. Its "direct writers" category includes insurers that distribute through the Internet, exclusive/captive agents, direct response, and affinity groups.

- In 2010 direct writers accounted for 51.4 percent of P/C insurance net premiums written and agency writers accounted for 47.2 percent, according to A.M. Best.*

- In the personal lines market, direct writers accounted for 70.7 percent of net premiums written in 2010 and agency writers accounted for 29.1 percent. Direct writers accounted for 69.8 percent of the homeowners market and agency writers accounted for 29.9 percent. Direct writers accounted for 71.1 percent of the personal auto market and agency writers accounted for 28.8 percent.*

- Agency writers accounted for 66.9 percent of commercial P/C net premiums written and direct writers accounted for 30.3 percent.*

*Unspecified distribution channels accounted for the remainder.

Traditionally, there has been a distinction between agents and brokers, with agents (whether captive or independent) representing the insurance company and brokers representing the client. Recently, the line between agencies and brokers has blurred, with intermediary firms operating as brokers and agents, depending on their jurisdiction and the type of risk.

TOP TEN COMMERCIAL INSURANCE BROKERS OF U.S. BUSINESS BY REVENUES, 2010[1]

($ millions)

Rank	Company	Brokerage revenues
1	Marsh & McLennan Cos. Inc.	$4,662.2
2	Aon Corp.	4,242.4
3	Willis Group Holdings P.L.C.	1,650.0
4	Wells Fargo Insurance Services USA Inc.	1,649.5
5	Arthur J. Gallagher & Co.	1,557.2
6	BB&T Insurance Services Inc.	1,078.6
7	Brown & Brown Inc.	964.0
8	USI Holdings Corp.	632.2
9	Lockton Cos. L.L.C.[2]	578.8
10	Hub International Ltd.	510.3

[1]Companies that derive more than 50 percent of revenues from commercial retail brokerage or employee benefits.
[2] Fiscal year ending April 30.

Source: Business Insurance, July 18, 2011.

Property/Casualty Insurance Industry Concentration

According to ISO, concentration in the property/casualty insurance sector as measured by the Herfindahl-Hirschman Index increased from 229 in 1980 to 357 in 2008, dipped to 351 in 2009, and then rebounded to 357 in 2010. The U.S. Department of Justice classifies any market with an HHI under 1,000 as unconcentrated and any market with an HHI over 1,800 as highly concentrated.

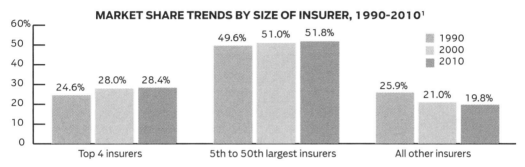

MARKET SHARE TRENDS BY SIZE OF INSURER, 1990-2010[1]

[1]Based on net premiums written, excluding state funds. Source: ISO.

Premiums by Line

In 2010 commercial lines net premiums written totaled $204.5 billion, or 48.0 percent, of property/casualty net premiums written. Personal lines totaled $221.6 billion, or 52.0 percent.

NET PREMIUMS WRITTEN BY LINE, PROPERTY/CASUALTY INSURANCE, 2008-2010[1]
($ millions)

| Lines of insurance | 2008 | 2009 | 2010 | Percent change from prior year | | | Percent of total, 2010 |
				2008	2009	2010	
Private passenger auto							
Liability	$94,536.0	$94,823.6	$97,674.4	-0.6%	0.3%	3.0%	22.9%
Collision and comprehensive	64,082.8	62,543.0	62,589.2	-0.8	-2.4	0.1	14.7
Total private passenger auto	158,618.8	157,366.6	160,263.6	-0.7	-0.8	1.8	37.6
Commercial auto							
Liability	17,832.6	16,574.5	16,238.3	-6.0	-7.1	-2.0	3.8
Collision and comprehensive	5,990.3	5,347.3	4,878.1	-10.0	-10.7	-8.8	1.1
Total commercial auto	23,822.9	21,921.8	21,116.4	-7.0	-8.0	-3.7	5.0
Fire	9,904.9	10,099.7	10,216.6	1.4	2.0	1.2	2.4
Allied lines	7,708.5	7,736.3	7,493.8	10.6	0.4	-3.1	1.8
Multiple peril crop	5,077.6	3,962.0	3,501.6	39.2	-22.0	-11.6	0.8
Federal flood[2]	3.2	21.0	6.1	-80.6	553.5	-70.7	[3]

(table continues)

NET PREMIUMS WRITTEN BY LINE, PROPERTY/CASUALTY INSURANCE, 2008-2010[1] (Cont'd)
($ millions)

Lines of insurance	2008	2009	2010	Percent change from prior year 2008	2009	2010	Percent of total, 2010
Farmowners multiple peril	$2,583.0	$2,608.7	$2,750.8	6.6%	1.0%	5.4%	0.6%
Homeowners multiple peril	56,404.9	57,679.7	61,303.4	1.5	2.3	6.3	14.4
Commercial multiple peril	30,223.9	28,866.8	28,847.0	-3.1	-4.5	-0.1	6.8
Mortgage guaranty	5,367.7	4,570.1	4,246.7	3.4	-14.9	-7.1	1.0
Ocean marine	3,094.3	2,935.7	2,738.9	-5.0	-5.1	-6.7	0.6
Inland marine	9,367.6	8,648.9	8,503.4	-3.8	-7.7	-1.7	2.0
Financial guaranty	3,171.6	1,793.4	1,371.9	4.4	-43.5	-23.5	0.3
Medical malpractice	9,521.1	9,206.6	9,092.3	-4.3	-3.3	-1.2	2.1
Earthquake	1,250.3	1,285.6	1,434.9	0.2	2.8	11.6	0.3
Accident and health[4]	7,156.3	6,705.9	7,506.8	0.8	-6.3	11.9	1.8
Workers compensation	36,523.0	32,009.9	31,479.3	-10.0	-12.4	-1.7	7.4
Excess workers compensation	926.5	941.1	799.5	NA	1.6	-15.0	0.2
Products liability	2,777.6	2,366.0	2,050.5	-15.9	-14.8	-13.3	0.5
Other liability[5]	38,484.5	36,031.1	35,678.5	-6.5	-6.4	-1.0	8.4
Aircraft	1,329.3	1,222.8	1,103.5	-24.5	-8.0	-9.8	0.3
Fidelity	1,140.6	1,105.4	1,077.9	-8.5	-3.1	-2.5	0.3
Surety	4,960.3	4,837.6	4,853.5	3.2	-2.5	0.3	1.1
Burglary and theft	160.6	152.0	167.1	-0.1	-5.3	9.9	[3]
Boiler and machinery	1,729.1	1,801.9	1,718.2	-0.7	4.2	-4.6	0.4
Credit	1,413.3	1,224.5	1,344.8	0.6	-13.4	9.8	0.3
Warranty	2,086.9	1,757.3	1,864.1	NA	-15.8	6.1	0.4
International	289.0	142.5	130.0	111.5	-50.7	-8.8	[3]
Reinsurance[6]	13,845.3	12,566.4	12,275.1	5.9	-9.2	-2.3	2.9
Other lines[7]	999.7	1,307.0	1,143.9	-66.2	30.7	-12.5	0.3
Total, all lines[8]	**$439,942.2**	**$422,874.5**	**$426,080.1**	**-1.5%**	**-3.9%**	**0.8%**	**100.0%**

[1]After reinsurance transactions, excluding state funds. [2]Provided by FEMA through participating private insurers. [3]Less than 0.1 percent. [4]Premiums from certain insurers that write health insurance but file financial statements with state regulators on a property/casualty basis. [5]Coverages protecting against legal liability resulting from negligence, carelessness or failure to act. [6]Only includes nonproportional reinsurance, an arrangement in which a reinsurer makes payments to an insurer whose losses exceed a predetermined amount. [7]Includese miscellaneous coverages. [8]May not match total premiums shown elsewhere in this book because of the use of different exhibits from SNL Financial LC. NA=Data not available.

Source: SNL Financial LC.

PREMIUMS WRITTEN BY LINE, PROPERTY/CASUALTY INSURANCE, 2010
($ billions)

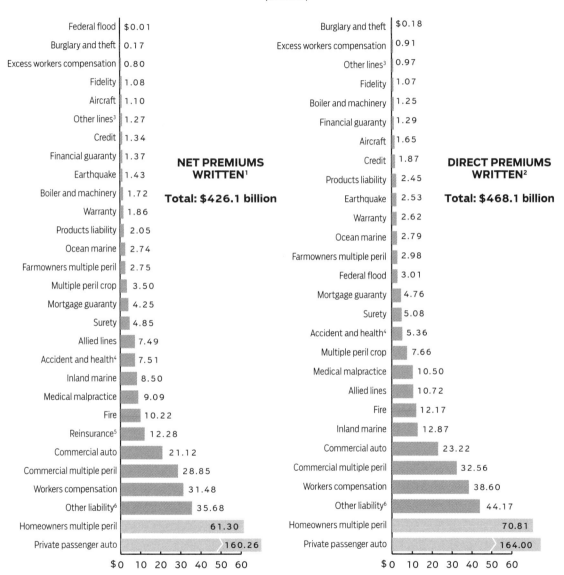

NET PREMIUMS WRITTEN[1]

Total: $426.1 billion

Line	$ billions
Federal flood	$0.01
Burglary and theft	0.17
Excess workers compensation	0.80
Fidelity	1.08
Aircraft	1.10
Other lines[3]	1.27
Credit	1.34
Financial guaranty	1.37
Earthquake	1.43
Boiler and machinery	1.72
Warranty	1.86
Products liability	2.05
Ocean marine	2.74
Farmowners multiple peril	2.75
Multiple peril crop	3.50
Mortgage guaranty	4.25
Surety	4.85
Allied lines	7.49
Accident and health[4]	7.51
Inland marine	8.50
Medical malpractice	9.09
Fire	10.22
Reinsurance[5]	12.28
Commercial auto	21.12
Commercial multiple peril	28.85
Workers compensation	31.48
Other liability[6]	35.68
Homeowners multiple peril	61.30
Private passenger auto	160.26

DIRECT PREMIUMS WRITTEN[2]

Total: $468.1 billion

Line	$ billions
Burglary and theft	$0.18
Excess workers compensation	0.91
Other lines[3]	0.97
Fidelity	1.07
Boiler and machinery	1.25
Financial guaranty	1.29
Aircraft	1.65
Credit	1.87
Products liability	2.45
Earthquake	2.53
Warranty	2.62
Ocean marine	2.79
Farmowners multiple peril	2.98
Federal flood	3.01
Mortgage guaranty	4.76
Surety	5.08
Accident and health[4]	5.36
Multiple peril crop	7.66
Medical malpractice	10.50
Allied lines	10.72
Fire	12.17
Inland marine	12.87
Commercial auto	23.22
Commercial multiple peril	32.56
Workers compensation	38.60
Other liability[6]	44.17
Homeowners multiple peril	70.81
Private passenger auto	164.00

[1]After reinsurance transactions, excluding state funds. [2]Before reinsurance transactions, includes some state funds. [3]Includes international and miscellaneous coverages. [4]Premiums from certain insurers that write health insurance but file financial statements with state regulators on a property/casualty rather than life/health basis. [5]Only includes nonproportional reinsurance, an arrangement in which a reinsurer makes payments to an insurer whose losses exceed a predetermined amount. [6]Coverages protecting against legal liability resulting from negligence, carelessness, or failure to act.

Source: SNL Financial LC.

Property Insurance Requirements for Mortgagors

Some lenders require borrowers to purchase homeowners insurance or other property insurance. Several states have passed laws that prohibit mortgage lenders from requiring a borrower to obtain property insurance coverage that exceeds the replacement value of the buildings and structures on the property as a condition for the loan. In states without such a law, borrowers might be forced to take out more coverage than they could be compensated for, as homeowners insurance only covers rebuilding costs, not the value of the land, in the event of a catastrophic fire or other covered peril.

Mortgage Guaranty Insurance

Private mortgage insurance (PMI), also known as mortgage guaranty insurance, guarantees that, in the event of a default, the insurer will pay the mortgage lender for any loss resulting from a property foreclosure, up to a specific amount. PMI, which is purchased by the borrower but protects the lender, is sometimes confused with mortgage life insurance, a life insurance product that pays off the mortgage if the borrower dies before the loan is repaid. Banks generally require PMI for all borrowers with down payments of less than 20 percent. The industry's combined ratio, a measure of profitability, deteriorated significantly in 2007 and 2008, reflecting the economic downturn and the subsequent rise in mortgage defaults. The combined ratio improved, or dropped, by 17.5 points in 2009 as conditions began to ease, and fell by another 3.4 points in 2010.

MORTGAGE GUARANTY INSURANCE, 2001-2010
($000)

Year	Net premiums written[1]	Annual percent change	Combined ratio[2]	Annual point change[3]
2001	$3,734,987	9.8%	52.0	4.7 pts.
2002	3,980,889	6.6	58.2	6.2
2003	4,315,463	8.4	67.5	9.3
2004	4,316,131	0.0	75.0	7.5
2005	4,429,402	2.6	71.8	-3.2
2006	4,563,852	3.0	71.8	-0.1
2007	5,189,894	13.7	129.5	57.7
2008	5,367,720	3.4	219.9	90.4
2009	4,570,092	-14.9	202.4	-17.5
2010	4,246,677	-7.1	199.0	-3.4

[1]After reinsurance transactions, excluding state funds.
[2]After dividends to policyholders. A drop in the combined ratio represents an improvement; an increase represents a deterioration.
[3]Calculated from unrounded data.

Source: SNL Financial LC.

TOP TEN MORTGAGE GUARANTY INSURANCE
GROUPS/COMPANIES BY DIRECT PREMIUMS WRITTEN, 2010[1]
($000)

Rank	Group/company	Direct premiums written	Market share
1	MGIC Investment Corp.	$1,079,369	22.6%
2	Radian Group Inc.	789,593	16.5
3	American International Group	727,227	15.2
4	PMI Group Inc.	707,685	14.8
5	Genworth Financial Inc.	655,122	13.7
6	Old Republic International Corp.	518,898	10.8
7	Triad Guaranty Inc.	216,016	4.5
8	CMG Mortgage Insurance Group	91,491	1.9
9	Essent US Holdings Inc.	219	[2]
10	Southern Pioneer P&C Insurance Co.	170	[2]

[1]Before reinsurance transactions.
[2]Less than 0.1 percent.

Source: SNL Financial LC.

Title Insurance

Title insurance protects the owner of property or the holder of a mortgage against loss in the event of a property ownership dispute. The sharp downturn in the realty market triggered a sharp drop in premiums in 2007 and 2008.

TITLE INSURANCE, 2001-2010
($000)

Year	Net premiums written	Annual percent change	Year	Net premiums written	Annual percent change
2001	$9,949,587	27.2%	2006	$16,568,820	-2.2%
2002	13,004,693	30.7	2007	14,227,111	-14.1
2003	17,036,936	31.0	2008	9,920,074	-30.3
2004	15,578,889	-8.6	2009	9,289,174	-6.4
2005	16,939,278	8.7	2010	9,446,438	1.7

Source: American Land Title Association.

Surety Bonds

Some kinds of insurance provide financial guarantees. The oldest type, a personal contract of suretyship, dates back to biblical times, when one person would guarantee the creditworthiness or the promise to perform of another. Surety bonds in modern times are primarily used to guarantee the performance of contractors.

Property/Casualty: Specialty Lines

A surety bond is a contract guaranteeing the performance of a specified obligation. Simply put, it is a three-party agreement under which one party, the surety company, answers to a second party, the owner, creditor or "obligee," for a third party's debts, default or nonperformance. Before it issues the bond, the insurer investigates the background and financial condition of the contractor to satisfy itself that the firm is capable of doing the job as set out in the contract. If the contractor fails to perform, the surety company is obligated to get the work completed or pay for the loss up to the bond "penalty." Surety bonds are generally required on large federal, state and local public works projects.

SURETY BONDS, 2001-2010
($000)

Year	Net premiums written[1]	Annual percent change	Combined ratio[2]	Annual point change[3]	Year	Net premiums written[1]	Annual percent change	Combined ratio[2]	Annual point change[3]
2001	$3,044,064	-8.5%	124.1	37.1 pts.	2006	$4,435,122	14.7%	81.7	-19.8 pts
2002	3,280,927	7.8	116.9	-7.2	2007	4,807,994	8.4	72.3	-9.3
2003	3,384,636	3.2	122.1	5.2	2008	4,960,255	3.2	66.9	-5.4
2004	3,821,170	12.9	119.8	-2.3	2009	4,837,598	-2.5	79.5	12.5
2005	3,866,026	1.2	101.5	-18.3	2010	4,853,548	0.3	70.6	-8.8

[1]After reinsurance transactions, excluding state funds.
[2]After dividends to policyholders. A drop in the combined ratio represents an improvement; an increase represents a deterioration.
[3]Calculated from unrounded data.
Source: SNL Financial LC.

TOP TEN SURETY GROUPS/COMPANIES BY DIRECT PREMIUMS WRITTEN, 2010[1]
($000)

Rank	Group/company	Direct premiums written	Market share
1	Travelers Companies Inc.	$867,822	16.7%
2	Liberty Mutual	751,166	14.5
3	Zurich Financial Services Ltd.	512,317	9.9
4	CNA Financial Corp.	406,462	7.8
5	Chubb Corp.	256,920	5.0
6	Hartford Financial Services	177,157	3.4
7	HCC Insurance Holdings Inc.	176,126	3.4
8	International Fidelity Insurance Co.	143,273	2.8
9	RLI Corp.	111,237	2.1
10	ACE Ltd.	109,531	2.1

[1]Before reinsurance transactions.
Source: SNL Financial LC.

Financial Guaranty Insurance

Financial guaranty insurance, also known as bond insurance, helps expand the financial markets by increasing borrower and lender leverage. Starting in the 1970s, surety bonds began to be used to guarantee the principal and interest payments on municipal obligations. This made the bonds more attractive to investors and at the same time benefited bond issuers because having the insurance lowered their borrowing costs. Initially, financial guaranty insurance was considered a special category of surety. It became a separate line of insurance in 1986.

Financial guaranty insurers are specialized, highly capitalized companies that traditionally have had the highest rating. The insurer's high rating attaches to the bonds, lowering the riskiness of the bonds to investors. With their credit rating thus enhanced, municipalities can issue bonds that pay a lower interest rate, enabling them to borrow more for the same outlay of funds. The high combined ratio beginning in 2007 reflects the crisis in financial markets.

FINANCIAL GUARANTY INSURANCE, 2001-2010
($000)

Year	Net premiums written[1]	Annual percent change	Combined ratio[2]	Annual point change[3]
2001	$1,913,150	33.4%	25.8	-11.3 pts.
2002	2,596,750	35.7	29.2	3.4
2003	3,506,363	35.0	24.8	-4.4
2004	3,118,566	-11.1	39.7	14.9
2005	3,006,829	-3.6	34.1	-5.6
2006	3,075,577	2.3	38.8	4.7
2007	3,038,967	-1.2	155.8	117.0
2008	3,171,561	4.4	422.5	266.7
2009	1,793,428	-43.5	101.2	-321.4
2010	1,371,908	-23.5	227.3	126.1

[1]After reinsurance transactions, excluding state funds.
[2]After dividends to policyholders. A drop in the combined ratio represents an improvement; an increase represents a deterioration.
[3]Calculated from unrounded data.

Source: SNL Financial LC.

TOP TEN FINANCIAL GUARANTY INSURANCE GROUPS/
COMPANIES BY DIRECT PREMIUMS WRITTEN, 2010[1]
($000)

Rank	Group/Company	Direct premiums written	Market share
1	Assured Guaranty Ltd.	$636,860	44.0%
2	MBIA Inc.	352,363	24.4
3	Ambac Financial Group Inc.	243,002	16.8
4	Financial Guaranty Insurance Co.	71,567	4.9
5	Syncora Holdings Ltd.	69,600	4.8
6	Radian Group Inc.	49,350	3.4
7	CIFG Assurance North America Inc.	20,249	1.4
8	Stonebridge Casualty Insurance Co.	3,000	0.2
9	ACA Financial Guaranty Corp.	487	[2]
10	Century Insurance Co. (Guam) Ltd.	32	[2]

[1]Before reinsurance transactions. [2]Less than 0.1 percent.
Source: SNL Financial LC.

Credit Insurance for Customer Defaults

Credit insurance protects merchants, exporters, manufacturers and other businesses that extend credit to their customers from losses or damages resulting from the nonpayment of debts owed them for goods and services provided in the normal course of business. Credit insurance facilitates financing, enabling insured companies to get better credit terms from banks. The high combined ratio beginning in 2007 reflects the crisis in financial markets.

CREDIT INSURANCE, 2001-2010
($000)

Year	Net premiums written[1]	Annual percent change	Combined ratio[2]	Annual point change[3]
2001	$575,214	-2.3%	90.7	11.4 pts.
2002	703,038	22.2	104.6	13.8
2003	568,502	-19.1	98.6	-6.0
2004	806,372	41.8	96.4	-2.2
2005	936,101	16.1	82.2	-14.2
2006	1,090,144	16.5	86.2	4.0
2007	1,405,439	28.9	129.2	43.0
2008	1,413,313	0.6	170.6	41.4
2009	1,224,472	-13.4	140.8	-29.8
2010	1,344,776	9.8	127.2	-13.6

[1]After reinsurance transactions, excluding state funds. [2]After dividends to policyholders. A drop in the combined ratio represents an improvement; an increase represents a deterioration. [3]Calculated from unrounded data.
Source: SNL Financial LC.

TOP TEN CREDIT INSURANCE GROUPS/COMPANIES BY DIRECT PREMIUMS WRITTEN, 2010[1]
($000)

Rank	Group/company	Direct premiums written	Market share
1	QBE Insurance Group Ltd.	$341,770	16.0%
2	Assurant Inc.	311,421	14.6
3	Allianz SE	212,572	10.0
4	American International Group	201,231	9.4
5	American National Insurance	152,060	7.1
6	Old Republic International Corp.	120,003	5.6
7	State National Companies Inc.	86,821	4.1
8	Arch Capital Group Ltd.	72,329	3.4
9	Coface North America Insurance Co.	71,254	3.3
10	Allstate Corp.	62,363	2.9

[1]Before reinsurance transactions.
Source: SNL Financial LC.

Reinsurance

Reinsurance is essentially insurance for insurance companies. It is a way for primary insurers to protect against unforeseen or extraordinary losses. Reinsurance also serves to limit liability on specific risks, to increase individual insurers' capacity to write business and to help insurers stabilize their business in the face of the wide swings in profit and loss margins that are inherent in the insurance business.

Reinsurance is an international business. According to the Reinsurance Association of America, 57.8 percent of the reinsurance purchased by U.S. insurance companies was written by foreign reinsurance companies in 2009. If the domicile of the reinsurance company's parent is taken into account, foreign (or foreign-owned) reinsurance companies accounted for 84.5 percent of the market. This is because many U.S. reinsurance companies are owned by foreign firms.

**TOP TEN U.S. PROPERTY/CASUALTY REINSURERS OF U.S. BUSINESS
BY GROSS PREMIUMS WRITTEN, 2010**
($000)

Rank	Company	Country of parent company	Gross premiums written
1	Swiss Reinsurance America Corporation	Switzerland	$4,365,550
2	National Indemnity Company (Berkshire Hathaway)[1]	U.S.	4,352,429
3	Transatlantic/Putnam Reinsurance Company	U.S.	3,675,627
4	Munich Reinsurance America Corp.[2]	Germany	3,620,278
5	Everest Reinsurance Company	Bermuda	3,379,194
6	XL Reinsurance America[3]	Bermuda	2,696,627
7	QBE Reinsurance Group, New York[4]	Australia	2,093,449
8	Odyssey America Re./Odyssey Reinsurance Corp.[5]	Canada	1,988,836
9	Berkley Insurance Company	U.S.	1,455,576
10	General Re Group[6]	U.S.	1,320,844
	Total, top ten reinsurers		**$28,948,410**
	Total, all reinsurers		**$34,507,904**

[1]Excludes assumptions from affiliated General Re Group.
[2]Includes Munich Re America, American Alternative Insurance Corporation and The Princeton Excess and Surplus Lines Insurance Co.
[3]Includes the net pooled share of the combined underwriting results of the XL America Group Pool.
[4]Includes the QBE Reinsurance Corporation, QBE Insurance Corporation and QBE Specialty Insurance Company.
[5]Includes Oyssey America Re, Clearwater Insurance, Clearwater Select, Hudson Insurance and Hudson Specialty Insurance Companies.
[6]North American Property/Casualty underwritten segment of General Re; excludes certain intercompany transactions and cessions to certain affiliates of Berkshire Hathaway.

Source: Reinsurance Association of America.

The Securitization of Insurance Risk: Catastrophe Bonds

Catastrophe (cat) bonds are one of a number of innovative risk transfer products that have emerged as an alternative to traditional insurance and reinsurance products. Insurers and reinsurers typically issue cat bonds through an issuer known as a special purpose vehicle, a company set up specifically for this purpose. Cat bonds pay high interest rates and diversify an investor's portfolio because natural disasters occur randomly and are not associated with economic factors. Depending on how the cat bond is structured, if losses reach the threshold specified in the bond offering, the investor may lose all or part of the principal or interest.

In 2010 cat bonds representing $4.6 billion of risk capital were issued, marking a 35.6 percent increase over 2009, according to an analysis by GC Securities. Cat bond activity further accelerated during the first quarter of 2011, with $1.02 billion in new issuances. This was a significant rise from the $300 million issued during the first quarter of 2010 and marked the most active first quarter on record for new issuances. A string of devastating disasters during first-quarter 2011, including the Great Tohoku Japan earthquake, Cyclone Yasi in Australia and the Christchurch earthquake in New Zealand, took a toll on the market, causing a decline in valuations of catastrophe bonds during the second half of March.

TOP TEN CATASTROPHE BOND TRANSACTIONS, 2010
($ millions)

Rank	Special purpose vehicle	Sponsor	Risk amount	Peril	Risk location
1	Lodestone Re Ltd. 2010-2	National Union (Chartis)	$450.0	Multiple	U.S.
2	Lodestone Re Ltd.	National Union (Chartis)	425.0	Multiple	U.S.
3	Residential Re 2010	USAA	405.0	Multiple	U.S.
4	Calypso Capital Limited	AXA Global P&C	€275.0	Windstorm	Europe
5	Merna Re II Ltd.	State Farm	350.0	U.S. earthquake	U.S.
6	Johnston Re Ltd. Series 2010-1	NC JUA/IUA[1]	305.0	Hurricane	U.S.
7	Residential Re 2010-II	USAA	300.0	Multiple	U.S.
8	Montana Re Ltd. 2010-1	Flagstone Re	210.0	Multiple	Multiple
9	Caelus Re II Limited	Nationwide	185.0	Multiple	U.S.
10	Foundation Re III Ltd.	Hartford Fire Insurance Co.	180.0	Hurricane	U.S.

[1]Sponsored through Munich Re.

Source: GC Securities and Guy Carpenter & Company, LLC.

Property/Casualty: Capital Markets

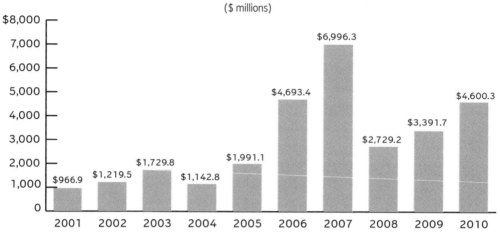

CATASTROPHE BONDS, ANNUAL RISK CAPITAL ISSUED, 2001-2010
($ millions)

Source: GC Securities and Guy Carpenter & Company, LLC.

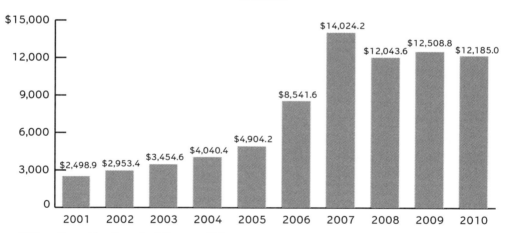

CATASTROPHE BONDS, RISK CAPITAL OUTSTANDING, 2001-2010
($ millions)

Source: GC Securities and Guy Carpenter & Company, LLC.

Life/Health: Financial

Whether measured by premium income or by assets, traditional life insurance is no longer the primary business of many companies in the life/health insurance industry. Today, the emphasis has shifted to the underwriting of annuities. Annuities are contracts that accumulate funds and/ or pay out a fixed or variable income stream. An income stream can be for a fixed period of time or over the lifetimes of the contract holder and his or her beneficiaries. Nevertheless, traditional life insurance products such as universal life and term life for individuals as well as group life remain an important part of the business, as do disability income and health insurance. Life insurers invest primarily in corporate bonds but also significantly in corporate equities. Besides annuities and life insurance products, life insurers may offer other types of financial services such as asset management.

LIFE/HEALTH INSURER FINANCIAL ASSET DISTRIBUTION, 2006-2010
($ billions)

	2006	2007	2008	2009	2010
Total financial assets	**$4,685.3**	**$4,949.7**	**$4,515.5**	**$4,823.9**	**$5,176.3**
Checkable deposits and currency	56.1	58.3	82.8	50.7	51.7
Money market fund shares	23.3	21.6	39.2	33.7	21.0
Credit market instruments	2,786.4	2,871.2	2,882.8	3,022.6	3,174.2
Open market paper	28.7	41.7	38.3	49.8	40.9
U.S. government securities	465.3	453.5	471.9	505.4	532.2
Treasury	87.9	70.6	105.7	133.5	152.0
Agency- and GSE[1]-backed securities	377.4	382.9	366.2	371.9	380.2
Municipal securities	36.6	41.4	47.1	73.1	113.3
Corporate and foreign bonds	1,819.5	1,862.6	1,817.0	1,914.7	2,027.1
Other loans and advances	132.6	145.8	166.1	153.5	143.2
Mortgages	303.8	326.2	342.4	326.1	317.5
Corporate equities	1,364.8	1,464.6	1,001.7	1,208.5	1,402.6
Mutual fund shares	148.8	188.4	121.0	140.8	155.7
Miscellaneous assets	303.3	342.9	380.1	357.6	360.3

[1]Government-sponsored enterprise.

Source: Board of Governors of the Federal Reserve System, June 9, 2011.

Financial Results

2010 was a challenging year for the life/annuity/health insurance industry. Annuity premiums rose 27 percent, but life insurance premiums slipped 16 percent. Reserve adjustments on reinsurance ceded (down $90.8 billion vs. 2009) pruned $29.3 billion from income. Pre-tax operating income slid 12.9 percent vs. 2009 but still topped $53 billion. The industry posted net realized capital losses for the fourth year in a row, at $16 billion in 2010, though this was smaller than in 2008 and 2009. Unrealized capital losses were another $16.4 billion. Nevertheless, in 2010 the industry paid roughly the same amount of policyholder dividends as in 2009, increased its benefit payments and earned net income of $28 billion.

LIFE/HEALTH INSURANCE INDUSTRY INCOME ANALYSIS, 2006-2010
($ millions, end of period)

Income statement	2006	2007	2008	2009	2010	Percent change, 2009-2010[1]
Premiums, consideration and deposits						
Life insurance	$145.1	$138.3	$142.8	$120.5	$101.7	-15.6%
Annuities	298.5	310.4	323.0	225.4	286.3	27.0
Accident and health	131.9	143.5	156.6	162.4	171.5	5.6
Credit life and credit accident and health	2.1	2.2	2.1	1.6	1.6	-2.0
Supplementary contracts and other premiums, consideration and deposits	-0.9	16.8	0.8	0.5	23.1	4,166.0
Total premiums, consideration and deposits	**$576.6**	**$611.2**	**$625.2**	**$510.4**	**$582.6**	**14.1%**
Net investment income earned	161.5	168.0	162.2	156.6	164.0	4.7
Reserve adjustments: reinsurance ceded	-4.7	-22.4	17.8	61.5	-29.3	-147.6
Fee income: investment management and separate account contracts	20.2	22.9	21.2	20.4	23.4	14.7
Other income	32.0	35.3	18.3	27.8	33.8	21.8
Total revenue	**$785.6**	**$815.1**	**$844.7**	**$776.7**	**$774.5**	**-0.3%**
Benefits	214.2	228.3	240.2	244.1	248.1	1.6
Surrenders	272.0	305.2	291.6	228.7	216.7	-5.2
Increase in reserves and deposits	69.8	35.3	144.2	99.0	96.2	-2.9
Commissions	49.7	50.7	51.7	48.9	49.2	0.6
General and administrative expense	49.3	52.1	53.6	54.2	56.9	4.9
Net transfers to separate accounts	61.0	66.1	22.7	11.1	29.3	163.6
Policyholder dividends	16.5	17.5	17.7	15.0	15.0	[2]
Income tax	11.0	11.5	-0.1	10.7	9.0	-16.0
Net realized capital gains (losses)	6.5	-1.5	-50.9	-28.7	-16.0	44.3
Net income	37.0	31.6	-52.3	21.5	28.1	30.5
Pre-tax operating income	41.4	44.6	-1.4	61.0	53.1	-12.9

[1]Calculated from unrounded data.
[2]Less than 0.1 percent.

Source: SNL Financial LC.

TOP U.S. LIFE/HEALTH INSURANCE GROUPS BY REVENUES, 2010[1]

($ millions)

Rank	Group	Revenues	Assets
1	MetLife	$52,717	$730,906
2	Prudential Financial	38,414	539,854
3	New York Life Insurance	34,947	199,646
4	TIAA-CREF	32,225	417,332
5	Massachusetts Mutual Life Insurance	25,647	188,449
6	Northwestern Mutual	23,384	180,038
7	Aflac	20,732	101,039
8	Lincoln National	10,411	193,824
9	Unum Group	10,193	57,308
10	Genworth Financial	10,089	112,395
11	Guardian Life Insurance Co. of America	10,051	46,122
12	Principal Financial	9,159	145,631
13	Reinsurance Group of America	8,262	29,082
14	Thrivent Financial for Lutherans	7,471	62,760
15	Mutual of Omaha Insurance	5,724	24,986
16	Pacific Life	5,603	115,992
17	Western & Southern Financial Group	4,921	36,465

[1]Revenues for insurance companies include premium and annuity income, investment income and capital gains or losses but exclude deposits. Based on companies and categories in the Fortune 500. Each company is assigned only one category, even if it is involved in several industries.

Source: Fortune.

Life Insurance Ownership

Fifty-three percent of all people in the United States were covered by some type of life insurance in 2010, according to LIMRA's 2011 *Life Insurance Ownership Study*. Other findings include:

- Only one-third of Americans are covered by individual life insurance, the lowest level in 50 years.
- 56 percent of all workers had group life insurance coverage through their employers in 2010, up from 48 percent in 2004.
- Insured individuals owned an average of $154,000 in life insurance coverage in 2010, compared with an average amount of $102,300 for people covered by group policies.
- The average amount of individual life insurance people carry decreased by $12,000 in 2010, compared with a $6,000 decline in group coverage.

Distribution Channels

Life insurance was once sold primarily by career life agents, captive agents that represent a single insurance company, and by independent agents, who represent several insurers. Now, life insurance is also sold directly to the public by mail, telephone and through the Internet. In addition, in the 1980s insurers began to market annuities and term life insurance through banks and financial advisors, professional groups and the workplace. A large portion of variable annuities, and a small portion of fixed annuities, are sold by stockbrokers. In 2010 independent agents held 46 percent of the new individual life insurance sales market, followed by affiliated (i.e., captive) agents with 42 percent, direct marketers with 4 percent and others, including stockbrokers, accounting for the remaining 8 percent, according to LIMRA. In 2010, 26 percent of adults said they would prefer to purchase life insurance via the Internet, or other direct channels, according to LIMRA.

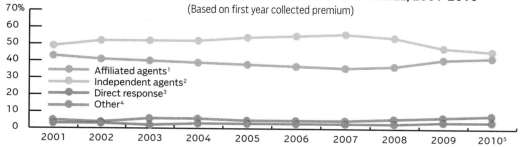

LIFE INDIVIDUAL MARKET SHARE BY DISTRIBUTION CHANNEL, 2001-2010
(Based on first year collected premium)

- Affiliated agents[1]
- Independent agents[2]
- Direct response[3]
- Other[4]

[1]Includes career, multiline exclusive and home service agents. [2]Includes brokers and personal producing general agents. [3]No producers are involved. Does not include direct marketing efforts involving agents. [4]Includes stockbrokers, financial institutions, worksite and other channels. [5]Estimate.
Source: LIMRA's *U.S. Individual Life Insurance Sales Survey*, LIMRA estimates.

- Worksite marketing is the selling of voluntary (employee-paid) insurance and financial products at the worksite. The products may be on either an individual or group platform and are usually paid through periodic payroll deductions.

- Worksite sales of life and health insurance totaled $5.24 billion in 2010, down by about 3 percent from 2009.

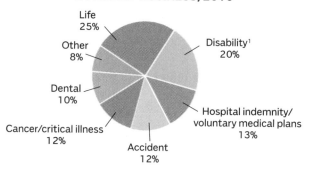

WORKSITE LIFE INSURANCE SALES BY LINE OF BUSINESS, 2010

- Life 25%
- Other 8%
- Dental 10%
- Cancer/critical illness 12%
- Accident 12%
- Hospital indemnity/ voluntary medical plans 13%
- Disability[1] 20%

[1]Short-term and long-term disability.
Source: Eastbridge Consulting Group, Inc.

Premiums by Line

Measured by premiums written, annuities are the largest life/health product line, followed by life insurance and health insurance (also referred to in the industry as accident and health). Life insurance policies can be sold on an individual, or "ordinary," basis or to groups such as employees and associations. Accident and health insurance includes medical expense, disability income and long-term care. Other lines include credit life, which pays the balance of a loan if the borrower dies or becomes disabled, and industrial life, small policies whose premiums are generally collected by an agent on a weekly basis.

DIRECT PREMIUMS WRITTEN BY LINE, LIFE/HEALTH INSURANCE INDUSTRY, 2006-2010
($ millions)

Lines of insurance	2006 Direct premiums written[1]	Percent of total	2009 Direct premiums written[1]	Percent of total	2010 Direct premiums written[1]	Percent of total
Annuities						
Ordinary individual annuities	$193,426,691	31.6%	$195,668,021	31.3%	$189,782,325	30.0%
Group annuities	117,152,669	19.2	108,215,782	17.3	109,572,588	17.3
Total	**$310,579,360**	**50.8%**	**$303,883,803**	**48.6%**	**$299,354,913**	**47.3%**
Life						
Ordinary life	129,199,580	21.1	121,062,285	19.4	125,535,790	19.8
Group life	35,182,751	5.8	29,807,040	4.8	30,459,708	4.8
Credit life (group and individual)	1,555,389	0.3	1,248,617	0.2	1,254,440	0.2
Industrial life	239,583	[2]	197,329	[2]	180,646	[2]
Total	**$166,177,302**	**27.2%**	**$152,315,270**	**24.4%**	**$157,430,584**	**24.9%**
Accident and health[3]						
Group	78,015,194	12.8	89,437,736	14.3	91,353,029	14.4
Other	55,482,684	9.1	78,195,632	12.5	83,870,645	13.3
Credit	1,430,649	0.2	978,694	0.2	947,319	0.1
Total	**$134,928,528**	**22.1%**	**$168,612,061**	**27.0%**	**$176,170,993**	**27.8%**
All other lines	59	[2]	1,375	[2]	2,077	[2]
Total, all lines[4]	**$611,685,248**	**100.0%**	**$624,812,509**	**100.0%**	**$632,958,567**	**100.0%**

[1]Before reinsurance transactions.
[2]Less than 0.1 percent.
[3]Does not include accident and health premiums reported on the property/casualty and health annual statements.
[4]Does not include deposit-type funds.

Source: SNL Financial LC.

Annuities

There are several types of annuities. Fixed annuities guarantee that a specific sum of money will be paid in the future, generally as a monthly benefit, for as long as the annuitant lives. The value of variable annuities fluctuates with the performance of an underlying investment portfolio. The equity-indexed annuity is a hybrid product, with features of fixed and variable annuities. Annuities play a key role in financing retirement for many Americans. (See also Retirement Assets: Annuities, page 50.)

TOP TEN WRITERS OF GROUP ANNUITIES BY DIRECT PREMIUMS WRITTEN, 2010
($000)

Rank	Group	Direct premiums written	Market share
1	ING Groep N.V.	$7,755,005	15.7%
2	Prudential Financial Inc.	6,449,944	13.0
3	Great-West Insurance Group	4,901,006	9.9
4	American International Group	4,347,140	8.8
5	AXA	3,993,000	8.1
6	TIAA-CREF	3,780,709	7.6
7	Sun Life Financial Inc.	3,289,259	6.6
8	Lincoln National Corp.	2,663,232	5.4
9	MetLife Inc.	2,072,818	4.2
10	Jackson National Life Group	1,904,919	3.8

Source: SNL Financial LC.

TOP TEN WRITERS OF INDIVIDUAL ANNUITIES BY DIRECT PREMIUMS WRITTEN, 2010
($000)

Rank	Group	Direct premiums written	Market share
1	MetLife Inc.	$24,367,159	13.5%
2	Prudential Financial Inc.	18,047,805	10.0
3	Jackson National Life Group	15,732,654	8.7
4	Lincoln National Corp.	11,180,832	6.2
5	Allianz SE	10,285,600	5.7
6	American International Group	8,557,339	4.8
7	New York Life Insurance Group	8,133,126	4.5
8	TIAA-CREF	7,021,041	3.9
9	Ameriprise Financial Inc.	6,625,530	3.7
10	Aviva Plc	5,796,478	3.2

Source: SNL Financial LC.

TOP TEN WRITERS OF ANNUITIES BY DIRECT PREMIUMS WRITTEN, 2010[1]

($000)

Rank	Group	Direct premiums written	Market share
1	MetLife Inc.	$26,439,976	11.5%
2	Prudential Financial Inc.	24,497,749	10.7
3	Jackson National Life Group	17,638,173	7.7
4	Lincoln National Corp.	13,844,064	6.0
5	American International Group	12,904,479	5.6
6	TIAA-CREF	10,801,750	4.7
7	ING Groep N.V.	10,767,457	4.7
8	Allianz SE	10,285,600	4.5
9	New York Life Insurance Group	8,323,765	3.6
10	AXA	6,922,432	3.0

[1]Includes individual and group annuities.

Source: SNL Financial LC.

Credit Life Insurance

Credit life insurance, a form of decreasing term insurance, protects creditors such as banks. The borrower pays the premium, generally as part of the credit transaction, to cover the outstanding loan in the event he or she dies. The face value of a policy decreases as the loan is paid off until both equal zero. When loans are paid off early, premiums for the remaining term are returned to the policyholder. Credit accident and health, a similar product, provides a monthly income in the event the borrower becomes disabled.

CREDIT LIFE, AND CREDIT ACCIDENT AND HEALTH INSURANCE DIRECT PREMIUMS WRITTEN, 2001-2010

($000)

Year	Credit life	Credit accident and health
2001	$2,263,822	$2,208,732
2002	1,784,067	1,883,150
2003	1,416,684	1,554,623
2004	1,526,154	1,554,325
2005	1,607,682	1,522,843
2006	1,564,313	1,442,644
2007	1,631,538	1,407,625
2008	1,563,238	1,251,054
2009	1,247,760	964,781
2010	1,247,848	930,578

Source: SNL Financial LC.

Private Health Insurance

Health insurance, also referred to in the insurance industry as accident and health insurance, includes coverage for medical expenses, disability and long-term care. Health insurance companies reported direct premiums written of $394.7 billion in 2010, according to SNL Financial. Life/health and property insurers also write this coverage, accounting for an additional $157.0 billion and $8.0 billion in direct premiums, respectively, in 2010. This brought total private health insurance premiums to $559.7 billion in 2010. The number of people without health insurance coverage rose from 46.3 million in 2008 to 50.7 million in 2009, while the percentage increased from 15.4 percent to 16.7 percent over the same period.

- According to the U.S. Census Bureau's latest health insurance survey, 16.3 percent of the U.S. population lacked coverage in 2010, up from 16.1 percent in 2009.

- Between 2009 and 2010, the number of people covered by private health insurance decreased from 196.2 million to 195.9 million, while the number covered by government health insurance climbed from 93.2 million to 95.0 million.

- Between 2009 and 2010 the number covered by employment-based health insurance declined from 170.8 million to 169.3 million. The number with Medicaid coverage increased from 47.8 million to 48.6 million.

THE NATION'S HEALTHCARE DOLLAR: 2009
WHERE IT CAME FROM

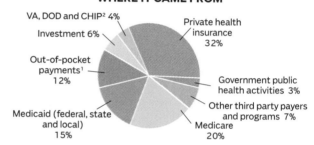

VA, DOD and CHIP[2] 4%
Investment 6%
Out-of-pocket payments[1] 12%
Private health insurance 32%
Government public health activities 3%
Other third party payers and programs 7%
Medicare 20%
Medicaid (federal, state and local) 15%

[1]Includes co-payments, deductibles, and any amounts not covered by health insurance.
[2]Department of Veterans Affairs, Department of Defense and Children's Health Insurance Program.

Source: Centers for Medicare and Medicaid Services, Office of the Actuary, National Health Statistics Group.

HEALTH INSURANCE COVERAGE STATUS
AND TYPE OF COVERAGE, 2006-2010
(000)

Year	Total U.S. population	Uninsured		Insured		
		Number of people	Percent of population	Private health insurance	Government health insurance	Individuals with some form of insurance
2006	296,824	45,214	15.2	203,942	80,343	251,610
2007	299,106	44,088	14.7	203,903	83,147	255,018
2008	301,483	44,780	14.9	202,626	87,586	256,702
2009	304,280	48,985	16.1	196,245	93,245	255,295
2010	306,110	49,904	16.3	195,874	95,003	256,206

[1]Includes individuals with some form of insurance (government, private or a combination of both). Source: U.S. Census Bureau.

TOP TEN HEALTH INSURANCE GROUPS BY DIRECT PREMIUMS WRITTEN, 2010[1]

($ billions)

Rank	Group	Direct premiums written	Market share
1	WellPoint Inc.	$42.1	10.9%
2	UnitedHealth Group Inc.	41.1	10.6
3	Health Care Services Corporation	20.2	5.2
4	Humana Inc.	12.4	3.2
5	Highmark Inc.	11.6	3.0
6	Aetna Inc.	10.0	2.6
7	Coventry Health Care Inc.	9.8	2.5
8	EmblemHealth Inc.	9.7	2.5
9	Kaiser Foundation Health Plan Inc.	9.5	2.5
10	Independence Blue Cross	9.3	2.4

[1]Based on health insurer annual statement data. Does not include health insurance data from the property/casualty and life/health annual statements.

Source: SNL Financial LC.

- Private health insurers' direct premiums written totaled $395 billion in 2010. Life/health and property/casualty insurers wrote an additional $165 billion of health coverage, bringing the total to $560 billion, according to data from SNL Financial.

Health Savings Accounts

Established in 2003 by the Medicare Modernization Act, health savings accounts (HSAs) are designed to give consumers financial incentives to manage their own healthcare expenses. An individual's HSA must be coupled with a high-deductible health plan (HDHP). HSA funds may be used to cover current and future healthcare costs.

HEALTH SAVINGS ACCOUNT ENROLLMENT (COVERED LIVES), 2008-2011[1]

	January 2008	January 2009	January 2010	January 2011
Individual market	1,502,000	1,832,000	2,053,000	2,358,497
Small group market	1,816,000	2,429,000	2,970,000	2,779,208
Large group market	2,777,000	3,752,000	4,986,000	6,299,460
Other group[2]	13,000	NA	NA	NA
Other[3]	10,000	NA	NA	NA
Total	**6,118,000**	**8,103,000**	**10,009,000**	**11,437,165**

[1]Includes health savings accounts (HSAs) and high-deductible health plans (HDHPs).
[2]Enrollment data for companies that did not break down their group membership into large and small group categories. [3]Enrollment data for companies that did not provide a breakdown of enrollees by market category. NA=Data not available.

Source: America's Health Insurance Plans.

- According to America's Health Insurance Plans, 11.4 million people were covered by HSA/HDHP products in January 2011, up from 10 million in January 2010.

- Overall, preferred provider organizations (PPO) products (92 percent) were the most popular product types among HSA/HDHP participants.

Long-Term Care Insurance

Long-term care (LTC) insurance pays for services to help individuals who are unable to perform certain activities of daily living without assistance or who require supervision due to a cognitive impairment such as Alzheimer's disease. According to the U.S. Department of Health and Human Services (HHS), 70 percent of individuals over age 65 will require at least some type of long-term care services during their lifetime. A 2011 study by Prudential Financial suggests that the need for LTC insurance will increase in the coming years as the baby boomer generation ages. The study projects that over the next 20 years, the number of Americans age 65 and older will more than double to 71 million, comprising roughly 20 percent of the U.S. population.

Nearly 5 million people were covered by long-term care insurance in 2010, according to a study by LIMRA International. The average first-year premium for individual LTC coverage purchased in 2010 was $2,235, up 2 percent from 2009. The average age of someone buying long-term care insurance today is about 60, according to the HHS. For those who purchase policies offered at work, the average age at which they buy is about 50.

INDIVIDUAL LONG-TERM CARE INSURANCE, 2010[1]

- The number of policyholders and new premiums grew by 11 percent and 13 percent, respectively, in 2010 from a year ago.

	Lives	Percent change, 2010	Premium ($ millions)	Percent change, 2010
New business	234,816	11%	$525	13%
In-force[2]	4,800,000	1	8,850	2

[1]Based on LIMRA International's Individual LTC Sales survey, representing over 95% of the individual LTC market.
[2]Includes estimates for non-participants.

Source: LIMRA International.

Overview

Banking, the largest sector within the financial services industry, includes all depository institutions, from commercial banks and thrifts (savings and loan associations and savings banks) to credit unions. In their role as financial intermediaries, banks use the funds they receive from depositors to make loans and mortgages to individuals and businesses, seeking to earn more on their lending activities than it costs them to attract depositors. However, in so doing they must manage many risk factors, including interest rates, which can result in a mismatch of assets and liabilities. Over the past decade, many banks have diversified and expanded into new business lines such as credit cards, stock brokerage and investment management services. Some have also moved into the insurance business, selling annuities and life insurance products in particular, often through the purchase of insurance agencies. (See Chapter 4: Convergence.)

Regulation

In July 2010 Congress passed the Dodd-Frank Wall Street Reform and Consumer Protection Act, sweeping legislation that dramatically changed the way that financial services companies operate in the U.S. and how they serve their customers. The act established a Financial Stability Oversight Council (FSOC) charged with identifying threats to the financial stability of the United States. The council, which is chaired by the Secretary of the Treasury, consists of 10 voting members and five nonvoting members, and brings together federal financial regulators, state regulators and an insurance expert appointed by the President. Among its responsibilities, the FSOC has authority to designate a nonbank financial firm for enhanced supervision.

Since 1863 banks have had the choice of whether to be regulated by the federal government or the states. National banks are chartered and supervised by the Office of the Comptroller of the Currency (OCC), part of the U.S. Treasury. Thrift institutions, including savings and loans associations and savings banks, can be federally chartered or state chartered and subject to state regulation. The Dodd-Frank Act phased out the Office of Thrift Supervision (OTS) and shifted its responsibilities to other federal agencies. Regulation of federal thrift institutions was moved from the OTS to the OCC. The OTS's responsibilities regarding state savings institutions were moved to the Federal Deposit Insurance Corporation and its powers regarding thrift holding companies were moved to the Federal Reserve.

The OCC conducts on-site reviews of national banks, federal savings associations and federal thrifts and provides supervision of these institutions' operations. It also analyzes investments and sensitivity to market risk for all national banks and federal thrifts with less than $10 billion in assets. Depository institutions with assets over $10 billion will be overseen by the new Consumer Financial Protection Bureau (CFPB) created by Dodd-Frank. Subsidiaries and all other affiliates of these institutions also fall under the CFPB's authority. These some 100 institutions collectively hold more than 80 percent of the banking industry's assets. (See page 213 for a detailed summary of the Dodd-Frank Act.)

Bank Holding Companies

A bank holding company (BHC) is any company (not necessarily a bank) that has direct or indirect control of at least one bank. Under the Bank Holding Company Act of 1956 and its amendments, the Federal Reserve supervises all BHCs, regardless of whether the bank subsidiary is a state or national bank. The act stipulated that BHCs may engage in, establish or acquire subsidiaries that engage in nonbanking activities closely related to banking, as determined by the Federal Reserve. The act was amended by the Gramm-Leach-Bliley Act (GLB) of 1999, which allows a BHC that meets specified eligibility requirements to become a financial holding company (FHC) and thereby engage in expanded financial activities, including securities underwriting and dealing, insurance agency and underwriting activities, and merchant banking activities. GLB also allows securities firms and insurance companies to acquire a bank and thereby become a BHC eligible for FHC status. (See Convergence, page 55.) The 2010 Dodd-Frank Act increases the Federal Reserve's oversight of bank holding companies with total consolidated assets of at least $50 billion. It also contains provisions requiring that FHCs remain "well capitalized and well maintained."

BANK HOLDING COMPANIES (BHCs) WITH ASSETS OVER $50 BILLION, 2010

($ billions)

Rank	Institution	Assets	Rank	Institution	Assets
1	Bank of America Corporation	$2,268	19	American Express Company	$146
2	JPMorgan Chase & Co.	2,118	20	Regions Financial Corporation	132
3	Citigroup Inc.	1,914	21	Citizens Financial Group, Inc.	130
4	Wells Fargo & Company	1,258	22	Fifth Third Bancorp	111
5	Goldman Sachs Group, Inc.	911	23	RBC USA Holdco Corporation	99
6	Morgan Stanley	808	24	KeyCorp	92
7	MetLife, Inc.	731	25	Northern Trust Corporation	84
8	Taunus Corporation	373	26	UnionBanCal Corporation	79
9	HSBC North America Holdings Inc.	344	27	BancWest Corporation	73
10	U.S. Bancorp	308	28	Harris Financial Corp.	70
11	PNC Financial Services Group, Inc.	264	29	M&T Bank Corporation	68
12	Bank of New York Mellon Corporation	247	30	Discover Financial Services	64
13	Capital One Financial Corporation	198	31	BBVA USA Bancshares, Inc.	63
14	TD Bank US Holding Company	177	32	Comerica Incorporated	54
15	SunTrust Banks, Inc.	173	33	Huntington Bancshares Incorporated	54
16	Ally Financial Inc.	172	34	Zions Bancorporation	51
17	State Street Corporation	159	35	CIT Group Inc.	51
18	BB&T Corporation	157	36	Marshall & Ilsley Corporation	51

Source: SNL Financial LC.

Troubled Asset Relief Program

In October 2008, in a response to a massive credit crisis and the failure or near collapse of several large institutions, Congress enacted the Emergency Economic Stabilization Act. The act established the Troubled Asset Relief Program (TARP), a landmark rescue plan for banks and other qualifying financial services firms. As of July 2011 taxpayers had recovered 76 percent, or $314 billion, of the $413 billion TARP funds that had been disbursed.

Deposit Insurance

The Federal Deposit Insurance Corporation (FDIC) was created in 1933 to restore confidence in the banking system following the collapse of thousands of banks during the Great Depression. The FDIC, which is an independent agency within the federal government, protects against the loss of deposits if an FDIC-insured commercial bank or savings association fails. The basic insurance amount, $100,000 per depositor per insured bank, was raised temporarily to $250,000 as part of the federal government's 2008 rescue program for the financial services industry. The Dodd-Frank Act, enacted in July 2010, made the increase permanent.

During the savings and loan crisis of the late 1980s and early 1990s, over 1,000 institutions holding over $500 billion failed, leading to a broad restructuring of the industry. The economic downturn that began in 2008 spawned an increase in bank failures. Twenty-five banks, with assets of $371.9 billion, failed in 2008, following three failures in 2007 and none during the previous two years. In 2009 there were 140 failures, the highest number since 1992, when 179 banks failed. Bank failures increased again in 2010, rising to 157. Assets of these failed institutions totaled $92 billion, down from $170 billion the previous year.

NUMBER OF BANK FAILURES, 2001- 2010[1]

Year	Number of failures	Year	Number of failures
2001	4	2006	0
2002	11	2007	3
2003	3	2008	25
2004	4	2009	140
2005	0	2010	157

■ 63 FDIC-insured banks failed in the United States during the first eight months of 2011.

[1]Based on failures of banks and savings and loan associations insured by the FDIC.

Source: Federal Deposit Insurance Corporation (FDIC).

TOP TEN BANK AND THRIFT DEALS ANNOUNCED IN 2010[1]
($ millions)

Rank	Buyer	Target (State)	Deal value2
1	BMO Financial Group	Marshall & Ilsley Corporation (WI)	$5,799.0
2	Hancock Holding Company	Whitney Holding Corporation (LA)	1,768.4
3	First Niagara Financial Group, Inc.	NewAlliance Bancshares, Inc. (CT)	1,498.0
4	M&T Bank Corporation	Wilmington Trust Corporation (DE)	351.3
5	Nara Bancorp, Inc.	Center Financial Corporation (CA)	286.3
6	Toronto-Dominion Bank	South Financial Group, Inc. (SC)	191.6
7	United Bankshares, Inc.	Centra Financial Holdings, Inc. (WV)	185.4
8	Eastern Bank Corporation	Wainwright Bank & Trust Company (MA)	162.8
9	Berkshire Hills Bancorp, Inc.	Legacy Bancorp, Inc. (MA)	112.8
10	Community Bank System, Inc.	Wilber Corporation (NY)	101.8

[1]Target is a U.S.-domiciled bank or thrift. List does not include terminated deals.
[2]At announcement.

Source: SNL Financial LC.

TOP TEN FEDERALLY CHARTERED AND STATE-CHARTERED BANKS BY ASSETS, 2010[1]
($ billions)

Rank	Federally chartered bank[2]	Total assets	State-chartered bank	State	Total assets
1	JPMorgan Chase Bank, National Association	$1,632	The Bank of New York Mellon	NY	$182
2	Bank of America, National Association	1,482	SunTrust Bank	GA	163
3	Citibank, National Association	1,154	State Street Bank and Trust Company	MA	156
4	Wells Fargo Bank, National Association	1,102	Branch Banking and Trust Company	NC	151
5	U.S. Bank National Association	302	Regions Bank	AL	128
6	PNC Bank, National Association	257	Fifth Third Bank	OH	109
7	FIA Card Services, National Association	197	Goldman Sachs Bank USA	NY	90
8	HSBC Bank USA, National Association	181	The Northern Trust Company	IL	70
9	TD Bank, National Association	169	Ally Bank	UT	70
10	Citibank (South Dakota), N.A.	143	Manufacturers and Traders Trust Company	NY	67

[1]As of December 31, 2010.
[2]Chartered by the Office of the Comptroller of the Currency.

Source: Federal Deposit Insurance Corporation.

Profitability

In their efforts to maximize profits, commercial banks and other depository institutions must balance credit quality and future economic conditions with liquidity needs and regulatory mandates.

PROFITABILITY OF SAVINGS BANKS, COMMERCIAL BANKS AND CREDIT UNIONS, 2006-2010

| Year | Return on equity | | Return on average assets |
	Savings banks	Commercial banks	Credit unions
2006	8.68%	13.02%	0.82%
2007	1.08	9.12	0.63
2008	-7.75	1.31	-0.05
2009	1.31	-0.99	0.18
2010	5.92	5.99	0.51

Source: Federal Deposit Insurance Corporation; National Credit Union Administration.

NET INCOME OF COMMERCIAL BANKS, SAVINGS INSTITUTIONS AND CREDIT UNIONS, 2001-2010
($ millions)

| Year | Amount | | | Percent change from prior year | | |
	Commercial banks[1]	Savings institutions[1]	Credit unions[2]	Commercial banks	Savings institutions	Credit unions
2001	$73,215.3	$13,279.2	$4,492.0	4.2%	24.1%	NA
2002	89,132.0	15,243.4	5,663.0	21.7	14.8	26.1%
2003	102,578.0	18,056.0	5,779.0	15.1	18.5	2.0
2004	104,724.0	18,246.0	5,789.0	2.1	1.1	0.2
2005	114,016.0	19,894.0	5,658.0	8.9	9.0	-2.3
2006	128,217.0	17,025.0	5,723.0	12.5	-14.4	1.1
2007	97,630.0	2,362.0	4,737.0	-23.9	-86.1	-17.2
2008	15,308.0	-10,759.0	-167.0	-84.3	-555.5	-103.5
2009	-12,296.0	1,677.0	1,673.0	-180.3	[3]	[3]
2010	79,166.0	8,332.0	4,586.0	[3]	396.8	174.1

[1]FDIC-insured.
[2]Federally insured credit unions.
[3]Not applicable.
NA=Data not available.

Source: Federal Deposit Insurance Corporation; National Credit Union Administration.

Assets

- Assets of credit unions grew 3.3 percent from 2009 to 2010. Commercial bank assets grew 0.3 percent. Savings institution assets fell 0.8 percent.

FINANCIAL ASSETS OF BANKING INSTITUTIONS, 1980-2010
($ billions, end of year)

Year	Commercial banks	Savings institutions	Credit unions
1980	$1,481.7	$792.4	$67.6
1990	3,337.8	1,323.0	217.2
2000	6,708.6	1,217.7	441.1
2005	9,843.7	1,789.4	685.7
2007	11,879.0	1,815.0	758.7
2008	14,056.3	1,523.5	812.4
2009	14,288.2	1,253.7	882.7
2010	14,336.1	1,244.1	912.0

Source: Board of Governors of the Federal Reserve System, June 9, 2011.

Credit Markets

Until about 1950, commercial banks dominated the credit market. While depository institutions continue to be the leading holders of credit assets, asset shares of federal mortgage pools, government-sponsored corporations and asset-backed securities issuers generally have risen steadily over the past two decades.

CREDIT MARKET ASSET HOLDINGS, 2006-2010[1]
($ billions, amount outstanding, end of year)

	2006	2007	2008	2009	2010	Percent of total, 2010
Financial sectors						
Monetary authority	$778.9	$740.6	$986.0	$1,987.7	$2,259.2	4.3%
Commercial banking	8,040.9	8,782.1	9,425.5	9,016.9	9,187.2	17.5
U.S.-chartered commercial banks	7,144.1	7,666.8	8,197.9	8,070.3	8,267.3	15.8
Foreign banking offices in the U.S.	761.6	963.3	1,063.7	782.7	753.1	1.4
Bank holding companies	36.0	59.1	73.0	75.8	97.9	0.2
Banks in U.S.-affiliated areas	99.3	92.8	90.9	88.1	68.9	0.1
Savings institutions	1,533.2	1,596.1	1,320.0	1,070.4	1,081.0	2.1
Credit unions	622.7	657.9	697.9	731.0	744.3	1.4
Property/casualty insurance companies	864.1	869.3	853.4	886.7	890.6	1.7
Life insurance companies	2,786.4	2,871.2	2,882.8	3,022.6	3,174.2	6.1
Private pension funds	758.3	860.8	951.4	1,063.0	1,171.0	2.2

(table continues)

CREDIT MARKET ASSET HOLDINGS, 2006-2010[1] (Cont'd)
($ billions, amount outstanding, end of year)

	2006	2007	2008	2009	2010	Percent of total, 2010
State and local govt retirement funds	$808.0	$820.3	$833.5	$824.7	$816.5	1.6%
Federal govt retirement funds	84.3	96.1	120.3	127.7	138.7	0.3
Money market mutual funds	1,560.8	1,936.4	2,675.0	2,031.0	1,621.0	3.1
Mutual funds	1,932.0	2,203.1	2,276.4	2,657.2	3,031.4	5.8
Closed-end funds	171.8	170.9	129.9	139.2	143.5	0.3
Exchange-traded funds	20.7	34.0	57.0	102.9	132.6	0.3
GSEs[2]	2,590.5	2,829.5	3,033.6	2,699.7	6,333.1	12.1
Agency- and GSE[2]-backed mortgage pools	3,841.1	4,464.4	4,961.4	5,376.7	1,139.5	2.2
ABS issuers	4,087.6	4,429.0	4,036.4	3,286.2	2,299.5	4.4
Finance companies	1,811.6	1,828.2	1,755.9	1,532.6	1,482.8	2.8
Real Estate Investment Trusts	265.8	244.7	180.8	182.7	217.9	0.4
Brokers and dealers	583.4	803.1	717.4	525.3	557.5	1.1
Funding corporations	363.5	309.2	999.9	764.4	869.7	1.7
Total financial sectors	**$33,505.7**	**$36,547.1**	**$38,894.6**	**$38,028.5**	**$37,291.1**	**71.2%**
Total domestic nonfinancial sectors[3]	**$5,648.5**	**$6,223.5**	**$6,035.8**	**$6,452.3**	**$6,691.0**	**12.8%**
Rest of the world	**$6,199.7**	**$7,272.6**	**$7,503.1**	**$7,784.7**	**$8,417.4**	**16.1%**
Total credit market assets held	**$45,353.9**	**$50,043.2**	**$52,433.4**	**$52,265.5**	**$52,399.5**	**100.0%**

[1]Excluding corporate equities and mutual fund shares. [2]Government-sponsored enterprise. [3]Includes household, federal and local governments, and selected nonfinancial and nonfarm business sectors.
Source: Board of Governors of the Federal Reserve System, June 9, 2011.

EMPLOYMENT IN THE BANKING INDUSTRY, 2006-2010
(000)

Year	Commercial banks	Savings banks	Credit unions	Total
2006	1,322.9	236.7	242.4	1,802.0
2007	1,351.4	225.7	246.3	1,823.5
2008	1,357.5	207.6	250.1	1,815.2
2009	1,316.9	191.6	245.3	1,753.8
2010	1,308.4	183.1	241.9	1,733.4

Source: U.S. Department of Labor, Bureau of Labor Statistics.

- In 2010, employment fell 4.4 percent at savings institutions, 1.4 percent at credit unions and 0.6 percent at commercial banks. Overall, banking industry employment fell by 1.2 percent.

Bank Branches

Consolidation has substantially reduced the number of commercial banking institutions but has r
reduced consumers' access to their deposits as the number of bank offices and ATMs continues to
grow. There are also fewer savings institutions and offices than in 1995, and the number of credit
unions dropped by 35 percent from 1995 to 2009.

NUMBER OF BANKING OFFICES BY TYPE OF BANK, 1995-2009

	1995	2000	2007	2008	2009	2010
All banking offices[1]	**92,686**	**95,808**	**105,375**	**106,967**	**107,104**	**105,856**
Commercial bank offices	65,321	71,337	83,360	85,283	88,061	87,723
Number of institutions	10,166	8,477	7,350	7,203	6,995	6,676
Savings institution offices	15,637	14,136	13,903	13,867	11,479	10,784
Number of institutions	2,082	1,623	1,244	1,227	1,180	1,135
Credit unions	11,687	10,316	8,101	7,806	7,554	7,339
U.S. branches of foreign banks	41	19	11	11	10	10

[1]Includes commercial bank and savings institution offices, credit unions and U.S. branches of foreign banks.
Source: Federal Deposit Insurance Corporation; National Credit Union Administration.

ASSETS OF FOREIGN BANKING OFFICES IN THE UNITED STATES, 2006-2010[1]

($ billions, end of year)

	2006	2007	2008	2009	2010
Total financial assets	**$828.2**	**$1,048.0**	**$1,624.8**	**$1,267.8**	**$1,337.5**
Reserves at Federal Reserve	0.6	1.0	239.0	284.1	350.8
Total bank credit	946.8	1,151.4	1,126.0	844.2	843.2
U.S. government securities	81.9	87.5	86.0	93.5	93.5
Treasury	26.8	30.4	35.5	61.4	66.2
Agency- and GSE[2] -backed securities	55.1	57.1	50.5	32.1	27.3
Corporate and foreign bonds	292.5	369.5	401.6	244.9	233.9
Total loans	572.3	694.4	638.4	505.9	515.9
Other bank loans	361.8	466.8	531.9	406.5	390.4
Mortgages	24.9	39.0	44.2	37.8	35.4
Security credit	185.6	188.6	62.3	61.6	90.1
Customers' liability on acceptances	0.4	0.5	0.0	0.0	0.0
Miscellaneous assets	-119.6	-104.9	259.8	139.5	143.5

[1]Branches and agencies of foreign banks, Edge Act and Agreement corporations and American Express Bank.
[2]Government-sponsored enterprise.
Source: Board of Governors of the Federal Reserve System, June 9, 2011.

Commercial Banks

Commercial banks vary greatly in size from the "money center" banks located in the nation's financial centers that offer a broad array of traditional and nontraditional banking services, including international lending, to the smaller regional and local community banks engaged in more typical banking activities, such as consumer and business lending. Commercial banks receive revenue from many sources, including check writing, trust account management fees, investments, loans and mortgages. A growing number of banks also receives revenue from consumer use of Internet banking services.

In 2010 all but the largest banks (i.e., those with assets greater than $10 billion) reported fewer institutions compared with 2009. There were 202 fewer commercial banks with assets less than $100 million in 2010 than in 2009. The number of banks with $100 million to $1 billion in assets dropped by 104 banks in 2010, and banks in the $1 billion to $10 billion asset range fell by five banks. There were 86 banks with assets of more than $10 billion in 2010, up from 85 in 2009. (See Concentration, page 125.)

Assets and Liabilities

A bank's assets and liabilities are managed in order to maximize revenues and maintain liquidity. The lending sector's susceptibility to changes in interest rates, domestic and international economies, and credit quality can make revenue streams unpredictable. Banks hold substantial amounts of U.S. Treasury and government agency obligations, which are highly liquid, although the asset mix includes equity as well as other asset classes.

ASSETS OF FDIC-INSURED COMMERCIAL BANKS, 2010

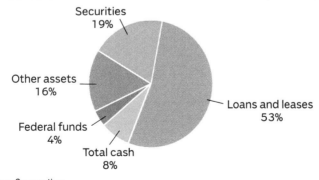

Source: Federal Deposit Insurance Corporation.

ASSETS AND LIABILITIES OF FDIC-INSURED COMMERCIAL BANKS GROUPED BY ASSET SIZE, 2010

($ millions, end of year)

	Total commercial banks	By asset size			
		Less than $100 million	$100 million to $1 billion	$1 billion or more	Foreign offices
Number of institutions	6,530	2,328	3,693	509	NA
Total assets	**$12,066,353**	**$132,179**	**$1,058,965**	**$10,875,209**	**$1,626,028**
Cash and funds due from depository institutions	923,122	13,267	79,538	830,317	224,091
Interest-bearing	738,297	8,565	58,486	671,247	NA
Securities	2,351,646	30,007	213,881	2,107,758	NA
Federal funds sold and re-repos[1]	454,321	4,409	16,028	433,885	NA
Net loans and leases	6,377,184	77,322	680,541	5,619,322	425,376
Loan loss allowance	217,700	1,410	14,151	202,139	NA
Assets held in trading accounts[2]	720,648	12	157	720,479	414,265
Bank premises and fixed assets	110,676	2,317	20,213	88,146	NA
Other real estate owned	46,718	1,062	12,091	33,565	NA
Intangible assets	373,222	422	5,351	367,450	NA
All other assets	708,815	3,362	31,165	674,288	NA
Total liabilities and capital	**$12,066,353**	**$132,179**	**$1,058,965**	**$10,875,209**	**NA**
Total liabilities	**$10,701,415**	**$117,124**	**$953,083**	**$9,631,208**	**$1,972,534**
Deposits, total	8,514,350	112,272	884,767	7,517,311	1,549,615
Interest-bearing	6,793,338	93,182	750,676	5,949,480	1,465,719
Federal funds purchased and repos[1]	528,417	716	17,812	509,889	NA
Trading liabilities	287,407	0	15	287,391	NA
Other borrowed money	919,993	3,337	42,693	873,962	NA
Subordinated notes and debentures	144,823	8	365	144,450	NA
All other liabilities	306,426	791	7,431	298,205	NA
Total equity capital	**$1,364,938**	**$15,055**	**$105,882**	**$1,244,001**	**NA**
Perpetual preferred stock	6,499	54	683	5,763	NA
Common stock	46,393	2,214	12,247	31,932	NA
Surplus	1,026,524	7,285	53,288	965,951	NA
Undivided profits	258,876	5,500	39,573	213,803	NA

[1]Short-term agreements to sell and repurchase government securities by a specified date at a set price. [2]The foreign office component of "assets held in trading accounts" is only available for institutions with $1 billion or more in total assets or $2 billion or more in off-balance sheet contracts. NA=Data not available.

Source: Federal Deposit Insurance Corporation.

Deposits

In the depository process, banks pay interest to depositors and gain income by lending and investing deposits at higher rates. Banks must balance the generation of revenue from these deposits with the maintenance of liquidity, according to FDIC guidelines. The impact of these guidelines on the banking industry is similar to that of statutory accounting practices on the insurance industry—both serve to promote solvency.

DEPOSITS, INCOME AND EXPENSES OF FDIC-INSURED COMMERCIAL BANKS, 2006-2010
($ millions, end of year)

	2006	2007	2008	2009	2010
Number of institutions	7,384	7,266	7,070	6,823	6,516
Total deposits (domestic and foreign) individuals, partnerships, corps.	**$5,991,024**	**$6,485,480**	**$7,172,255**	**$7,420,458**	**$7,689,406**
U.S. government	3,727	4,898	3,853	3,742	3,616
States and political subdivisions	286,564	322,662	350,854	381,075	386,178
All other	392,912	434,378	490,059	466,372	383,703
Total domestic and foreign deposits	**$6,674,226**	**$7,247,418**	**$8,017,021**	**$8,271,646**	**$8,462,903**
Interest-bearing	5,465,215	6,053,457	6,593,729	6,712,382	6,749,367
Noninterest-bearing	1,209,011	1,193,961	1,423,292	1,559,264	1,713,537
Domestic office deposits					
Demand deposits	507,795	504,432	637,800	642,986	689,734
Savings deposits	3,094,150	3,185,596	3,495,456	4,129,159	4,597,032
Time deposits	1,879,273	2,055,843	2,345,213	1,970,185	1,627,094
Total domestic deposits	**$5,481,218**	**$5,745,870**	**$6,478,469**	**$6,742,331**	**$6,913,859**
Transaction	703,808	695,226	839,342	892,293	945,384
Nontransaction	4,777,410	5,050,644	5,639,128	5,850,037	5,968,475
Income and expenses					
Total interest income	541,524	604,687	524,603	477,278	477,643
Total interest expense	259,277	304,149	207,352	120,058	88,007
Net interest income	282,247	300,538	317,252	357,220	389,636
Total noninterest income (fees, etc.)	216,759	210,290	193,247	241,662	217,105
Total noninterest expense	288,349	312,042	328,765	371,099	356,609
Provision for loan and lease losses	25,154	56,471	151,358	229,239	144,386
Pretax net operating income	185,503	142,315	30,376	-1,456	105,745
Securities gains (losses)	-1,346	-567	-14,443	-1,411	8,284
Income taxes	59,231	42,649	6,196	3,942	33,123
Net extraordinary items	2,648	-1,741	5,446	-3,841	-566
Net income	127,573	97,358	15,183	-11,432	79,704

Source: Federal Deposit Insurance Corporation.

Investments

SECURITIES OF FDIC-INSURED COMMERCIAL BANKS, GROUPED BY ASSET SIZE, 2010

($ millions, end of year)

	Total commercial banks	By asset size[1]		
		Less than $100 million	$100 million to $1 billion	$1 billion or more
Securities (debt and equity)	**$2,351,646**	**$30,007**	**$213,881**	**$2,107,758**
Securities held-to-maturity (amortized cost)	127,779	3,878	18,456	105,445
Securities available-for-sale (fair value)	2,223,867	26,129	195,425	2,002,313
By security type[2]:				
U.S. government securities	1,488,103	20,145	148,009	1,319,949
U.S. Treasury securities	185,959	955	6,227	178,777
U.S. government obligations	1,302,144	19,190	141,782	1,141,172
Securities issued by states and political subdivisions	171,140	8,759	54,410	107,971
Asset-backed securities	129,274	23	508	128,743
Other domestic debt securities[3]	67,751	595	5,212	61,944
Foreign debt securities[3]	239,315	4	267	239,044
Equity securities	14,773	145	1,028	13,601
Other items[2]				
Pledged securities	1,085,314	10,480	96,094	978,740
Mortgage-backed securities	1,283,995	8,427	84,994	1,190,575
Certificates of participation in pools of residential mortgages	743,681	6,140	52,521	685,019
Issued or guaranteed by the U.S.	738,562	6,122	52,461	679,979
Privately issued	5,119	19	60	5,040
Collateralized mortgage obligations and REMICs[4]	489,580	2,217	31,734	455,628
Issued by FNMA and FHLMC[5]	334,424	1,993	28,410	304,022
Privately issued by GNMA[6]	155,155	225	3,324	151,606

[1]Grouped by asset size and insurance fund membership.
[2]Includes held-to-maturity securities at amortized cost and available-for-sale securities at fair value.
[3]Institutions with less than $100 million in total assets include "foreign debt securities" in "other domestic debt securities."
[4]Real estate mortgage investment conduits (REMICs).
[5]Federal National Mortgage Association (Fannie Mae) and Federal Home Mortgage Corporation (Freddie Mac). Includes REMICs.
[6]Government National Mortgage Association (Ginnie Mae).

Source: Federal Deposit Insurance Corporation.

Concentration

As a result of consolidation over the past two decades, small banks are dropping in number and in percentage of assets and deposits held. A large share of the nation's banking business is held by a relatively small number of big banks.

COMMERCIAL BANK CONCENTRATION BY ASSET SIZE, 2006 AND 2010
($ billions, end of year)

	Less than $100 million	Percent of total	$100 million to $1 billion	Percent of total	$1 billion to $10 billion	Percent of total	Greater than $10 billion	Percent of total	Total banks
2006									
Number of institutions reporting	3,246	43.9%	3,662	49.5%	406	5.5%	88	1.2%	7,402
Total assets	$170.4	1.7	$1,039.6	10.3	$1,076.3	10.7	$7,804.3	77.3	$10,090.6
Total deposits	141.0	2.1	847.5	12.6	767.6	11.4	4,975.3	73.9	6,731.4
Return on assets	0.95%	NA	1.24%	NA	1.35%	NA	1.35%	NA	1.33%
Return on equity	7.38	NA	12.20	NA	12.65	NA	13.40	NA	13.06
2010									
Number of institutions reporting	2,325	35.6%	3,694	56.6%	424	6.5%	86	1.3%	6,529
Total assets	$131.9	1.1	$1,058.6	8.8	$1,090.4	9.0	$9,786.6	81.1	$12,067.6
Total deposits	112.0	1.3	884.0	10.4	841.9	9.9	6,676.3	78.4	8,514.3
Return on assets	0.36%	NA	0.34%	NA	0.19%	NA	0.75%	NA	0.66%
Return on equity	3.06	NA	3.35	NA	1.67	NA	6.78	NA	5.99

NA=Not applicable.

Source: Federal Deposit Insurance Corporation.

TOP TWENTY U.S. COMMERCIAL BANKS BY REVENUES, 2010
($ millions)

Rank	Company	Revenues
1	Bank of America Corp.	$134,194
2	J.P. Morgan Chase & Co.	115,475
3	Citigroup	111,055
4	Wells Fargo	93,249
5	Goldman Sachs Group	45,967
6	Morgan Stanley	39,320
7	American Express	30,242
8	U.S. Bancorp	20,518
9	Capital One Financial	19,067
10	Ally Financial	17,373
11	PNC Financial Services Group	17,096
12	Bank of New York Mellon Corp.	14,929
13	BB&T Corp.	11,072
14	SunTrust Banks	10,072
15	State Street Corp.	9,716
16	Discover Financial Services	8,241
17	Regions Financial	8,220
18	Fifth Third Bancorp	7,218
19	CIT Group	6,363
20	KeyCorp	5,458

Source: Fortune.

TOP TWENTY-FIVE U.S. COMMERCIAL BANKS BY ASSETS, 2010
($ millions)

Rank	Company	City, State	Assets
1	JPMorgan Chase Bank, National Association	Columbus, OH	$1,631,621
2	Bank of America, National Association	Charlotte, NC	1,482,278
3	Citibank, National Association	Las Vegas, NV	1,154,293
4	Wells Fargo Bank, National Association	Sioux Falls, SD	1,102,278
5	U.S. Bank, National Association	Cincinnati, OH	302,260
6	PNC Bank, National Association	Wilmington, DE	256,639
7	FIA Card Services, National Association	Wilmington, DE	196,749
8	Bank of NY Mellon	New York, NY	181,855
9	HSBC Bank USA, National Association	McLean, VA	181,118
10	TD Bank, National Association	Wilmington, DE	168,749
11	Suntrust Bank	Atlanta, GA	162,510
12	State Street Bank & Trust Company	Boston, MA	155,529
13	Branch Banking and Trust Company	Winston-Salem, NC	150,828
14	Citibank SD, National Association	Sioux Falls, SD	142,350
15	Chase Bank USA, National Association	Newark, DE	131,083
16	Regions Bank	Birmingham, AL	128,373
17	Capital One, National Association	McLean, VA	126,901
18	Fifth Third Bank	Cincinnati, OH	108,972
19	RBS Citizens, National Association	Providence, RI	107,836
20	Goldman Sachs Bank USA	New York, NY	89,447
21	Keybank, National Association	Cleveland, OH	88,592
22	Union Bank, National Association	San Francisco, CA	78,675
23	Capital One Bank USA, National Association	Glen Allen, VA	72,203
24	Northern Trust Company	Chicago, IL	70,373
25	Ally Bank	Midvale, UT	70,284

Source: Board of Governors of the Federal Reserve System.

Thrift Institutions

Savings and loan associations and savings banks fall into the category of thrift institutions. Thrifts were originally established to promote personal savings through savings accounts and home ownership through mortgage lending, but now provide a range of services similar to many commercial banks.

At their peak in the late 1960s, there were more than 4,800 thrifts. But a combination of factors has reduced their ranks significantly. These include sharp increases in interest rates in the late 1970s, which immediately raised the cost of funds without a similar rise in earnings from thrifts' principal assets, long-term, fixed-rate mortgages. In addition, the recession of the early 1980s increased loan defaults. By 2010, due mostly to acquisitions by, or conversions to, commercial banks or other savings banks, the number of thrifts had fallen to 1,128.

The 2010 Dodd-Frank Act phased out the Office of Thrift Supervision (OTS) and shifted its responsibilities to other federal agencies. Regulation of federal thrift institutions was moved to the Office of the Comptroller of the Currency (OCC). The OTS's responsibilities regarding state savings institutions were moved to the Federal Deposit Insurance Corporation and its powers regarding thrift holding companies were moved to the Federal Reserve. The OCC conducts on-site reviews of national banks, federal savings associations and federal thrifts and provides supervision of these institutions' operations. It also analyzes investments and sensitivity to market risk for all national banks and federal thrifts with less than $10 billion in assets. Depository institutions, including thrifts, with assets over $10 billion will be overseen by the new Consumer Financial Protection Bureau created by Dodd-Frank.

SELECTED INDICATORS, FDIC-INSURED SAVINGS INSTITUTIONS, 2006-2010

	2006	2007	2008	2009	2010
Return on assets (%)	0.99	0.13	-0.72	0.14	0.67
Return on equity (%)	8.68	1.08	-7.75	1.31	5.92
Core capital (leverage) ratio (%)	10.28	9.97	8.04	9.50	10.43
Noncurrent assets plus other real estate owned to assets (%)	0.63	1.46	2.40	3.00	3.07
Net charge-offs to loans (%)	0.29	0.47	1.14	1.82	1.47
Asset growth rate (%)	-3.70	4.97	-17.53	-17.50	-0.82
Net interest margin (%)	2.87	2.94	2.77	3.20	3.35
Net operating income growth (%)	-9.84	-81.68	-456.82	120.41	283.78
Number of institutions reporting	1,279	1,251	1,219	1,173	1,128
Percentage of unprofitable institutions (%)	10.24	17.19	33.31	31.54	23.23
Number of failed institutions	0	1	5	20	18
Number of assisted institutions	0	0	1	2	0

Source: Federal Deposit Insurance Corporation.

OTS-REGULATED THRIFT INDUSTRY INCOME STATEMENT DETAIL, 2006-2010
($ millions, end of year)

	2006	2007	2008	2009	2010
Interest income	$90,805	$95,904	$74,910	$52,522	$42,201
Interest expense	49,871	55,283	36,827	19,889	13,370
Net interest income before provisions for losses	40,934	40,621	38,083	32,663	28,831
Provisions for losses for interest bearing assets[1]	3,768	11,638	39,338	19,564	9,705
Net interest income after provisions for losses	37,167	28,983	-1,254	13,069	19,126
Noninterest income[2]	25,678	20,121	18,634	17,142	17,699
Noninterest expense	38,665	47,371	38,746	27,669	26,545
Income before taxes and extraordinary items	1,733	-19,131	-21,366	2,541	10,280
Income taxes	8,292	2,383	-5,638	2,554	3,895
Other[3]	-39	1	-83	52	116
Net income	-6,598	-21,513	-15,812	-34	6,477
Other items					
Gross profits of profitable thrifts	16,342	11,425	-22,029	-9,587	NA
Gross profits of unprofitable thrifts	-492	-12,074	6,217	9,616	NA

[1]Loss provisions for noninterest-bearing assets are included in noninterest expense.
[2]Net gain (loss) on sale of assets is reported in noninterest income.
[3]Defined as extraordinary items, net of tax effect and of cumulative effect of changes in accounting principles. Extraordinary items are material events and transactions that are unusual and infrequent.
NA=Data not available

Source: U.S. Department of the Treasury, Office of Thrift Supervision (OTS).

BALANCE SHEET OF THE FEDERALLY INSURED THRIFT INDUSTRY, 2006-2010

($ millions, end of year)

	2006	2007	2008	2009	2010
Number of thrifts	1,279	1,251	1,219	1,173	1,128
Assets					
Cash and investment securities	$159,259	$186,345	$174,986	$200,768	$183,446
Mortgage-backed securities	223,422	264,586	211,726	184,670	200,708
1 to 4 family loans	828,639	840,255	637,644	435,544	419,881
Multifamily loans	86,710	92,112	56,416	55,486	57,845
Construction and land development	66,403	69,574	58,311	36,754	25,753
Nonresidential loans	93,852	104,248	111,100	109,825	112,662
Consumer loans	97,385	99,409	89,546	80,498	89,768
Commercial loans	79,560	74,637	82,165	68,313	74,599
Real estate owned	1,681	3,433	4,671	5,597	5,959
Other assets	132,985	123,346	105,750	85,886	82,998
Total assets	**$1,769,896**	**$1,857,945**	**$1,532,316**	**$1,263,342**	**$1,253,619**
Liabilities and equity					
Total liabilities	1,551,941	1,653,438	1,395,422	1,126,924	1,106,258
Deposits	1,093,800	1,105,535	953,534	893,635	908,608
FHLB advances	268,326	347,771	255,079	124,719	104,876
Other borrowings	152,096	161,805	156,959	90,066	75,329
Other liabilities	37,720	38,327	29,849	18,504	17,445
Equity capital	217,955	204,507	136,895	136,417	147,361
Total liabilities and equity	**$1,769,896**	**$1,857,945**	**$1,532,316**	**$1,263,342**	**$1,253,619**

Source: U.S. Department of the Treasury, Office of Thrift Supervision (OTS).

INVESTMENT SECURITIES OF FDIC-INSURED SAVINGS INSTITUTIONS, 2001-2010

($ millions, end of year)

Year	U.S. Treasury, agencies and corporations			States and political subdivisions	Other debt securities
	U.S. Treasury	U.S. agencies and corporations	Total[1]		
2001	$3,132.5	$147,723.7	$150,856.3	$4,105.2	$32,023.1
2002	2,677.1	176,991.2	179,668.3	5,280.0	30,348.8
2003	2,599.8	198,236.7	200,836.5	6,061.4	31,112.3
2004	2,632.8	196,352.0	198,984.8	6,769.1	55,634.3
2005	5,638.1	208,328.8	213,966.9	8,524.2	79,033.4
2006	5,543.0	183,457.5	189,000.5	11,477.8	93,438.0
2007	829.7	188,754.8	189,584.4	11,672.4	143,080.3
2008	779.3	168,100.5	168,879.8	7,531.8	98,334.1
2009	2,136.1	197,113.0	199,249.2	9,099.1	77,500.2
2010	1,459.3	214,886.6	216,345.9	10,592.3	69,504.8

Year	Equity securities	Less: contra accounts[2]	Less: trading accounts	Total investment securities[3]	Memo[4] mortgage-backed securities
2001	$8,425.9	$1.6	$1,512.9	$193,895.9	$139,095.9
2002	9,837.1	0.9	742.0	224,391.3	156,107.8
2003	9,254.6	0.3	1,025.5	246,238.8	170,612.0
2004	8,801.7	0.0	4,817.0	265,373.0	197,256.8
2005	7,783.0	0.1	12,845.0	296,462.4	224,087.7
2006	7,905.3	0.0	4,974.0	296,847.7	210,370.8
2007	7,244.8	0.0	6,734.1	344,847.9	249,463.7
2008	4,907.5	0.0	6,378.8	273,274.4	199,893.8
2009	5,092.9	0.0	4,581.2	286,360.2	173,413.0
2010	4,150.5	NA	205.1	300,388.5	189,249.9

[1]Components may not add to total.
[2]Balance in account that offsets another account. Reserves for loan losses, for example, offset the loan account.
[3]Book value.
[4]Represents mortgage-backed securities, included in other columns, on a consolidated basis.
NA=Data not available.

Source: Federal Deposit Insurance Corporation.

THRIFT INDUSTRY MORTGAGE LENDING ACTIVITY, 2001-2010
($ millions, end of year)

Year	Mortgage refinancing[1]	Mortgage loans outstanding	Mortgage-backed securities outstanding	Total mortgage portfolio	Mortgage portfolio as a percent of total assets
2001	$125,889	$578,974	$92,360	$671,333	68.66%
2002	218,585	599,747	90,232	689,979	68.69
2003	368,546	787,734	91,891	879,625	80.51
2004	240,807	878,715	157,125	1,035,841	79.27
2005	250,181	980,207	172,595	1,152,802	78.74
2006	210,790	909,522	167,346	1,076,868	76.35
2007	343,891	926,475	207,584	1,134,059	75.00
2008	173,796	668,677	166,303	834,980	70.00
2009	130,711	475,993	140,813	598,806	64.00
2010	85,758	437,425	158,042	595,467	64.00

[1] Full year.

Source: U.S. Department of the Treasury, Office of Thrift Supervision (OTS).

TOP TEN U.S. THRIFT COMPANIES BY ASSETS, 2010[1]
($ billions)

Rank	Company	Parent name	Assets
1	ING Bank, FSB	ING Groep N.V.	$87.8
2	Sovereign Bank	Banco Santander SA	72.3
3	Hudson City Savings Bank	Hudson City Bancorp, Inc.	60.6
4	Charles Schwab Bank	Charles Schwab Corporation	54.9
5	USAA Federal Savings Bank	USAA Insurance Group	44.7
6	E*TRADE Bank	E*TRADE Financial Corporation	44.3
7	New York Community Bank	New York Community Bancorp, Inc.	38.9
8	American Express Bank, FSB	American Express Company	34.9
9	Citizens Bank of Pennsylvania	HM Treasury	32.3
10	OneWest Bank, FSB	IMB Management Holdings, LP	27.2

[1] Data based on regulatory financials of savings banks and savings institutions.

Source: SNL Financial LC.

TOP TEN U.S. THRIFT COMPANIES BY REVENUES, 2010[1]

($ millions)

Rank	Company	Revenues
1	American Express Bank, FSB	$6,197.7
2	GE Money Bank	3,971.9
3	USAA Federal Savings Bank	3,264.6
4	Sovereign Bank	2,596.3
5	OneWest Bank, FSB	2,051.3
6	E*TRADE Bank	1,892.5
7	ING Bank, FSB	1,535.4
8	New York Community Bank	1,456.5
9	Hudson City Savings Bank	1,340.7
10	Charles Schwab Bank	1,128.7

[1]Based on regulatory filings of savings banks and savings institutions.

Source: SNL Financial LC.

Remittances

Remittances, money from immigrants sent back to their homes, totaled over $180 billion in 2009, according to the World Bank. The flow of such funds from immigrants from Latin America and the Caribbean to their families back home, at about $60 billion, was at basically the same level in 2010 as in 2009, marking the end of the downward trend resulting from the 2008-2009 global financial and economic crisis, according to a study by the Inter-American Development Bank (IADB). Remittances to selected Latin American countries rose by 0.2 percent from 2009 to 2010, after falling 15.0 percent in the previous year. Mexico was the recipient of the largest amount of remittances in 2010, $21.3 billion. The IADB said that while it expects the trend toward recovery in remittances to continue in 2011 it does not predict that the total will reach the levels attained before the crisis. An earlier IADB study found that in 2009 most respondents sent the money through transfers (65 percent of participants); the remainder sent the money through travelers and other informal means (14 percent), the Internet (2 percent) and banks (20 percent, up from 7 percent the previous year).

REMITTANCES TO SELECTED LATIN AMERICAN COUNTRIES, 2009-2010
($ millions)

Country	2009	2010	Percent change
Mexico	$21,132	$21,271	0.7%
Brazil	4,746	4,044	-14.8
Colombia	4,134	4,023	-2.7
Guatemala	3,912	4,127	5.5
El Salvador	3,465	3,540	2.2
Dominican Republic	2,790	2,908	4.2
Peru	2,665	2,534	-4.9
Honduras	2,483	2,529	1.9
Ecuador	2,495	2,324	-6.9
Jamaica	1,798	1,911	6.3
Other	9,180	9,689	5.5
Total	**$58,800**	**$58,900**	**0.2%**

Source: Inter-American Development Bank/MIF.

The United States tops the list of countries from which immigrants send money back to their families overseas, as tracked by the World Bank. In 2009, immigrants in the United States sent $48 billion overseas, down 1.1 percent from 2008 but almost twice as much as the next highest country, Saudi Arabia, with $26 billion in remittances in 2009.

TOP TEN COUNTRIES, BY REMITTANCES SENT OVERSEAS, 2008-2009
Total amount ($ millions)

Rank	Remittance outflows	2008	2009[1]	Percent change
1	United States	$48,829	$48,308	-1.1%
2	Saudi Arabia	21,696	25,969	19.7
3	Switzerland	18,982	19,562	3.1
4	Russian Federation	26,145	18,613	-28.8
5	Germany	14,951	15,924	6.5
6	Italy	12,716	12,986	2.1
7	Spain	14,755	12,646	-14.3
8	Luxembourg	10,832	10,556	-2.5
9	Kuwait	10,323	9,912	-4.0
10	Netherlands	8,280	8,142	-1.7
	Total	**$187,510**	**$182,619**	**-2.6%**

[1]Estimates based on the International Monetary Fund's Balance of Payments Statistics Yearbook 2008.
Source: World Bank.

Credit Unions

Credit unions, generally set up by groups of individuals with a common link, such as membership in a labor union, are not-for-profit financial cooperatives that offer personal loans and other consumer banking services. Originating in Europe, the first credit union in this country was formed in Manchester, New Hampshire, in 1909. Credit unions now serve nearly 90 million people in the United States.

In 1934 President Roosevelt signed the Federal Credit Union Act into law, authorizing the establishment of federally chartered credit unions in all states. The purpose of the federal law was "to make more available to people of small means credit for provident [provisions for the future] purposes through a national system of cooperative credit..." In 1970 the National Credit Union Administration, which charters and supervises credit unions, was created along with the National Credit Union Share Insurance Fund, which insures members' deposits. Individual credit unions are served by 28 federally insured corporate credit unions, which provide investment, liquidity and payment services for their members.

FEDERAL CREDIT UNIONS AND FEDERALLY INSURED STATE-CHARTERED CREDIT UNIONS, 1980-2009
(End of year)

	1980	1990	2000	2007	2008	2009
Operating credit unions						
Federal	12,440	8,511	6,336	4,847	4,714	4,589
State	4,910	4,349	3,980	2,959	2,840	2,750
Number of failed institutions	239	164	29	18	28	18
Members (000)						
Federal	24,519	36,241	43,883	49,100	49,600	50,100
State	12,338	19,454	33,705	39,500	40,300	40,400
Assets ($ millions)						
Federal	$40,092	$130,073	$242,881	$447,124	$482,684	$500,075
State	20,870	68,133	195,363	364,132	402,069	414,395
Loans outstanding ($ millions)						
Federal	26,350	83,029	163,851	309,277	311,154	306,300
State	14,852	44,102	137,485	256,720	261,285	258,600
Shares ($ millions)						
Federal	36,263	117,892	210,188	373,366	408,832	427,600
State	18,469	62,082	169,053	307,762	343,835	358,900

Source: National Credit Union Administration.

- From 1980 to 2009 federal and federally insured state credit union assets grew from $61 billion to $885 billion. In 2009 assets increased by $74 billion, or 9.1 percent, from 2008.

- There are currently fewer than 500 nonfederally insured state-chartered credit unions.

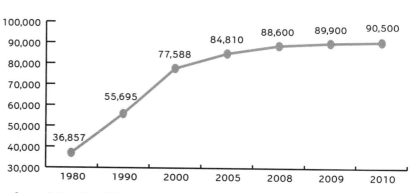

CREDIT UNION MEMBERS, 1980-2010
(000)

Source: National Credit Union Administration.

ASSETS AND LIABILITIES OF CREDIT UNIONS, 2006-2010
($ billions, end of year)

	2006	2007	2008	2009	2010
Total financial assets	$716.2	$758.7	$812.4	$882.7	$912.0
Reserves at Federal Reserve	0.0	0.0	4.7	22.8	36.9
Checkable deposits and currency	44.4	43.3	37.6	39.1	32.8
Time and savings deposits	17.0	17.0	28.3	37.8	43.2
Federal funds and security repos[1]	5.1	2.5	-2.3	0.1	0.0
Credit market instruments	622.7	657.9	697.9	731.0	744.3
Open market paper	1.0	0.4	0.0	0.0	0.0
U.S. government securities	79.9	78.8	91.7	125.0	164.0
Treasury	7.4	10.4	8.8	14.2	18.4
Agency- and GSE[2]-backed securities	72.5	68.4	82.9	110.8	145.6
Corporate and foreign bonds	30.6	34.6	25.7	18.6	0.0
Other loans and advances	26.8	26.9	29.6	32.3	33.1
Home mortgages	249.7	281.5	314.7	317.9	320.8
Consumer credit	234.5	235.7	236.2	237.2	226.5
Mutual fund shares	2.1	2.1	2.0	1.3	1.5
Miscellaneous assets	24.9	35.9	44.2	50.6	53.4

(table continues)

ASSETS AND LIABILITIES OF CREDIT UNIONS, 2006-2010 (Cont'd)
($ billions, end of year)

	2006	2007	2008	2009	2010
Total liabilities	**$648.7**	**$688.2**	**$742.7**	**$815.3**	**$840.9**
Shares/deposits	620.6	652.3	697.4	769.4	803.8
Checkable	72.6	73.7	75.3	86.9	92.4
Small time and savings	483.0	508.7	551.7	655.1	681.3
Large time	65.0	69.9	70.4	27.3	30.1
Other loans and advances	18.9	32.3	40.6	26.5	26.1
Miscellaneous liabilities	9.2	3.6	4.7	19.4	11.0

[1]Security repurchase agreements; short-term agreements to sell and repurchase government securities at a specified date and at a set price.
[2]Government-sponsored enterprise.
Source: Board of Governors of the Federal Reserve System, June 9, 2011.

CREDIT UNION DISTRIBUTION BY ASSET SIZE, 2009[1]
(End of year)

Asset size ($ millions)	Number of credit unions	Percent change from Dec. 2008	Assets ($ millions)	Percent change from Dec. 2008
$0 to $0.2	115	-13.5%	$13	-17.6%
$0.2 to $0.5	212	-3.2	74	-4.0
$0.5 to $1	259	-12.2	192	-12.0
$1 to $2	433	-5.0	645	-4.2
$2 to $5	872	-8.0	2,994	-7.3
$5 to $10	980	-5.8	7,183	-6.1
$10 to $20	1,114	-0.5	16,006	-0.7
$20 to $50	1,361	-3.5	43,774	-4.7
$50 to $100	840	5.9	58,903	5.1
$100 to $200	575	-0.5	80,711	0.4
$200 to $500	466	-1.5	147,225	-0.9
$500 to $1,000	209	1.5	146,032	0.8
More than $1,000	169	6.3	430,384	7.5
Total	**7,605**	**-2.9%**	**$934,134**	**3.3%**

[1]From Credit Union Call Reports.
Source: Credit Union National Association.

TOP TEN U.S. CREDIT UNIONS BY ASSETS, 2009[1]
($ millions)

Rank	Company	Assets
1	Navy Federal Credit Union	$44,198.4
2	State Employees'	21,463.2
3	Pentagon	14,894.9
4	Boeing Employees	9,180.7
5	SchoolsFirst	8,497.4
6	The Golden 1	7,748.7
7	Alliant	7,592.4
8	Security Service	6,167.9
9	Star One	5,431.6
10	American Airlines	5,192.8

[1]Federally insured credit unions.

Source: National Credit Union Administration.

Overview

The securities industry consists of securities brokers and dealers, investment banks and advisers, and stock exchanges. Together, these entities facilitate the flow of funds from investors to companies and institutions seeking to finance expansions or other projects. Firms that make up the securities sector may specialize in one segment of the business or engage in a wide range of activities that includes brokerage, asset management and advisory services, as well as investment banking and annuity sales.

Investment banking involves the underwriting of new debt securities (bonds) and equity securities (stocks) issued by private or government entities to finance new projects. Investment banks buy the new issues and, acting essentially as wholesalers, sell them, primarily to institutional investors such as banks, mutual funds and pension funds. Investment banks are sometimes referred to as securities dealers or broker/dealers because many also participate in the financial market as retailers, selling to individual investors. The primary difference between a broker and dealer is that dealers buy and sell securities for their own account, whereas brokers act as intermediaries for investors who wish to purchase or sell securities. Dealers make money by selling at a slightly higher price than they paid. Like underwriters and wholesalers, they face the risk that the securities in their inventory will drop in price before they can resell them.

In 2008 massive mortgage and real estate investment losses led to an upheaval in the securities industry, which included the takeover of Bear Stearns by JP Morgan Chase and the collapse of Lehman Brothers, the largest bankruptcy in U.S. history. Also in 2008 Morgan Stanley and Goldman Sachs got regulatory approval to convert to traditional bank holding companies (BHCs). Both now have financial holding company status, which expands the financial services activities that BHCs are permitted.

Regulation

The Dodd-Frank Wall Street Reform and Consumer Protection Act, the massive financial services regulatory overhaul enacted in July 2010, has key implications for the securities industry, including provisions that affect the regulation of capital market transactions, credit agencies, hedge funds and derivatives. A year after its passage, legislators were still hammering out the details of how and when many of the law's provisions would be implemented.

Securities and Exchange Commission: The Securities and Exchange Commission (SEC), established by Congress in 1934, regulates the U.S. securities markets. Its mission is to protect investors and maintain the integrity of the market by enacting new regulations and interpreting and enforcing existing laws. The Dodd-Frank Act enhanced the SEC's enforcement authority in a number of areas, including antifraud actions and the servicing of subpoenas. The act exempts indexed annuities from SEC regulation, thus keeping them under the purview of state insurance departments.

The Financial Industry Regulatory Authority: The Financial Industry Regulatory Authority (FINRA) is the largest nongovernmental regulator of the securities industry. Its members include all securities firms doing business in the United States. Its role is to promote investor protection through such activities as registering and examining securities firms, enforcing federal securities laws, rule writing and dispute resolution. The body was formed in 2007 through the consolidation of the enforcement and arbitration functions of the New York Stock Exchange with those of FINRA's predecessor organization, the National Association of Securities Dealers (NASD).

NUMBER OF FINANCIAL INDUSTRY REGULATORY AUTHORITY (FINRA) REPORTING FIRMS, 2001-2010

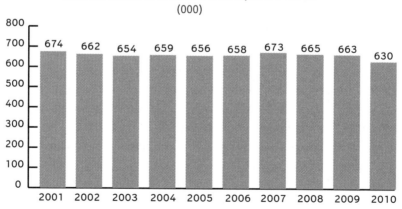

Source: Securities Industry and Financial Markets Association.

NUMBER OF FINANCIAL INDUSTRY REGULATORY AUTHORITY (FINRA) REGISTERED REPRESENTATIVES, 2001-2010
(000)

Source: Securities Industry and Financial Markets Association.

Mergers and Acquisitions

The largest 2010 securities deal, AXA's acquisition of a portfolio of private equity funds, totaled $1.9 billion, in contrast to 2009's largest deal, Wells Fargo & Company's purchase of Prudential's $4.5 billion stake in Wells Fargo Advisors.

TOP TEN SECURITIES AND INVESTMENT FIRMS MERGERS AND ACQUISITIONS, 2010[1]

($ millions)

Rank	Buyer	Industry	Target	Industry	Deal value[2]
1	AXA	Insurance	Portfolio of private equity funds	Asset manager	$1,900.0
2	JPMorgan Chase & Co.	Bank	RBS Sempra Commodities' global metals, oil and European energy businesses	Broker/dealer	1,710.0
3	Man Group Plc	Asset manager	GLG Partners, Inc.	Asset manager	1,522.2
4	Affiliated Managers Group, Inc.	Asset manager	Pantheon Ventures Inc.	Asset manager	1,000.0
5	Intercontinental-Exchange, Inc.	Broker/dealer	Climate Exchange plc	Broker/dealer	588.4
6	Hanwha Group	Not classified	Prudential's units	Asset manager	425.3
7	Stifel Financial Corp.	Broker/dealer	Thomas Weisel Partners Group, Inc.	Broker/dealer	354.0
8	Bank of New York Mellon Corporation	Bank	BHF Asset Servicing GmbH	Broker/dealer	344.3
9	Investor group	Not classified	Artemis Investment Management, Ltd.	Asset manager	326.2
10	Sprott Inc.	Asset manager	Global Companies	Asset manager	244.2

[1]Securities and investments firm is either buyer or target. List does not include terminated deals.
[2]At announcement.

Source: SNL Financial LC.

- Bank purchases of securities firms accounted for 24 percent of securities industry mergers and acquisitions from 2006 to 2010. (See also Chapter 4: Convergence.)

MERGERS AND ACQUISITIONS OF U.S. SECURITIES FIRMS, 2006-2010[1]

	2006	2007	2008	2009	2010
Number of deals	169	188	182	178	168
Purchased by banks and thrifts	51	49	45	43	22

[1]Target is a U.S.-domiciled securities and investment firm. List does not include terminated deals.
Source: SNL Financial LC.

Profitability

SECURITIES INDUSTRY PRETAX RETURN ON EQUITY, 2001-2010[1]
(Percent)

- The security industry's return on equity was 16.2 percent in 2010, down from 45.4 percent in 2009.

- The 2008 return on equity (negative 38.5 percent) was the lowest in the 29 years that the Securities Industry and Financial Markets Association has kept records.

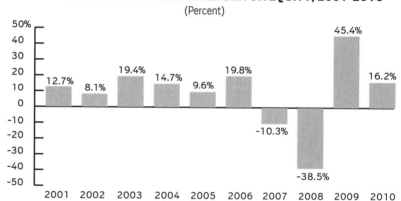

[1]New York Stock Exchange reporting firms doing public business in the United States.
Source: Securities Industry and Financial Markets Association.

SECURITIES INDUSTRY PRETAX PROFIT/LOSS, 2001-2010[1]
($ billions)

- The securities industry posted a pretax profit of $25.1 billion in 2010, following a record high of $58.6 billion in 2009.

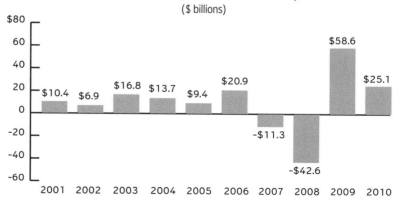

[1]New York Stock Exchange reporting firms doing public business in the United States.
Source: Securities Industry and Financial Markets Association.

FINANCIAL DATA OF NYSE-REPORTING FIRMS, 2010[1]

($ millions)

Revenue	
Commissions	$25,002
Trading gain (loss)	16,678
Investment account gain (loss)	375
Underwriting	20,344
Margin interest	3,796
Mutual fund sales	5,307
Asset management fees	20,646
Research	73
Commodities	2,577
Other revenue related to the securities business	50,649
Other revenue	14,322
Total revenue	**$159,767**
Expenses	
Total compensation	$66,858
Registered representative compensation	26,189
Clerical employee compensation	39,224
Total floor costs	8,073
Communications expense	4,985
Data processing (EDP) costs	2,372
Occupancy and equipment costs	5,540
Promotional costs	1,022
Interest expense	19,568
Losses from error accounts and bad debts	250
Regulatory fees and expenses	1,338
Nonrecurring charges	62
Other expenses	24,607
Total expenses	**$134,674**
Pretax net income (loss)	**$25,092**

[1]New York Stock Exchange reporting firms doing public business in the United States.

Source: NYSE Euronext; Securities Industry and Financial Markets Association.

ASSETS AND LIABILITIES OF SECURITIES BROKER/DEALERS, 2006-2010
($ billions)

	2006	2007	2008	2009	2010
Total financial assets	$2,741.7	$3,092.0	$2,217.2	$2,084.2	$2,075.1
Checkable deposits and currency	80.5	105.0	120.1	90.7	96.9
Credit market instruments	583.4	803.1	717.4	525.3	557.5
Open market paper	64.3	87.1	65.7	41.5	36.2
U.S. government securities	71.0	230.2	433.2	233.9	244.3
Treasury	-67.0	-60.0	190.6	123.0	94.5
Agency- and GSE[1]-backed securities	138.0	290.2	242.6	110.9	149.8
Municipal securities	50.9	50.1	38.7	35.4	40.0
Corporate and foreign bonds	355.5	382.8	123.8	171.3	184.3
Other loans and advances	41.7	52.8	55.9	43.2	52.6
Corporate equities	186.4	224.8	109.2	124.2	117.2
Security credit	292.1	325.5	164.8	203.0	278.2
Miscellaneous assets	1,599.4	1,633.7	1,105.7	1,141.0	1,025.3
Total liabilities	$2,669.1	$3,020.5	$2,146.3	$1,998.5	$1,987.7
Security repos[2] (net)	1,071.8	1,147.3	586.9	470.9	404.7
Credit market instruments	68.8	64.8	142.6	92.9	129.7
Corporate bonds	68.8	64.8	97.1	92.9	129.7
Other bank loans	0.0	0.0	45.5	0.0	0.0
Trade payables	48.3	45.8	21.2	70.1	18.1
Security credit	957.8	1,200.9	963.6	888.2	936.6
Customer credit balances	655.7	866.4	742.7	668.6	694.3
From banks	302.2	334.5	221.0	219.6	242.3
Taxes payable	2.8	2.2	2.5	5.7	3.6
Miscellaneous liabilities	519.5	559.5	429.5	470.8	495.0
Foreign direct investment in U.S.	61.0	63.7	60.2	85.2	100.4
Due to affiliates	596.5	560.4	626.1	1,158.5	1,142.8
Other	-137.9	-64.6	-256.8	-773.0	-748.2

[1]Government-sponsored enterprise.
[2]Security repurchase agreements: short-term agreements to sell and repurchase government securities at a specified date and at a set price.

Source: Board of Governors of the Federal Reserve System, June 9, 2011.

SECURITIES INDUSTRY EMPLOYMENT BY FUNCTION, 2006-2010
(000)

	2006	2007	2008	2009	2010
Securities, commodity contracts, investments (total industry)	**818.3**	**848.6**	**864.2**	**811.3**	**800.9**
Securities and commodity contracts, brokerages and exchanges	510.6	518.8	516.2	475.7	468.6
Securities brokerage	300.1	302.9	301.5	283.9	279.7
Other financial investment activities	307.8	329.7	348.0	335.6	332.3
Miscellaneous intermediation	23.7	24.0	26.1	25.4	24.2
Portfolio management	121.0	129.3	141.3	135.1	132.3
Investment advice	121.3	130.1	133.5	131.6	133.3
All other financial activities	41.8	46.3	47.2	43.4	42.4

Source: U.S. Department of Labor, Bureau of Labor Statistics.

TOTAL CAPITAL OF NYSE REPORTING FIRMS, 2001-2010
($ billions)

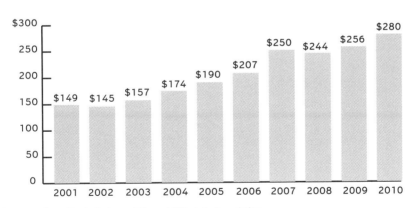

Source: NYSE Euronext; Securities Industry and Financial Markets Association.

EQUITY CAPITAL OF NYSE REPORTING FIRMS, 2001-2010
($ billions)

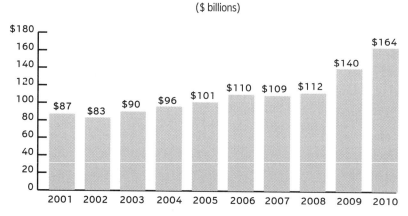

Source: NYSE Euronext; Securities Industry and Financial Markets Association.

TOP FIVE U.S. SECURITIES FIRMS BY REVENUES, 2010[1]
($ millions)

Rank	Company	Revenues
1	KKR	$9,668
2	BlackRock	8,612
3	Franklin Resources	5,853
4	Charles Schwab	4,474
5	NYSE Euronext	4,425

[1]Based on all securities firms in the Fortune 500.
Source: Fortune.

TOP TEN PUBLICLY TRADED U.S. SECURITIES AND INVESTMENT COMPANIES BY ASSETS, 2010[1]
($ millions, end of year)

Rank	Company	Assets
1	Goldman Sachs Group, Inc.[2]	$911,332
2	Morgan Stanley[2]	807,698
3	BlackRock, Inc.	178,459
4	Charles Schwab Corporation	92,568
5	Annaly Capital Management, Inc.	83,027
6	Brookfield Asset Management Inc.	78,131
7	MF Global Holdings Ltd.	50,966
8	KKR & Co. L.P.	38,391
9	Jefferies Group, Inc.	36,727
10	IntercontinentalExchange, Inc.	26,642

[1]Includes assets managers, investment companies and broker/dealers.
[2]Financial holding company. Classified as a securities firm by SNL Financial LC on the basis of its business model.

Source: SNL Financial LC.

Capital Markets

Investment Banking

Investment banks underwrite securities for the business community and offer investment advice. The type of equity deals they bring to market reflects a variety of factors including investor sentiment, the economy and market cycles. Examples of how these market factors drive this segment of the securities business include the rise and retreat of technology stocks; the varying levels of initial public offerings, where new stock issues are first offered to the public; and fluctuations in merger and acquisition activity.

In 2008 the crisis in the U.S. financial markets led to a shake up in the investment banking industry. Following the collapse of the giant investment bank Lehman Brothers, Goldman Sachs and Morgan Stanley opted to convert to bank holding companies.

CORPORATE UNDERWRITING, 2006-2010
($ billions)

Year	Value of U.S. corporate underwritings			Number of U.S. corporate underwritings		
	Debt	Equity	Total	Debt	Equity	Total
2006	$2,793.0	$190.6	$2,983.6	5,814	812	6,626
2007	2,488.2	247.5	2,735.7	4,557	825	5,382
2008	933.8	242.6	1,176.4	1,390	377	1,767
2009	1,118.2	264.2	1,382.4	1,505	942	2,447
2010	1,218.4	261.6	1,480.0	1,799	1,071	2,870

Source: Thomson Reuters; Securities Industry and Financial Markets Association.

CORPORATE AND GOVERNMENT EQUITY AND DEBT, 2001-2010
($ billions, end of year)

Year	Corporate equities[1]	Corporate bonds[2]	Total U.S. government securities[3]	Municipal bonds
2001	$15,628.6	$5,577.9	$8,341.8	$1,603.4
2002	12,438.3	6,255.7	9,146.1	1,762.8
2003	16,638.5	7,047.2	9,977.6	1,900.4
2004	18,940.1	7,921.8	10,455.2	2,030.9
2005	20,636.1	8,693.6	10,842.5	2,225.8
2006	24,339.3	9,981.8	11,354.1	2,403.2
2007	25,576.0	11,435.0	12,496.9	2,618.8
2008	15,638.1	11,016.5	14,504.9	2,680.2
2009	20,101.4	11,434.4	15,888.7	2,808.9
2010	22,961.6	11,332.2	16,959.7	2,925.3

[1]Market value.
[2]Includes foreign bonds.
[3]Includes Treasury and agency- and government-sponsored enterprise-backed securities.

Source: Board of Governors of the Federal Reserve System, June 9, 2011.

Municipal Bonds

Municipal bonds are debt obligations issued by state or local governments to raise funds for general government needs (general obligation bonds) or special projects (revenue bonds). The average daily trading volume of these bonds nearly tripled from $8.8 billion in 2000 to $26.5 billion in 2007. Volume dropped to $15.0 billion in 2009 from $21.8 billion in 2008 and remained at that level in 2010.

There are a variety of types of municipal bonds. Revenue bonds are used to fund projects that will eventually create revenue directly, such as a toll plaza. The principal and interest on revenue bonds are paid out of the revenues of the local government operation that issued the bonds. General obligation bonds are unsecured bonds; the principal and interest are backed by the "full faith and credit" of the local government and paid for out of the municipality's general revenues.

Municipal bonds are usually sold in blocks to securities dealers, who either submit competitive bids for the bonds or negotiate a sale price. Negotiation is the prevailing form when the issuer is new to the financial markets or when the issue is particularly complex. Negotiation enables the underwriting dealer to become familiar with the issuer and the bonds and to help the municipality structure a complex issue. In some cases, new issues of municipal bonds are sold through private placements, in which issuers sell the bonds directly to investors, without a public offering.

NUMBER AND VALUE OF LONG-TERM MUNICIPAL BOND UNDERWRITINGS, 2001-2010[1]
($ billions)

Year	Revenue bonds		General obligation bonds		Private placement bonds		Total municipal bonds	
	Value	Number	Value	Number	Value	Number	Value	Number
2001	$183.2	6,457	$101.4	6,874	$3.1	455	$287.7	13,786
2002	229.4	6,505	125.4	7,552	2.7	341	357.5	14,398
2003	238.2	6,688	140.6	8,065	3.9	277	382.7	15,030
2004	227.8	6,022	129.1	7,295	2.9	286	359.8	13,603
2005	262.4	6,108	144.0	7,664	1.8	176	408.2	13,948
2006	267.5	5,921	114.6	6,537	4.4	284	386.5	12,742
2007	294.3	5,994	130.1	6,263	4.9	372	429.3	12,629
2008	277.1	4,713	110.3	5,658	4.2	315	391.5	10,686
2009	251.9	4,227	155.2	7,081	2.7	189	409.8	11,497
2010	283.4	5,307	147.3	8,258	2.4	160	433.1	13,725

[1]Excludes taxable municipal bonds and bonds with maturities under 13 months.

Source: Thomson Reuters; Securities Industry and Financial Markets Association.

Private Placements

Private placement is the sale of stocks, bonds or other securities directly to an institutional investor such as an insurance company. If the purchase is for investment purposes, as opposed to resale purposes, the transaction does not have to be registered with the Securities and Exchange Commission, as public offerings do.

PRIVATE PLACEMENTS, 2006-2010
($ billions)

Year	Value of U.S. private placements			Number of U.S. private placements		
	Debt	Equity	Total	Debt	Equity	Total
2006	$524.0	$76.2	$600.2	2,721	738	3,459
2007	579.6	139.9	719.5	2,031	980	3,011
2008	169.0	127.8	296.8	528	862	1,390
2009	164.2	33.9	198.0	517	520	1,037
2010	154.4	34.9	189.3	546	671	1,217

Source: Thomson Reuters; Securities Industry and Financial Markets Association.

FOREIGN HOLDINGS OF U.S. SECURITIES, 2001-2010
($ billions, end of year)

Year	Stocks	Corporate bonds	Treasuries[1]	Total
2001	$1,441.0	$1,018.7	$1,599.3	$4,059.0
2002	1,221.6	1,123.0	1,916.1	4,260.7
2003	1,674.6	1,330.0	2,168.8	5,173.4
2004	1,904.6	1,558.9	2,688.8	6,152.3
2005	2,039.1	1,762.9	2,997.3	6,799.3
2006	2,448.1	2,320.5	3,389.8	8,158.4
2007	2,812.2	2,719.1	3,958.8	9,490.1
2008	1,806.7	2,354.0	4,658.3	8,819.0
2009	2,427.9	2,489.3	4,864.4	9,781.6
2010	3,071.3	2,446.7	5,544.3	11,062.3

[1]Includes agency issues.

Source: Board of Governors of the Federal Reserve System, June 9, 2011.

U.S. HOLDINGS OF FOREIGN SECURITIES, 2001-2010
($ billions, end of year)

Year	Stocks[1]	Bonds	Total
2001	$1,612.7	$557.1	$2,169.8
2002	1,374.0	702.7	2,076.7
2003	2,079.4	868.9	2,948.3
2004	2,560.4	985.0	3,545.4
2005	3,317.7	1,011.6	4,329.3
2006	4,329.0	1,275.5	5,604.5
2007	5,248.0	1,587.1	6,835.1
2008	2,748.4	1,237.3	3,985.7
2009	3,977.4	1,493.6	5,471.0
2010	4,399.1	1,582.1	5,981.2

[1]Market value.

Source: Board of Governors of the Federal Reserve System, June 9, 2011.

Asset-Backed Securities

Asset-backed securities (ABS) are bonds that represent pools of loans of similar types, duration and interest rates. By selling their loans to ABS packagers, the original lenders recover cash quickly, enabling them to make more loans. The asset-backed securities market increased significantly from 1999 to 2007, but growth decreased for the three consecutive years ending in 2010. Asset-backed securities may be insured by bond insurers. In 2010, 80 percent of ABSs consisted of bundled mortgages, compared with 66 percent in 2009. See also Chapter 9, Mortgage Industry.

ASSET-BACKED SECURITY SOURCES, 2006 AND 2010

2006

Trade receivables 3%
Business loans 6%
Treasury securities 1%
Agency securities[2] 9%
Consumer loans 16%
Mortgages[1] 66%

2010

Trade receivables 2%
Treasury securities 2%
Consumer loans 6%
Agency securities[2] 1%
Business loans 10%
Mortgages[1] 80%

[1]Mortgages backing privately issued pool securities and CMOs.
[2]Securities of federal mortgage pools backing privately issued collateralized mortgage obligations (CMOs). In CMOs, mortgage principal and interest payments are separated into different payment streams to create bonds that repay capital over differing periods of time.

Source: Board of Governors of the Federal Reserve System, June 9, 2011.

Asset-Backed Securities/Derivatives

ASSET-BACKED SECURITY SOURCES, 2001-2010
($ billions, end of year)

Year	Agency securities[1]	Mortgages[2]	Consumer loans	Business loans	Trade receivables	Treasury securities	Total
2001	$211.4	$725.1	$597.8	$127.7	$89.1	$0.5	$1,751.7
2002	286.5	836.0	630.4	144.0	83.5	0.9	1,981.3
2003	368.7	1,009.5	594.8	149.2	92.3	2.8	2,217.4
2004	361.1	1,446.1	571.5	168.1	102.6	8.0	2,657.5
2005	330.4	2,131.4	609.9	188.3	99.8	27.7	3,387.6
2006	355.3	2,761.5	661.1	253.4	108.3	56.4	4,195.9
2007	381.6	2,936.0	683.7	341.9	111.7	85.8	4,540.6
2008	353.5	2,584.5	646.4	379.8	95.5	72.2	4,131.9
2009	126.0	2,199.7	577.9	328.7	61.3	53.9	3,347.4
2010	18.3	1,887.0	131.7	222.2	51.8	40.3	2,351.3

[1]Securities of federal mortgage pools backing privately issued collateralized mortgage obligations (CMOs). In CMOs, mortgage principal and interest payments are separated into different payment streams to create bonds that repay capital over differing periods of time.
[2]Mortgages backing privately issued pool securities and CMOs.

Source: Board of Governors of the Federal Reserve System, June 9, 2011.

Derivatives

Financial derivatives are contracts that derive their value from the performance of an underlying financial asset, such as publicly traded securities and foreign currencies. They are used as hedging instruments to protect against changes in asset value. There are many kinds of derivatives, including futures, options and swaps. Futures and options contracts are traded on the floors of exchanges. Swaps are over-the-counter, privately negotiated agreements between two parties. The number of futures contracts traded on U.S. exchanges more than quadrupled from 629 million in 2001 to 2.9 billion in 2008, dropped to 2.3 billion in 2009 and rebounded to 2.8 billion in 2010.

Credit derivatives are contracts that lenders, large bondholders and other investors can purchase to protect against credit risks. One such derivative, credit default swaps (CDSs), protects lenders when companies do not pay their debt. The swaps are contracts between two parties: the buyer of the credit protection and the seller, i.e., the firm offering protection. Their workings are similar to insurance. Under the contract the buyer makes payments to the seller over an arranged period of time. The seller pays only if there is a default or other credit problem. Either the buyer or the seller can sell the contract to a third party. These instruments are often valued based on computer models; the actual value at settlement might be quite different from the modeled value. Banks, insurance companies and hedge funds create and trade the CDSs, which are largely unregulated and experienced enormous growth from 2004 to 2007 but declined sharply in the three subsequent years.

Bond insurers now issue protection in the form of CDSs in addition to their traditional bond insurance coverage. According to the Bank for International Settlements, the CDS market dropped from $58.2 trillion in 2007 to $29.9 trillion in 2010, based on data from The Group of Ten (G10), made up of eleven industrial countries (Belgium, Canada, France, Germany, Italy, Japan, the Netherlands, Sweden, Switzerland, the United Kingdom and the United States) which work together on economic and financial matters.

CREDIT DEFAULT SWAPS MARKET, 2004-2010[1]

($ billions , end of year)

Year	Amount outstanding[2]	Percent change
2004	$6,395.7	NA
2005	13,908.3	117.5%
2006	28,650.3	106.0
2007	58,243.7	103.3
2008	41,882.7	-28.1
2009	32,692.7	-21.9
2010	29,897.6	-8.5

[1]Based on over-the-counter derivatives data from the G10 countries (11 countries). [2]Notional principal value outstanding. Notional value is the underlying (face) value. NA=Data not available.
Source: Bank for International Settlements.

NUMBER OF FUTURES CONTRACTS TRADED ON U.S. EXCHANGES, 2001-2010

(millions)

Year	Interest rate	Agricultural commodities	Energy products	Foreign currency	Equity indices	Precious metals	Non-precious metals	Other	Total
2001	342.2	72.3	72.5	21.7	107.2	9.6	2.9	0.7	629.2
2002	418.8	79.2	92.1	23.5	221.5	12.4	2.9	1.0	851.3
2003	509.6	87.9	91.9	33.6	296.7	16.9	3.2	3.1	1,043.0
2004	704.2	101.8	109.5	51.1	330.0	21.3	3.3	2.9	1,324.0
2005	870.5	116.4	140.5	84.8	406.8	23.4	4.0	6.5	1,652.9
2006	1,034.6	157.5	190.9	114.0	500.4	34.3	3.3	1.1	2,043.9
2007	1,333.1	193.3	240.9	143.0	659.3	44.1	3.8	19.2	2,644.6
2008	1,213.1	215.4	285.9	155.8	904.9	56.2	4.6	13.0	2,852.5
2009	854.6	196.6	313.1	156.3	744.7	48.8	6.4	4.8	2,328.1
2010	1,123.0	239.5	350.6	229.1	740.6	4.8	63.8	10.4	2,764.8

Source: Futures Industry Association; Securities Industry and Financial Markets Association.

Securities

Derivatives

NUMBER OF OPTIONS CONTRACTS TRADED ON U.S. EXCHANGES, 2001-2010
(millions)

- The number of options contracts traded on U.S. exchanges rose by 9.3 percent in 2010, following a 2.8 percent decline in 2009 and a 26.8 percent rise in 2008.

Year	Equity	Stock index	Foreign currency	Interest rate	Futures	Total
2001	701.1	79.6	0.6	[1]	168.2	949.4
2002	679.4	100.6	0.4	[1]	213.1	993.6
2003	789.2	118.3	0.3	0.1	221.7	1,129.5
2004	1032.4	149.3	0.2	0.1	289.2	1,471.2
2005	1,292.2	211.8	0.2	0.1	368.0	1,872.2
2006	1,717.7	310.0	0.1	0.2	501.5	2,529.4
2007	2,379.1	267.9	2.8	[1]	583.6	3,233.5
2008	3,284.8	292.2	5.6	[1]	518.9	4,101.5
2009	3,367.0	244.1	1.6	[1]	374.5	3,987.1
2010	3,610.4	287.8	0.8	[1]	457.3	4,356.4

[1]Fewer than 50,000 interest rate contracts traded.

Source: Options Clearing Corporation; Futures Industry Association; Securities Industry and Financial Markets Association.

GLOBAL DERIVATIVES MARKET, 2001-2010[1]
($ billions)

Year	Exchange-traded	Over-the-counter	Total
2001	$23,755	$111,178	$134,933
2002	23,831	141,665	165,497
2003	36,701	197,167	233,867
2004	46,521	258,628	305,149
2005	57,258	299,261	356,519
2006	69,399	418,131	487,530
2007	79,088	585,932	665,020
2008	57,744	598,147	655,892
2009	73,118	603,900	677,017
2010	67,946	601,048	668,995

[1]Notional principal value outstanding. Notional value is the underlying (face) value.

Source: Bank for International Settlements; Securities Industry and Financial Markets Association.

Exchanges

Exchanges are markets where sales of securities and commodities are transacted. Most stock exchanges are auction markets where stocks are traded through competitive bidding in a central location. The oldest stock exchanges in the United States are the New York Stock Exchange (NYSE) and the American Stock Exchange (AMEX). In 2008 AMEX was acquired by NYSE Euronext, a holding company for a number of exchanges in the U.S. and Europe, including the NYSE.

Stocks are also traded in dealer markets. Most transactions in a dealer market are between principals acting as dealers for their own accounts rather than between brokers acting as agents for buyers and sellers. One example is the NASDAQ, the first electronic stock market, introduced in 1971. NASDAQ's dealer markets have come to more closely resemble auction markets. As with auction markets, companies must meet size and earnings requirements to trade on NASDAQ.

Over-the-counter (OTC) stocks are another segment of the securities market. Securities transactions are conducted through a telephone and computer network connecting dealers, rather than on the floor of an exchange. OTC stocks, which dropped by 21 percent from 3,006 securities in September 2010 to 2,385 in September 2011, are traditionally those of smaller companies that do not meet the listing requirements of NYSE, AMEX or NASDAQ. OTC trading rules are written and enforced by the Financial Industry Regulatory Authority (FINRA). The Dow Jones Industrial Average, a price-weighted average of a collection of industrial stocks, was introduced in 1896 and is still widely used as an indicator of stock prices today.

NUMBER OF EXCHANGE LISTED COMPANIES, 2001-2010

Year	NASDAQ	NYSE	AMEX[1]
2001	4,109	2,798	691
2002	3,663	2,783	698
2003	3,333	2,755	700
2004	3,271	2,768	725
2005	3,208	2,767	812
2006	3,247	2,764	821
2007	3,158	2,805	812
2008	2,954	3,507	644
2009	2,852	4,014	NA
2010	2,784	3,923	NA

[1]Acquired by NYSE Euronext on October 1, 2008.
NA=Data not available.

Source: New York Stock Exchange, Inc.; The NASDAQ Stock Market, Inc.; American Stock Exchange LLC; Securities Industry and Financial Markets Association.

Exchanges

The New York Stock Exchange Composite Index rose 10.8 percent in 2010 after increasing by 24.8 percent in 2009. The Dow Jones Industrial Average rose 11.0 percent in 2010, after increasing by 18.8 percent in 2009. The NYSE and Dow Jones indices dropped by 40.9 percent and 33.8 percent, respectively, in 2008 at the height of the recession.

EXCHANGE ACTIVITIES, 2001-2010

Year	NYSE		AMEX		NASDAQ	
	Reported share volume (millions)	Value of shares traded ($ millions)	Share volume (millions)	Value of shares traded ($ millions)	Share volume (millions)	Value of shares traded ($ millions)
2001	307,509	$10,489,323	16,317	$817,042	471,217	$10,934,572
2002	363,136	10,311,156	16,063	642,183	441,706	7,254,595
2003	352,398	9,692,316	16,919	563,438	424,745	7,057,440
2004	367,098	11,618,151	16,513	884,100	453,930	8,727,498
2005	403,764	14,125,304	19,500	1,267,300	448,175	9,965,442
2006	453,291	17,140,500	44,515	2,364,800	500,264	11,675,879
2007	531,947	21,866,800	54,027	4,394,100	537,263	15,115,541
2008	660,168	20,855,441	146,202	6,817,600	571,613	15,104,864
2009	549,644	11,767,400	113,276	4,208,600	560,637	10,458,851
2010	444,524	11,968,700	87,249	4,025,500	552,293	12,750,993

Source: New York Stock Exchange, Inc; American Stock Exchange LLC; The NASDAQ Stock Market, Inc; Securities Industry and Financial Markets Association.

STOCK MARKET PERFORMANCE INDICES, 2001-2010
(End of year)

Year	DJIA[1]	S&P 500	NYSE Composite	AMEX Composite	NASDAQ Composite
2001	10,021.50	1,148.08	6,236.39	847.61	1,950.40
2002	8,341.63	879.82	5,000.00	824.38	1,335.51
2003	10,453.92	1,111.92	6,440.30	1,173.55	2,003.37
2004	10,783.01	1,211.92	7,250.06	1,434.34	2,175.44
2005	10,717.50	1,248.29	7,753.95	1,759.08	2,205.32
2006	12,463.15	1,418.30	9,139.02	2,056.43	2,415.29
2007	13,264.82	1,468.36	9,740.32	2,409.62	2,652.28
2008	8,776.39	903.25	5,757.05	1,397.53	1,577.03
2009	10,428.05	1,115.10	7,184.96	1,824.95	2,269.15
2010	11,577.51	1,257.64	7,964.02	2,208.38	2,652.87

[1]Dow Jones Industrial Average.

Source: Securities Industry and Financial Markets Association.

Mutual Funds

A mutual fund is a pool of assets that is managed by professional investment managers. Embraced as an investment vehicle by people who do not want to actively manage their investment accounts but who believe they can earn higher returns in the securities markets than through traditional savings bank products, mutual funds have experienced tremendous growth. In 1940 there were only 68 funds and about 300,000 shareholder accounts. By 1990 there were 3,000 funds and 62 million accounts, with a trillion dollars in assets. In 2010, 7,581 funds had 292 million shareholder accounts and $11.8 trillion in assets, up from $11.1 trillion in 2009. According to the Investment Company Institute, the trade association for the mutual fund industry, 51.6 million households, or 43.9 percent of all U.S. households, owned mutual funds in 2010, up from 43.0 percent in 2009.

Mutual funds are regulated by the Investment Company Act of 1940, which defines, among other things, the responsibilities of mutual fund companies to the public and requirements regarding financial reporting, governance and fiduciary duties. Mutual fund managers have a substantial presence in the securities markets as they trade and manage the securities within the funds they oversee. For further information on mutual funds, see Chapter 3, Retirement Funds.

MUTUAL FUND INDUSTRY NET ASSETS, NUMBER OF FUNDS AND SHAREHOLDER ACCOUNTS, 1940-2010
(End of year)

Year	Total net assets ($ billions)	Number of funds	Number of shareholder accounts[1] (000)
1940	$0.45	68	296
1960	17.03	161	4,898
1970	47.62	361	10,690
1980	134.76	564	12,088
1985	495.39	1,528	34,098
1990	1,065.19	3,079	61,948
1995	2,811.29	5,725	131,219
2000	6,964.63	8,155	244,705
2005	8,891.11	7,974	275,479
2006	10,397.94	8,118	288,596
2007	12,002.28	8,027	292,590
2008	9,603.60	8,022	264,599
2009	11,120.20	7,685	269,224
2010	11,820.68	7,581	292,109

[1]Number of shareholder accounts includes a mix of individual and omnibus accounts.
Source: Investment Company Institute.

- In 2010 mutual funds accounted for 35 percent of private pension fund assets, up from 33 percent in 2009, according to the U.S. Federal Reserve.

- Mutual funds owned 20.7 percent of U.S. corporate equities in 2010, up slightly from 20.6 percent in 2009, according to the U.S. Federal Reserve.

MUTUAL FUND INDUSTRY NET ASSETS BY TYPE OF FUND, 1985-2010
($ billions, end of year)

Year	Equity funds	Hybrid funds	Bond funds	Taxable money market funds	Tax-exempt money market funds	Total
1985	$111.3	$17.6	$122.7	$207.6	$36.3	$495.4
1990	239.5	36.1	291.3	414.6	83.8	1,065.2
1995	1,249.1	210.3	598.9	631.3	121.7	2,811.3
2000	3,961.9	346.3	811.2	1,611.4	233.9	6,964.6
2005	4,942.7	564.4	1,357.3	1,690.5	336.4	8,891.1
2006	5,914.1	650.3	1,495.1	1,969.4	369.0	10,397.9
2007	6,518.8	716.7	1,681.0	2,617.7	468.1	12,002.3
2008	3,705.6	498.3	1,567.5	3,338.6	493.7	9,603.6
2009	4,957.0	639.2	2,208.1	2,917.0	398.9	11,120.2
2010	5,667.4	741.1	2,608.3	2,473.9	330.0	11,820.7

Source: Investment Company Institute.

NUMBER OF MUTUAL FUNDS BY TYPE, 1985-2010
(End of year)

Year	Equity funds	Hybrid funds	Bond funds	Taxable money market funds	Tax-exempt money market funds	Total
1985	562	103	403	350	110	1,528
1990	1,099	193	1,046	505	236	3,079
1995	2,139	412	2,177	676	321	5,725
2000	4,385	523	2,208	704	335	8,155
2005	4,586	504	2,014	593	277	7,974
2006	4,769	507	1,995	573	274	8,118
2007	4,764	488	1,970	545	260	8,027
2008	4,827	492	1,920	534	249	8,022
2009	4,653	471	1,857	476	228	7,685
2010	4,585	478	1,866	442	210	7,581

Source: Investment Company Institute.

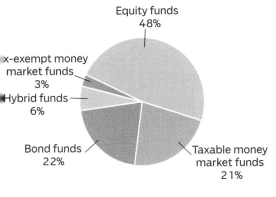

**MUTUAL FUND INDUSTRY NET
ASSETS BY TYPE OF FUND, 2010**

Equity funds
48%

x-exempt money
market funds
3%

Hybrid funds
6%

Bond funds
22%

Taxable money
market funds
21%

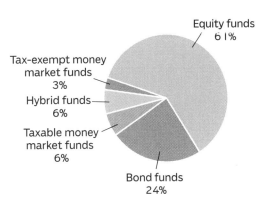

**NUMBER OF MUTUAL FUNDS
BY TYPE OF FUND, 2010**

Equity funds
61%

Tax-exempt money
market funds
3%

Hybrid funds
6%

Taxable money
market funds
6%

Bond funds
24%

Source: Investment Company Institute.

TOP TEN MUTUAL FUND COMPANIES BY ASSETS, 2010[1]
($000)

Rank	Company	Total net assets
1	Vanguard Group	$1,287,463,442
2	Fidelity Investments	1,216,499,002
3	Capital Research & Management	988,877,058
4	PIMCO Funds	420,242,286
5	JP Morgan Chase & Co.	406,266,879
6	Franklin Templeton Investments	343,199,708
7	BlackRock Funds	304,930,165
8	Federated Investors	272,425,550
9	Bank of New York Mellon/Dreyfus	258,135,565
10	T. Rowe Price	242,536,070

[1]As of August 31, 2010. Includes members of Investment Company Institute only.

Source: Investment Company Institute, Washington, D.C., 2010.

Global Mutual Fund Assets

The U.S. mutual fund market, with $11.8 trillion in assets under management at year-end 2010, is the largest in the world, accounting for 48 percent of the $24.7 trillion in mutual fund assets worldwide, according to the Investment Company Institute.

GLOBAL MUTUAL FUND ASSETS, 2010

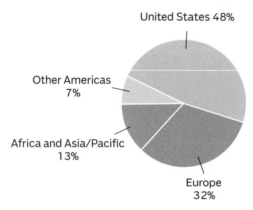

Source: Investment Company Institute.

Overview

Finance companies, which supply credit to businesses and consumers, are often categorized as nondepository institutions, along with mortgage bankers and brokers, because they make loans without taking in deposits. They acquire funds to make these loans largely by issuing commercial paper and bonds, and securitizing their loans. As financial intermediaries, finance companies compete with banks, savings institutions and credit unions. In terms of assets, the sector is twice as large as the credit union sector, about the same size as thrifts and one-fifth as large as commercial banks. Accounts receivable—the amount of money that is owed to a business—rather than assets or revenues, determine a company's standing within the industry.

Finance companies are diverse. Captive finance companies—which are generally affiliated with motor vehicle or appliance manufacturers—finance dealer inventories and consumer purchases of their products, sometimes at below-market rates. Consumer finance companies make loans to consumers who want to finance purchases of large household items such as furniture, make home improvements or refinance small debts. Business finance companies offer commercial credit, making loans secured by the assets of the business to wholesalers and manufacturers and purchasing accounts receivable at a discount. Increasingly, finance companies are participating in the real estate market. They also offer credit cards and engage in motor vehicle, aircraft and equipment leasing.

TOP TEN SPECIALTY LENDER MERGERS AND ACQUISITIONS, 2010[1]
($ millions)

Rank	Buyer	Buyer's industry	Target	Deal value[2]
1	Toronto-Dominion Bank	Bank	Chrysler Financial Corp.	$6,300.0
2	General Motors Corporation	Not classified	AmeriCredit Corp.	3,325.4
3	Banco Santander SA	Bank	Consumer mortgage business of General Electric	2,000.0
4	Grupo Aval Acciones y Valores S.A.	Not classified	BAC-Credomatic GECF, Inc.	1,900.0
5	Ocwen Financial Corporation	Specialty lender	Home equity servicing business of Barclays PLC	1,300.0
6	General Electric Capital Corporation	Specialty lender	BAC-Credomatic Holding Company Ltd.	633.0
7	Discover Financial Services	Specialty lender	Student Loan Corporation of Citigroup Inc.	600.0
8	Canadian Imperial Bank of Commerce	Bank	CIT Business Credit Canada Inc.	312.7
9	Investor group	Not classified	Red Capital Group	200.0
10	Dollar Financial Corp.	Specialty lender	Purpose U.K. Holdings Limited	195.0

[1]Target is a U.S.-domiciled specialty lender. List does not include terminated deals.
[2]At announcement.

Source: SNL Financial LC.

Finance Companies

Overview

ASSETS AND LIABILITIES OF FINANCE COMPANIES, 2006-2010[1]

($ billions, end of year)

	2006	2007	2008	2009	2010
Total financial assets	**$1,891.3**	**$1,911.2**	**$1,851.7**	**$1,662.5**	**$1,590.0**
Checkable deposits and currency	15.8	16.2	16.5	17.0	15.3
Time and savings deposits	47.4	48.6	49.4	51.0	45.9
Credit market instruments	1,811.6	1,828.2	1,755.9	1,532.6	1,482.8
Corporate and foreign bonds	184.8	189.4	192.4	198.6	179.0
Other loans and advances	498.0	523.0	539.9	448.9	441.0
Mortgages	594.4	531.9	447.9	397.4	344.2
Consumer credit	534.4	584.1	575.8	487.8	518.6
Miscellaneous assets	16.4	18.2	30.0	61.9	46.0
Total liabilities	**$1,876.8**	**$1,949.6**	**$1,880.5**	**$1,630.3**	**$1,536.7**
Credit market instruments	1,144.2	1,279.6	1,200.3	1,044.1	962.1
Open market paper	165.3	123.5	100.9	62.1	63.8
Corporate bonds	849.7	974.1	924.5	837.5	818.7
Other bank loans	129.2	182.0	174.9	144.5	79.6
Taxes payable	17.0	15.5	15.4	12.7	12.9
Miscellaneous liabilities	715.7	654.4	664.8	573.6	561.7
Foreign direct investment in U.S.	51.1	62.7	57.7	58.8	59.4
Investment by parent	338.5	321.4	313.0	280.5	264.6
Other	326.0	270.3	294.0	234.3	237.7
Consumer leases not included above[2]	106.0	122.9	111.1	85.4	72.7

[1]Includes retail captive finance companies and mortgage companies.
[2]Receivables from operating leases, such as consumer automobile leases, are booked as current income when payments are received and are not included in financial assets (or household liabilities). The leased automobile is a tangible asset.

Source: Board of Governors of the Federal Reserve System, June 9, 2011.

FINANCE COMPANY EMPLOYMENT, 2006-2010
(000)

	2006	2007	2008	2009	2010
Nondepository credit intermediation	**776.3**	**715.9**	**632.7**	**571.5**	**556.9**
Credit card issuing	117.5	112.1	108.1	101.5	99.6
Sales financing	108.7	108.9	104.9	91.4	82.2
Other nondepository credit intermediation	550.1	494.9	419.7	378.7	375.1
Consumer lending	117.8	118.9	109.9	97.0	92.7
Real estate credit	351.4	292.2	225.8	200.0	199.4
Miscellaneous nondepository credit intermediation	80.9	83.8	84.1	81.7	83.0

Source: U.S. Department of Labor, Bureau of Labor Statistics.

BUSINESS AND CONSUMER FINANCE COMPANIES' RETURN ON EQUITY, 2007-2010[1]

	Business finance companies' return on average equity[2]		Consumer finance companies' return on average equity[3]	
Year	Median	Average	Median	Average
2007	11.74%	15.90%	11.67%	-1.90%
2008	9.28	-4.71	7.36	18.71
2009	6.29	0.22	11.08	1.75
2010	7.62	5.83	15.32	5.08

[1]Net income as a percentage of average equity.
[2]Includes 35 public and private commercial lenders; excludes government-sponsored enterprises (GSEs), mortgage real estate investment trusts (REITs) and real estate companies.
[3]Includes 36 public and private consumer lenders; excludes GSEs, REITs and real estate companies.

Source: SNL Financial LC.

Receivables

TOTAL RECEIVABLES OUTSTANDING AT FINANCE COMPANIES, 2006-2010[1]
($ billions, end of year)

	2006	2007	2008	2009	2010
Total	**$2,014.8**	**$2,057.2**	**$1,926.3**	**$1,626.8**	**$1,492.0**
Consumer	818.6	883.3	832.5	696.4	640.9
Real estate	614.0	573.7	486.5	435.0	377.0
Business	582.2	600.1	607.3	495.4	474.1

[1]Includes finance company subsidiaries of bank holding companies but not retailers and banks. Includes owned receivables (carried on the balance sheet of the institution) and managed receivables (outstanding balances of pools upon which securities have been issued; these balances are no longer carried on the balance sheets of the loan originator).

Source: Board of Governors of the Federal Reserve System.

Finance Companies

BUSINESS RECEIVABLES OUTSTANDING AT FINANCE COMPANIES, 2006-2010

($ billions, end of year)

| | 2006 | 2007 | 2008 | 2009 | 2010 | Percent of total | | | | |
						2006	2007	2008	2009	2010
Total	$585.2	$602.2	$608.3	$495.6	$474.3	100.0%	100.0%	100.0%	100.0%	100.0%
Motor vehicles	105.1	105.7	95.1	63.4	68.1	18.0	17.6	15.6	12.8	14.4
Retail loans	17.1	16.4	12.8	10.1	9.3	2.9	2.7	2.1	2.0	2.0
Wholesale loans[1]	55.7	56.9	51.3	37.0	43.3	9.5	9.4	8.4	7.5	9.1
Leases	32.3	32.4	31.0	16.3	15.4	5.5	5.4	5.1	3.3	3.2
Equipment	299.5	328.2	347.0	296.9	307.1	51.2	54.5	57.0	59.9	64.7
Loans	102.4	111.4	115.9	92.2	113.1	17.5	18.5	19.1	18.6	23.8
Leases	197.1	216.9	231.1	204.7	194.0	33.7	36.0	38.0	41.3	40.9
Other business receivables[2]	93.5	89.0	97.8	88.6	65.9	16.0	14.8	16.1	17.9	13.9
Securitized assets[3]	87.2	79.3	68.4	46.8	33.2	14.9	13.2	11.2	9.4	7.0
Motor vehicles	38.0	33.6	27.4	12.4	5.9	6.5	5.6	4.5	2.5	1.2
Retail loans	3.0	2.6	2.4	3.0	2.1	0.5	0.4	0.4	0.6	0.4
Wholesale loans	34.9	30.9	25.0	9.4	3.8	6.0	5.1	4.1	1.9	0.8
Leases	0.1	0.1	0.0	0.0	0.0	[4]	[4]	[4]	[4]	[4]
Equipment	15.4	13.3	10.7	6.8	4.0	2.6	2.2	1.8	1.4	0.8
Loans	9.9	9.4	7.1	3.4	1.1	1.7	1.6	1.2	0.7	0.2
Leases	5.5	3.9	3.6	3.4	2.9	0.9	0.6	0.6	0.7	0.6
Other business receivables[2]	33.8	32.4	30.3	27.6	23.3	5.8	5.4	5.0	5.6	4.9

[1]Credit arising from transactions between manufacturers and dealers, also known as floor plan financing.
[2]Includes loans on commercial accounts receivable, factored commercial accounts, and receivable dealer capital; small loans used primarily for business or farm purposes; and wholesale and lease paper for mobile homes, recreation vehicles and travel trailers.
[3]Outstanding balances of pools upon which securities have been issued; these balances are no longer carried on the balance sheets of the loan originator.
[4]Less than 0.1 percent.

Source: Board of Governors of the Federal Reserve System.

CONSUMER RECEIVABLES OUTSTANDING AT FINANCE COMPANIES, 2006-2010
($ billions, end of year)

	2006	2007	2008	2009	2010
Total consumer	**$825.4**	**$891.1**	**$840.2**	**$703.0**	**$646.9**
Motor vehicle loans	259.8	261.5	247.7	205.6	185.1
Motor vehicle leases	106.0	122.9	111.1	85.4	72.7
Revolving[1]	79.9	86.0	74.4	46.4	71.9
Other[2]	194.7	236.5	253.7	235.8	261.5
Securitized assets[3]	185.1	184.1	153.3	129.9	55.5
Motor vehicle loans	112.8	110.7	85.1	67.3	50.4
Motor vehicle leases	3.6	3.1	2.7	2.3	2.0
Revolving	15.9	25.6	25.5	24.1	0.1
Other	52.8	44.7	40.0	36.2	3.0

[1]Excludes revolving credit reported as held by depository institutions that are subsidiaries of finance companies.
[2]Includes student loans, personal cash loans, mobile home loans and loans to purchase other types of consumer goods such as appliances, apparel, boats and recreational vehicles.
[3]Outstanding balances of pools upon which securities have been issued; these balances are no longer carried on the balance sheets of the loan originator.
Source: Board of Governors of the Federal Reserve System.

REAL ESTATE RECEIVABLES OUTSTANDING AT FINANCE COMPANIES, 2006-2010
($ billions, end of year)

	2006	2007	2008	2009	2010
Total real estate	**$614.8**	**$572.4**	**$483.9**	**$431.9**	**$374.4**
1 to 4 family	538.1	472.7	375.4	327.7	280.6
Other	56.2	59.1	72.5	69.7	63.6
Securitized real estate assets[1]	20.5	40.5	36.0	34.6	30.2
1 to 4 family	16.8	34.9	31.0	30.3	29.6
Other	3.7	5.6	5.0	4.3	0.6

[1]Outstanding balances of pools upon which securities have been issued; these balances are no longer carried on the balance sheets of the loan originator.
Source: Board of Governors of the Federal Reserve System.

Demographic factors such as the size of various age groups and changes in disposable income as well as interest rates, the desirability of other investment options and economic conditions such as unemployment all influence the residential mortgage market.

The total mortgage market (including commercial and residential mortgages) fell 3.5 percent in 2010, following a 2.0 percent drop the previous year. The home mortgage holdings of several financial services sectors fell in 2010, including commercial banks (down 2.4 percent), savings institutions (down 4.0 percent), finance companies (down 14.4 percent) and life insurers (down 12.5 percent). Holdings by credit unions rose by 0.9 percent during the same period.

Home mortgage debt outstanding dropped by $330 billion to $10.5 trillion in 2010, following a $208 billion drop the previous year. These were the only two annual declines since recordkeeping began in 1945. In the 1990s the housing market entered a period of expansion, marked by a relaxation of mortgage underwriting requirements, the introduction of innovative mortgage products and a rise in median home prices. In 2006 conditions began to change. Home prices dropped, credit tightened and mortgage defaults rose. In 2007, 1.03 percent of all U.S. housing units received at least one foreclosure filing during the year, according to mortgage data firm RealtyTrac. By 2010 that figure had risen to 2.23 percent, or one out of every 45 U.S. housing units.

In September 2008 the federal government took over and put into conservatorship Fannie Mae and Freddie Mac, two government-sponsored enterprises (GSE) that own or guarantee about half the nation's residential mortgages. With the two giant GSEs under government control, the federal government's role in the mortgage market has increased. Freddie Mac, Fannie Mae and the Federal Housing Administration owned or guaranteed approximately 90 percent of single-family mortgage originations in 2010, according to figures in Harvard's 2011 State of the Nation's Housing Report.

Mortgages may be packaged as securities and sold to investors as products known as mortgage-backed securities (MBS). The number of such instruments rose during the housing boom, as they enabled investors and institutions around the world to invest in the U.S. housing market. As housing prices fell during the recession, major global financial institutions that had borrowed and invested heavily in MBSs reported significant losses, contributing to the credit crisis. Today, the MBS market is highly dependent on support from the federal government. GSE- and agency-backed MBSs accounted for 96 percent of issuances in 2010. Moreover, the U.S. Treasury purchased over $1 trillion in agency MBSs in 2009 and 2010 in order to provide support to mortgage and housing markets and to foster improved conditions in the financial markets.

HOME MORTGAGES BY HOLDER, 2006-2010[1]
($ billions, end of year)

	2006	2007	2008	2009	2010
Total assets	**$10,457.0**	**$11,167.5**	**$11,069.4**	**$10,861.5**	**$10,531.2**
Household sector	102.9	90.8	91.2	83.2	75.2
Nonfinancial corporate business	35.9	25.0	20.2	18.2	16.2
Nonfarm noncorporate business	12.7	15.4	14.3	13.2	12.5
State and local governments	84.9	88.5	87.0	91.9	93.9
Federal government	13.3	13.7	16.4	22.1	23.9
Commercial banking	2,082.1	2,210.5	2,248.1	2,261.3	2,207.2
Savings institutions	867.8	879.0	666.3	448.6	430.5
Credit unions	249.7	281.5	314.7	317.9	320.8
Life insurance companies	10.3	9.4	8.8	5.6	4.9
Private pension funds	1.3	1.2	1.3	2.0	2.1
State and local government retirement funds	5.2	3.5	3.4	3.3	3.4
GSEs[2,3]	457.6	447.9	455.9	444.1	4,705.8
Agency- and GSE[2]-backed mortgage pools[3]	3,749.1	4,371.8	4,864.0	5,266.5	1,068.8
ABS issuers	2,142.3	2,177.5	1,865.7	1,528.4	1,264.5
Finance companies	538.1	472.7	375.4	327.7	280.6
REITs[4]	103.7	79.2	36.7	27.5	21.0
Home equity loans included above[5]	1,066.2	1,130.9	1,114.3	1,032.1	949.7
Commercial banking	653.6	692.3	776.1	761.7	709.6
Savings institutions	137.6	180.5	119.5	80.0	74.0
Credit unions	86.9	94.1	98.7	94.6	88.2
ABS issuers	80.5	69.5	45.0	30.3	21.8
Finance companies	107.6	94.5	75.1	65.5	56.1

[1]Mortgages on 1 to 4 family properties.
[2]Government-sponsored enterprise.
[3]Beginning in 2010 Fannie Mae and Freddie Mac moved the unpaid balances of securitized mortgages onto their consolidated balance sheets, reflecting new accounting rules. In response to this shift, the data for years after 2009 are included on the Government-Sponsored Enterprises chart on page 173. (See "consolidated trusts.")
[4]Real Estate Investment Trusts.
[5]Loans made under home equity lines of credit and home equity loans by junior liens. Excludes home equity loans held by mortgage companies and individuals.

Source: Board of Governors of the Federal Reserve System, June 9, 2011.

TOTAL MORTGAGES, 2006-2010
($ billions, end of year)

	2006	2007	2008	2009	2010
Total mortgages	**$13,463.9**	**$14,515.9**	**$14,605.7**	**$14,320.3**	**$13,819.8**
Home	10,457.0	11,167.5	11,069.4	10,861.5	10,531.2
Multifamily residential	707.5	786.8	837.3	848.9	840.1
Commercial	2,191.3	2,448.9	2,565.4	2,475.4	2,316.3
Farm	108.0	112.7	133.6	134.5	132.3

Source: Board of Governors of the Federal Reserve System, June 9, 2011.

AVERAGE CONVENTIONAL SINGLE-FAMILY MORTGAGES, 2001-2010[1]
($000)

Year	Mortgage loan amount	Purchase price	Adjustable rate mortgage (ARM) share[2]
2001	$155.7	$215.5	12
2002	163.4	231.2	17
2003	167.9	243.4	18
2004	185.5	262.0	35
2005	211.9	299.8	30
2006	222.9	307.1	22
2007	224.7	300.5	11
2008	219.8	306.1	7
2009	217.8	307.3	3
2010	215.8	304.9	5

- Adjustable rate mortgages, loans in which the interest rate is adjusted periodically according to a pre-selected index, dropped from a high of 62 percent of mortgages in 1984 to just 5 percent of mortgages in 2010, according to the Federal Housing Finance Agency.

[1]National averages, all homes.
[2]ARM share is the percent of total volume of conventional purchase loans. Does not include interest-only mortgages.
[3]Insufficient sample size.

Source: Federal Housing Finance Agency, Monthly Interest Rate Survey.

Interest-Only Mortgages

Interest-only mortgages were an innovation that gained popularity in the early 2000s. In these arrangements, the borrower paid only the interest on the capital for a set term. After the end of that term, usually five to seven years, the borrower either refinanced, paid the balance in a lump sum or started paying off the principal, in which case the monthly payments rose. The vast majority of interest-only mortgages were adjustable rate mortgages, according to First American LoanPerformance. Originations of nonprime loans with so-called affordability features—such as interest-only loans or payment-option loans (which give the borrower a choice of payment options)—fell from almost 20 percent of originations in 2005 to less than 2 percent in 2008, according to Harvard's 2009 State of the Nation's Housing study. By 2009 such mortgages were virtually unavailable.

Foreclosures

The number of properties in some phase of foreclosure totaled over 2.9 million in 2010, up 2 percent, compared with 2009 and up 23 percent, compared with 2008, according to a report from RealtyTrac, an online marketplace for foreclosure properties. The report also shows that 2.23 percent of all U.S. housing units (one in 45) received at least one foreclosure filing during the year, up from 2.21 percent in 2009, 1.84 percent in 2008, 1.03 percent in 2007 and 0.58 percent in 2006.

TOP TEN STATES BY FORECLOSURE RATE, 2010

Rank	State	Percent of housing units with foreclosure filings[1]
1	Nevada	9.42%
2	Arizona	5.73
3	Florida	5.51
4	California	4.08
5	Utah	3.44
6	Georgia	3.25
7	Michigan	3.00
8	Idaho	2.98
9	Illinois	2.87
10	Colorado	2.51

[1]Foreclosure filings include foreclosure-related documents in all phases of foreclosure, including defaults, auction notices and repossessions by banks. One property may have more than one filing.

Source: RealtyTrac Inc., http://www.realtytrac.com/trendcenter.

Home Equity Mortgage Loans

Home equity loans, in which the borrower's home serves as collateral, are generally used for major items such as education, home improvements or medical bills, as opposed to day-to-day expenses. The dollar value of home equity loans outstanding dropped from $1.13 trillion in 2007 to $949.7 billion in 2010.

HOME EQUITY MORTGAGE LOANS BY HOLDER, 2006-2010[1]
($ billions, end of year)

	2006	2007	2008	2009	2010
Total	$1,066.2	$1,130.9	$1,114.3	$1,032.1	$949.7
Commercial banking	653.6	692.3	776.1	761.7	709.6
Savings institutions	137.6	180.5	119.5	80.0	74.0
Credit unions	86.9	94.1	98.7	94.6	88.2
Asset-backed security issuers	80.5	69.5	45.0	30.3	21.8
Finance companies	107.6	94.5	75.1	65.5	56.1

[1]Loans made under home equity lines of credit and home equity loans secured by junior liens, such as second mortgages, which are subordinate to another mortgage. Excludes home equity loans held by individuals.

Source: Board of Governors of the Federal Reserve System, June 9, 2011.

Subprime Loans

Subprime loans are offered to applicants with an incomplete or less than perfect credit record. The subprime interest rate is generally higher than the prevailing rate because of the additional risks involved in lending to less creditworthy applicants. During the housing boom years, which began in the 1990s, the subprime industry flourished, with lenders extending credit to borrowers previously unable to qualify for loans. By 2007 the tide had turned; subprime mortgages were harder to obtain and defaults were on the rise. The 2011 State of the Nation's Housing study from Harvard University's Joint Center for Housing Studies found that in 2010 the share of mortgage loans with subprime rates was 15.6 percent in U.S. Census tracts that were identified as areas with a high rate of foreclosures. This compares with 5.8 percent in all other Census tracts.

CHARACTERISTICS OF HIGH FORECLOSURE CENSUS TRACTS, 2010[1]

	High foreclosure tracts[2]	All other tracts
Number of housing units	1,859	2,005
Housing market characteristics		
Single-family share of housing units	65.7%	68.0%
Homeownership rate	55.6	66.4
Vacancy rate	18.7	11.0
Share of loans with subprime rates	15.6	5.8
Share of loans delinquent	17.3	7.4
Foreclosure rate	16.1	2.5

[1] Average or census track values.
[2] Census tracts with foreclosure rates of 10 percent or higher.
Source: The State of the Nation's Housing, 2011, Joint Center for Housing Studies, Harvard University.

Government-Sponsored Enterprises

Government-sponsored enterprises (GSEs) are privately owned, federally chartered corporations with a public purpose. They were created by Congress to assist groups of borrowers such as homeowners, mortgage lenders, students and farmers gain access to capital markets. Two of these entities, the Federal Home Loan Mortgage Corporation, known as Freddie Mac, and the Federal National Mortgage Association, known as Fannie Mae, were established (Freddie Mac in 1970 and Fannie Mae in 1983) to increase the supply of funds that mortgage lenders make available to home buyers. The institutions do not lend money to home buyers directly, but rather purchase home loans from lenders, which can then use the money to offer new loans to consumers. The loans may be packaged into securities, known as mortgage-backed securities, and sold to investors in what is known as the secondary market.

Although they are private corporations, Fannie Mae and Freddie Mac have an implicit guarantee of federal support. As the housing market entered a downturn in 2006, the two GSEs confronted steep rises in delinquencies and foreclosures. To reassure investors and provide continued liquidity in the housing market, the federal government stepped in to take control of Fannie Mae and Freddie Mac. The plan, announced by the U.S. Treasury in September 2008, put the firms into conservatorship, giving management control to the Federal Housing Finance Agency. The same year the Treasury injected more than $100 billion in capital into the two institutions. From January 2009 through March 2010, the U.S. Treasury bought $1.25 trillion of GSE debt securities and invested another $175 billion in the securities.

The role of GSEs in the residential mortgage market has increased since the economic downtown. In 2010 mortgages held or securitized by Freddie Mac and Fannie Mae accounted for $11.4 trillion, or 46.7 percent, of residential mortgage debt outstanding, up from 38.8 percent in 2006.

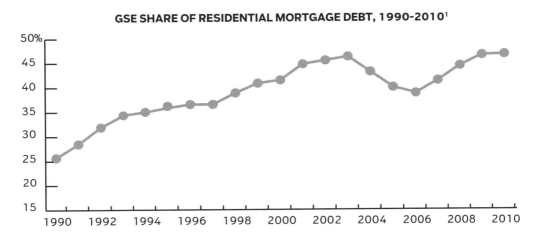

GSE SHARE OF RESIDENTIAL MORTGAGE DEBT, 1990-2010[1]

[1]Includes Fannie Mae and Freddie Mac. GSEs are government-sponsored enterprises.
Source: Federal Housing Finance Agency.

GOVERNMENT-SPONSORED ENTERPRISES (GSEs)[1], 2006-2010
($ billions, amounts outstanding, end of year)

	2006	2007	2008	2009	2010
Total financial assets	**$2,872.9**	**$3,174.3**	**$3,400.0**	**$3,013.8**	**$6,620.4**
Checkable deposits and currency	16.4	13.7	88.3	99.4	63.4
Time and savings deposits	33.9	46.6	68.5	25.7	26.1
Federal funds and security RPs[2] (net)	117.4	142.7	114.5	122.1	150.0
Credit market instruments	2,590.5	2,829.5	3,033.6	2,699.7	6,333.1
Open market paper	32.4	27.7	6.8	9.7	9.9
U.S. Government securitites	728.2	718.4	926.8	946.4	432.2
Treasury securities	14.2	15.5	16.8	21.9	55.2
Agency- and GSE[3]- backed securities	714.0	702.9	910.0	924.5	377.0
Municipal securities	36.1	33.3	31.3	29.1	24.9
Corporate and foreign bonds	481.7	464.4	386.6	310.8	293.9
Other loans and advances	704.9	942.6	980.7	695.9	551.3
Farm Credit System	63.5	75.5	80.3	80.0	87.3
Federal Home Loan Banks	641.4	867.1	900.5	615.9	464.0
Mortgages	607.2	643.1	701.4	707.7	5,021.0
Home	457.6	447.9	455.9	444.1	4,705.8
Consolidated trusts[4]	0.0	0.0	0.0	0.0	4,141.0
Other	157.6	447.9	455.9	444.1	564.8
Multifamily residential	105.4	147.7	187.7	204.4	256.5
Consolidated trusts[4]	0.0	0.0	0.0	0.0	75.4
Other	105.4	147.7	187.7	204.4	181.1
Farm	44.2	47.6	57.9	59.2	58.7
Miscellaneous assets	114.7	141.7	95.0	66.8	47.9
Total liabilities	**$2,781.2**	**$3,081.3**	**$3,394.1**	**$2,977.0**	**$6,589.1**
Credit market instruments	2,627.8	2,910.2	3,181.9	2,706.6	6,434.5
GSE[3] issues[5]	2,627.8	2,910.2	3,181.9	2,706.6	6,434.5
Consolidated trusts[4]	0.0	0.0	0.0	0.0	4216.4
Other	2,627.8	2,910.2	3,181.9	2,706.6	2218.1
Miscellaneous liabilities	153.4	171.1	212.1	270.4	154.6

[1]Federal Home Loan Banks, Fannie Mae, Freddie Mac, Federal Agricultural Mortgage Corportation, Farm Credit System, the Financing Corporation and the Resolution Funding Corporation. Beginning 2010 includes almost all Fannie Mae and Freddie Mac mortgage pools, previously included in the Agency and Government-Sponsored Enterprise (GSE)-Backed Mortgage Pools chart on page 175.
[2]Short-term agreements to sell and repurchase government securities by a specified date and at a set price.
[3]Government-sponsored enterprise.
[4]The unpaid balance of securitized mortgages Fannie Mae and Freddie Mac moved on to their balance sheets in 2010 in response to new accounting rules.
[5]Such issues are classified as agency- and GSE-backed securities.

Source: Board of Governors of the Federal Reserve System, June 9, 2011.

AGENCY- AND GOVERNMENT-SPONSORED ENTERPRISE (GSE)[1]-BACKED MORTGAGE POOLS, 2006-2010
($ billions, amounts outstanding, end of year)

	2006	2007	2008	2009	2010
Total financial assets	**$3,841.1**	**$4,464.4**	**$4,961.4**	**$5,376.7**	**$1,139.5**
Home mortgages	3,749.1	4,371.8	4,864.0	5,266.5	1,068.8
Multifamily residential mortgages	88.8	88.1	92.8	105.7	66.9
Farm mortgages	3.2	4.5	4.7	4.5	3.8
Total pool securities (liabilities)[2]	**$3,841.1**	**$4,464.4**	**$4,961.4**	**$5,376.7**	**$1,139.5**

[1]Federal Home Loan Banks, Fannie Mae, Freddie Mac, Federal Agricultural Mortgage Corporation and Farmers Home Administration pools. Beginning 2010, almost all Fannie Mae and Freddie Mac mortgage pools were consolidated into the Government-Sponsored Enterprises (GSEs) chart shown on page 173 in response to new accounting rules. Also includes agency- and GSE-backed mortgage pool securities used as collateral for agency- and GSE-backed collateralized mortgage obligations (CMOs) and privated issued CMOs. Excludes Federal Financing Bank holdings of pool securities.

[2]Such issues are classified as agency- and GSE-backed securities.

Source: Board of Governors of the Federal Reserve System, June 9, 2011.

TOTAL MORTGAGES HELD OR SECURITIZED BY FANNIE MAE AND FREDDIE MAC AS A PERCENTAGE OF RESIDENTIAL MORTGAGE DEBT OUTSTANDING, 2001-2010
($ millions)

Year	Fannie Mae	Freddie Mac	Combined GSEs[1]	Residential mortgage debt outstanding	Combined GSE share[1]
2001	$1,579,398	$1,150,723	$2,730,121	$6,102,611	44.7%
2002	1,840,218	1,297,081	3,137,299	6,896,266	45.5
2003	2,209,388	1,397,630	3,607,018	7,797,171	46.3
2004	2,325,256	1,505,531	3,830,787	8,872,741	43.2
2005	2,336,807	1,684,546	4,021,353	10,049,205	40.0
2006	2,506,482	1,826,720	4,333,202	11,163,068	38.8
2007	2,846,812	2,102,676	4,949,488	11,954,031	41.4
2008	3,081,655	2,207,476	5,289,131	11,906,478	44.4
2009	3,202,041	2,250,539	5,452,580	11,707,666	46.6
2010	3,156,192	2,164,859	5,321,051	11,387,676	46.7

[1]Fannie Mae and Freddie Mac combined. GSEs are government-sponsored enterprises.

Source: Federal housing Finance Agency.

MORTGAGE STATUS OF OWNER OCCUPIED HOUSING UNITS, 2009

Mortgages	
Number of owner occupied housing units with a mortgage	50,747,854
Percent of units of owner occupied housing with mortgage	67.8%
Mortgage status	Percent
With either a second mortgage or home equity loan, but not both	23.9%
Second mortgage only	6.3
Home equity loan only	17.6
Both second mortgage and home equity loan	1.0
No second mortgage and no home equity loan	75.1

Source: U.S. Census Bureau; American Community Survey.

Reverse Mortgages

Reverse mortgages are special mortgages that allow homeowners over age 61 to sell their homes to a bank in exchange for monthly payments, a lump sum or a line of credit. The Home Equity Conversion Mortgage (HECM) is the federally insured reverse mortgage product. It is insured by the Federal Housing Administration, a branch of the U.S. Department of Housing and Urban Development. HECMs now account for nearly all reverse mortgages.

REVERSE MORTGAGES: ANNUAL ORIGINATION VOLUME FOR HOME EQUITY CONVERSION MORTGAGES (HECMs), FISCAL YEAR 2007-2011[1]

- After increasing steadily since 2001, the volume of reverse mortgages declined in 2010 and 2011.

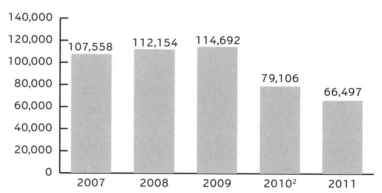

[1]HECMs are federally insured reverse mortgage products.
[2]Through July 2010; fiscal year ends September 30.
Source: National Reverse Mortgage Lenders Association.

CONVENTIONAL HOME PURCHASE LOANS ORIGINATED BY RACIAL/ETHNIC IDENTITY AND INCOME OF BORROWERS, 2006 AND 2010[1]

Race/ethnic identity	2006 Number	2006 Amount ($000)	2010 Number	2010 Amount ($000)
American Indian/Alaska native	35,868	$6,722,088	4,668	$706,615
Asian	302,275	76,956,869	107,117	30,976,644
Black or African American	550,729	84,331,152	34,153	5,153,314
Hispanic or Latino	893,134	163,222,889	66,720	10,663,253
White	4,627,989	846,788,394	1,058,849	219,212,213
Income[2]				
Less than 50%	262,994	21,463,059	96,964	8,146,458
50 to 79%	881,326	91,724,238	220,841	27,537,820
80 to 99%	706,603	88,899,576	144,590	23,021,390
100 to 119%	663,330	95,116,965	134,338	24,683,695
120% or more	3,344,741	798,624,058	720,989	206,971,387
Income not available	391,652	76,637,401	40,532	8,743,657

[1]Includes 1 to 4 family and manufactured homes.
[2]Percentage of metropolitan area median. Metropolitan area median is the median family income of the metropolitan area in which the property related to the loan is located.

Source: Federal Financial Institutions Examination Council.

Home Ownership

HOME OWNERSHIP RATES BY AGE OF HOUSEHOLDER, 2010
(Percent)

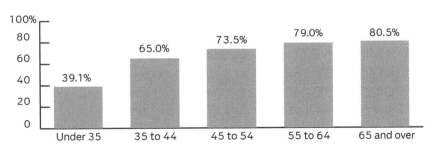

Source: U.S. Census Bureau; Housing Vacancy Survey.

SNAPSHOT OF HOUSING IN AMERICA, 2008-2010

	Percent change[1]	
	2008-2009	2009-2010
New single-family sales	-22.7%	-13.9%
Existing single-family sales	5.0	-5.7
Housing starts[2]	-38.8	5.9
Housing completions[2]	-29.1	-18.0
Median new single-family price	-6.3	0.7
Median existing single-family price	-12.1	-1.0
Home equity	-3.0	-8.0
Mortgage debt	-1.1	-4.2
Residential investment	-25.2	-4.9
Owner residential improvements	-6.4	0.9

[1]Calculated from unrounded data. Dollar values adjusted for inflation using the consumer price index for all items.
[2]Single- and multifamily units.

Source: The State of the Nation's Housing, 2011, Joint Center for Housing Studies, Harvard University.

Home Prices

In 2010 the national median existing single-family home price rose 0.2 percent to $172,900, after falling for three years running. The median represents the market price where half of the homes sold for more and half sold for less, and is an indicator of typical prices.

MEDIAN SALES PRICE OF EXISTING SINGLE FAMILY HOMES, 1975-2010

Year	Median sales price	Average annual percent change[1]	Year	Median sales price	Average annual percent change[1]
1975	$35,300	8.9%	2005	$219,600	12.4%
1980	62,200	12.0	2006	221,900	1.0
1985	75,500	4.0	2007	219,000	-1.3
1990	96,400	4.9	2008	198,100	-9.5
1995	114,600	3.5	2009	172,500	-12.9
2000	143,600	4.5	2010	172,900	0.2

[1]From prior year.

Source: National Association of Realtors.

U.S. HOME OWNERSHIP RATES BY RACE AND ETHNICITY, 2006-2010

	2006	2007	2008	2009	2010
All households	**68.8%**	**68.1%**	**67.8%**	**67.4%**	**66.9%**
Whites	75.8	75.2	75.0	74.8	74.4
Hispanics	49.7	49.7	49.1	48.4	47.5
Blacks	48.4	47.8	47.9	46.6	45.9
Asians/others	60.8	60.1	59.5	59.0	58.2

Source: U.S. Census Bureau.

HOME OWNERSHIP RATES BY REGION, 1960-2010

Year	United States	Northeast	Midwest	South	West
1960	62.1%	55.5%	66.4%	63.4%	62.2%
1970	64.2	58.1	69.5	66.0	60.0
1980	65.6	60.8	69.8	68.7	60.0
1990	63.9	62.6	67.5	65.7	58.0
2000	67.4	63.5	72.6	69.6	61.7
2001	67.8	63.7	73.1	69.8	62.6
2002	67.9	64.3	73.1	69.7	62.5
2003	68.3	64.4	73.2	70.1	63.4
2004	69.0	65.0	73.8	70.9	64.2
2005	68.9	65.2	73.1	70.8	64.4
2006	68.8	65.2	72.7	70.5	64.7
2007	68.1	65.0	71.9	70.1	63.5
2008	67.8	64.6	71.7	69.9	63.0
2009	67.4	64.0	71.0	69.6	62.6
2010	66.9	64.1	70.8	69.0	61.4

Source: U.S. Census Bureau, Housing Vacancy Survey.

Mortgage Finance and Housing

Home Ownership

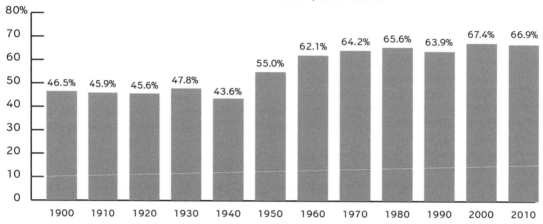

HOME OWNERSHIP RATES, 1900-2010

Year	Rate
1900	46.5%
1910	45.9%
1920	45.6%
1930	47.8%
1940	43.6%
1950	55.0%
1960	62.1%
1970	64.2%
1980	65.6%
1990	63.9%
2000	67.4%
2010	66.9%

Source: 1900-1950: U.S. Census Bureau, Census of Housing. 1960-present: U.S. Census Bureau, Housing Vacancy Survey.

SELECTED CHARACTERISTICS OF HOMEOWNERS, 2009

Race/origin of householder	As a percent of owner occupied housing units
White alone, not Hispanic or Latino	78.9%
Hispanic or Latino origin	8.2
Black or African American	8.0
Asian	3.4
Total owner occupied units	**74,843,004**
Household income in the past 12 months (in 2009 inflation-adjusted dollars)	
Less than $5,000	1.7%
$5,000 to $9,999	2.1
$10,000 to $14,999	3.6
$15,000 to $19,999	4.0
$20,000 to $24,999	4.4
$25,000 to $34,999	9.0
$35,000 to $49,999	13.7
$50,000 to $74,999	20.1
$75,000 to $99,999	14.8
$100,000 to $149,999	15.4
$150,000 or more	11.1
Median household income	$63,306

Source: U.S. Census Bureau; American Community Survey.

Information Technology

Information technology (IT) has transformed the financial services industry, making available many products and services that would have otherwise been impossible to offer. These range from asset-backed securities and automated teller machines (ATMs), introduced in the 1970s and 1980s, to more recent innovations such as online banking. At the same time, IT has improved efficiency and reduced labor costs.

The technology explosion has also radically changed the ways consumers shop for financial products, with many Americans now using the Internet for banking services and for researching and buying financial products. In 2010 about 80 percent of U.S. residents had Internet access at home, according to U.S. Census data. On a typical day, 12 percent of Internet users go online to get financial information and 26 percent do some form of banking, according to research by the Pew Internet and American Life Project.

HOUSEHOLD INTERNET USAGE BY STATE, 2010[1]

State	Anywhere	In the home	No internet use	Rank[2]
Alabama	74.18%	60.03%	25.82%	46
Alaska	88.64	78.67	11.36	2
Arizona	83.46	75.50	16.54	13
Arkansas	70.87	58.76	29.13	51
California	84.19	75.86	15.81	9
Colorado	82.68	74.78	17.32	18
Connecticut	81.95	76.49	18.05	20
Delaware	79.08	71.72	20.92	34
D.C.	80.95	73.40	19.05	23
Florida	79.93	72.02	20.07	26
Georgia	79.89	70.43	20.11	27
Hawaii	78.57	71.09	21.43	35
Idaho	84.12	75.54	15.88	10
Illinois	79.85	70.71	20.15	29
Indiana	74.73	61.29	25.27	44
Iowa	79.45	70.70	20.55	32
Kansas	84.78	76.38	15.22	6
Kentucky	72.02	61.27	27.98	49
Louisiana	74.94	62.81	25.06	43
Maine	81.72	73.36	18.28	21

(table continues)

HOUSEHOLD INTERNET USAGE BY STATE, 2010 [1](Con't)

State	Anywhere	In the home	No internet use	Rank[2]
Maryland	83.25	76.34	16.75	15
Massachusetts	83.82	77.53	16.18	11
Michigan	80.81	69.76	19.19	24
Minnesota	83.44	73.65	16.56	14
Mississippi	71.43	57.66	28.57	50
Missouri	78.21	67.82	21.79	37
Montana	75.74	65.33	24.26	42
Nebraska	82.54	71.25	17.46	19
Nevada	84.33	76.58	15.67	8
New Hampshire	86.35	80.98	13.65	4
New Jersey	82.86	74.76	17.14	17
New Mexico	76.77	62.60	23.23	40
New York	79.30	71.06	20.70	33
North Carolina	76.53	68.42	23.47	41
North Dakota	79.87	73.13	20.13	28
Ohio	78.44	67.47	21.56	36
Oklahoma	77.30	66.20	22.70	39
Oregon	86.18	78.31	13.82	5
Pennsylvania	78.13	70.21	21.87	38
Rhode Island	79.84	72.08	20.16	30
South Carolina	74.38	63.77	25.62	45
South Dakota	80.97	69.04	19.03	22
Tennessee	72.20	63.29	27.80	48
Texas	80.23	69.51	19.77	25
Utah	90.10	82.31	9.90	1
Vermont	83.52	74.69	16.48	12
Virginia	79.84	72.99	20.16	31
Washington	88.37	79.70	11.63	3
West Virginia	72.87	65.12	27.13	47
Wisconsin	83.15	73.69	16.85	16
Wyoming	84.35	74.40	15.65	7
United States	**80.23%**	**71.06%**	**19.77%**	

[1]As of January 2011. Based on the civilian noninstitutional population 16 years and older.
[2]Ranked on the percentage of population having Internet connection anywhere.

Source: U.S. Department of Commerce, National Telecommunications and Information Administration.

IT Spending

A 2011 survey by Celent projects that global information technology spending by financial services institutions will reach $363.8 billion in 2011, a 3.7 percent increase from the previous year. North American institutions accounted for 34.2 percent of 2011 spending, followed by Europe (33.6 percent), Asia-Pacific (26.4 percent) and Latin America/Africa (5.8 percent).

IT SPENDING BY THE NORTH AMERICAN FINANCIAL SERVICES INDUSTRY, 2009-2013[1]
($ billions)

	2009	2010	2011[1]	2012[1]	2013[1]	Compound annual growth	
						2009-2013	2010-2011
Banking	$50.3	$51.4	$53.4	$55.9	$58.3	3.8%	4.0%
Insurance	33.0	34.1	35.7	36.5	37.3	3.1	4.5
Securities and investments	31.8	33.0	35.2	37.0	39.5	5.6	6.5
Total	$115.0	$118.5	$124.3	$129.4	$135.1	4.1%	4.8%

[1]Data for 2011 to 2013 are estimated.

Source: Celent.

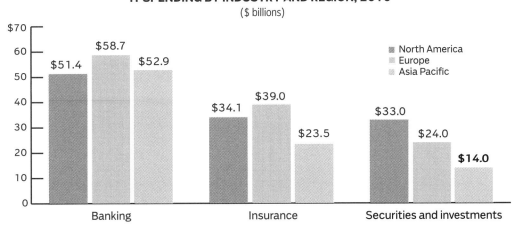

IT SPENDING BY INDUSTRY AND REGION, 2010[1]
($ billions)

Source: Celent.

Technology

Electronic Commerce

Seventy-seven percent of American adults use the Internet, according to 2010 Pew Internet and American Life Tracking surveys. Of those who use the Internet, 78 percent used the Web in 2010 to look for information about a service or product they were thinking of buying. This wide acceptance of the online marketplace is changing the way financial services products are researched and bought.

SELECTED INTERNET ACTIVITIES IN 2010[1]

Activity	Percent of Internet users
Look for health/medical information	83%
Get news	78
Look for information online about a service or product	78
Buy a product	66
Use an online social networking site such as Facebook	61
Do banking online	58
Get stock quotes or other financial info	37
Use Twitter or other status-update service	24

[1]Based on responses to various Pew Internet surveys conducted in 2010. Reflects activities conducted at any point during the year.

Source: Pew Internet and American Life Tracking surveys.

Online Securities Revenues

E-COMMERCE AND TOTAL REVENUES, SECURITIES AND COMMODITY CONTRACTS, 2008-2009
($ millions)

	Value of revenues				Percent change		E-commerce as a percent of total revenues	
	2008		2009					
	Total	E-commerce	Total	E-commerce	Total revenues	E-commerce revenues	2008	2009
Securities and commodity contracts, intermediation and brokerage	$202,520	$13,556	$286,348	$12,040	41.4%	-11.2%	6.7%	4.2%

Source: U.S. Department of Commerce, Census Bureau.

Online Banking

Online banking, a service provided by many banks, thrifts and credit unions, allows consumers to conduct banking transactions over the Internet using a personal computer, mobile telephone or handheld computer. In recent years online banks, which provide financial services solely over the Internet, have emerged. However, the distinctions between "brick and mortar" and online banks have diminished as traditional banks also offer online banking, and some formerly Internet-only banks have opened branches. Fifty-eight percent of adult Internet users did some banking online in 2010, up dramatically from 13 percent in 1998, according to surveys by Pew Research. A 2010 survey by the American Bankers Association found that for the second year in a row more bank customers (36 percent) prefer to do their banking online than by any other method. Survey results showed that the popularity of online banking was not exclusive to the youngest consumers; it is the preferred banking method for all bank customers under the age of 55. Consumers over 55 still prefer to visit their local branch (33 percent), followed by online banking (20 percent).

PREFERRED BANKING METHOD, ALL AGE GROUPS, 2010[1]

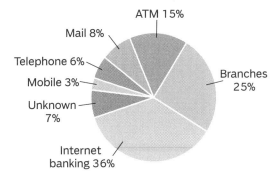

ATM 15%
Mail 8%
Telephone 6%
Mobile 3%
Unknown 7%
Internet banking 36%
Branches 25%

- 36 percent of bank customers preferred to bank online in 2010, up from 25 percent in 2009.

[1]Estimated.
Source: American Bankers Association.

Online Insurance Sales

Insurance distribution systems have evolved to encompass many of the new ways of transacting business online. Recent studies have shown the Internet playing an increasingly important role in the sales and distribution of life insurance and auto insurance.

Life Insurance Sales: One in four adults (25 percent) would prefer to purchase life insurance directly via the Internet, by mail or over the phone, according to the 2011 Insurance Barometer study by the Life and Health Insurance Foundation for Education (LIFE) Foundation and LIMRA. Sixty-four percent would prefer to buy their life insurance from an insurance or financial professional, down from 80 percent in 1996. Younger consumers showed the most interest in purchasing life insurance through the Internet. Among people age 25 to 44, 31 percent said they would prefer to buy directly, with three in four of those individuals citing the Internet as their preferred means of direct buying.

Auto Insurance Sales: The 2011 results of J.D. Power's annual auto survey of auto insurance consumers underscore the growing role of the Web in auto insurance sales. For the first time, a majority of new buyers of auto insurance initiated their policy purchase by applying for a rate quote online. More than one-half (54 percent) of insurance shoppers reported getting their quote online. While nearly one-half of all accepted Web quotes were closed by either an agent or call center representative, the study shows that customers are more often looking to websites in the early stages of the shopping process.

A 2011 survey by comScore found that online auto insurance channels continued to generate a high volume of insurance shopping activity in 2010, with 37 million quotes submitted and 2.9 million policies purchased over the year. This represents a 3 percent drop in quotes and a 1 percent rise in purchases, compared with the previous year. In 2009 online quote submission and purchasing rose by 21 percent and 22 percent, respectively. While the most popular method of initial auto insurance policy purchases for respondents continues to be through a local insurance agent, one in five respondents now report having purchased their initial policies online.

METHODS OF PURCHASING AUTO INSURANCE, 2009 AND 2011

	Percentage of respondents	
Purchase method	2009	2011
With a local agent in person	49%	43%
Online	15	20
With a local agent over the phone	18	18
Over the phone via a toll-free number	13	15
Work/other	5	3

Source: 2011 comScore Auto Insurance Survey.

Electronic Payments

Over the past quarter-century, electronic alternatives to the traditional way of paying bills by check have revolutionized the payments infrastructure. By 2006 debit card payments, which include both personal identification number (PIN) and signature, surpassed credit card payments to become the most frequently used electronic payment type, according to the Federal Reserve. Other choices such as Automated Clearing House (ACH) payments and electronic benefits transfer (EBT) have grown rapidly as well. EBTs give consumers more flexible access to Social Security, veterans' pensions and other benefits disbursed by the federal government.

Studies conducted by the Federal Reserve in 2004, 2007 and 2010 document the dramatic shift in payments away from paper-based checks and toward electronic payments. In 2003 there were 37.3 billion checks paid, compared with 44.2 billion electronic payments. In 2009 there were 24.5 billion check payments, compared with 84.5 billion electronic payments.

Automated Clearing House Network

Total payments processed through the Automated Clearing House (ACH), a national electronic payments network, reached 19.4 billion payments in 2009, up 3.4 percent from 2009 and 35 percent from 2005. Such payments include direct deposit of payroll, Social Security benefits and tax refunds, as well as direct payment of consumer bills, business-to-business payments and e-commerce payments. The majority (80.4 percent) of these payments were processed through the ACH network, a vast electronic funds transfer system whose transactions are processed by two ACH operators, the Federal Reserve and the Electronic Payments Network.

AUTOMATED CLEARING HOUSE ELECTRONIC PAYMENTS 2001-2010

Year	Volume (millions)	Percent change	Year	Volume (millions)	Percent change
2001	7,994	16.2%	2006	15,107	8.2%
2002	8,944	11.9	2007	17,105	13.2
2003	10,017	12.0	2008	18,285	6.9
2004	12,009	19.9	2009	18,760	2.6
2005	13,957	16.2	2010	19,406	3.4

- Consumer Internet ACH transactions were up 7.8 percent to 2.6 billion payments in 2010.

Source: NACHA - The Electronic Payments Association.

ELECTRONIC PAYMENTS, 2006-2009[1]

	2006	2009	Percent change 2006-2009	Compound annual growth rate
Volume (billions)	64.7	84.5	19.8%	9.3%
Value ($ trillions)	$34.1	$40.6	6.5	6.0
Average payment ($millions)	528.0	481.0	-8.9	NA

[1]Includes ACH, credit card, debit card and ATM transactions.
NA=Data not available.

Source: Federal Reserve System.

COMMERCIAL AND GOVERNMENT AUTOMATED CLEARING HOUSE ELECTRONIC PAYMENTS, 2009-2010

($ millions)

- The dollar amount of federal government ACH transactions increased by 3.0 percent to $4.42 trillion from 2009 to 2010.

Transaction volume	2009	2010	Percent change
Commercial	$17,550	$18,170	3.5%
Federal government	1,210	1,236	2.1
Total	$18,760	$19,406	3.4%

Source: NACHA - The Electronic Payments Association.

ATMs

The growth of online banking, electronic payments and deposits, and automated teller machine (ATM) usage has been driven by customer demand for greater convenience. ATMs were introduced in the mid-1970s. By 2009 there were some 425,000 ATMs in the United States, four times the number of bank and thrift branches. ATMs increasingly are being installed in places where consumers may want access to their money such as supermarkets, convenience stores and transportation terminals.

The ATM business consists of three major entities: ATM cardholders' banks, the ATM network that links banks in other locations and the owners of the ATM machines, which may or may not be banks. Most banks allow their own customers to withdraw money from their ATMs free of charge but charge a fee to other banks' customers. These charges help offset the cost of ATMs and fees banks must pay to the ATM network system.

A 2010 study on payment systems by the Federal Reserve found that there were 6.0 billion ATM withdrawals in 2009, with a total value of $647 billion, up from 5.8 billion withdrawals valued at $579 billion in 2006. The average ATM withdrawal increased slightly from $100 to $108 during the same period.

ATM WITHDRAWALS, 2006-2009

	2006	2009	Percent change	
			2006-2009	Compound annual growth rate
Number of ATM withdrawals (billions)	5.8	6.0	3.4%	0.9%
Value of ATM withdrawals ($ billions)	$578.8	$646.7	11.7	3.8
Average value ($millions)	100.0	108.0	8.0	2.9

Source: Federal Reserve System.

TOP TEN U.S. BANK OWNERS OF ATMS, 2011[1]

Rank	Owner	Number
1	Bank of America Corporation	17,817
2	JPMorgan Chase & Co.	16,443
3	Wells Fargo & Company	12,000
4	Citigroup Inc.[2]	9,812
5	PNC Financial Services Group, Inc.	6,707
6	U.S. Bancorp	5,086
7	SunTrust Banks, Inc.	2,919
8	BB&T Corporation	2,475
9	Regions Financial Corporation	2,132
10	M&T Bank Corporation[3]	1,855

[1]As of June, 2011 unless otherwise noted.
[2]As of December 31, 2002.
[3]As of September 30, 2010.

Source: SNL Financial LC.

WITHDRAWALS FROM BANK ATMS BY TYPE OF INSTITUTION, 2010

	Number (billions)	Value ($ billions)
Commercial banks	4.2	$478.5
Credit unions	1.4	132.2
Savings institutions	0.3	35.9
Total[1]	**6.0**	**$646.7**

[1]May not add to total due to rounding.

Source: Federal Reserve System.

As businesses increasingly depend on electronic data and computer networks to conduct their daily operations, growing pools of personal and financial information are being transferred and stored online. This can leave individuals exposed to privacy violations and financial institutions and other businesses exposed to potentially enormous liability, if and when a breach in data security occurs.

In 2000 the Federal Bureau of Investigation, the National White Collar Crime Center and the Bureau of Justice Assistance joined together to create the Internet Crime Complaint Center (IC3) to monitor Internet-related criminal complaints. In 2010, IC3 logged 303,809 complaints via its website, or about 25,000 complaints per month. The IC3 referred 121,710 of the complaints to federal, state or local law enforcement officials.

CYBER CRIME COMPLAINTS, 2006- 2010[1]

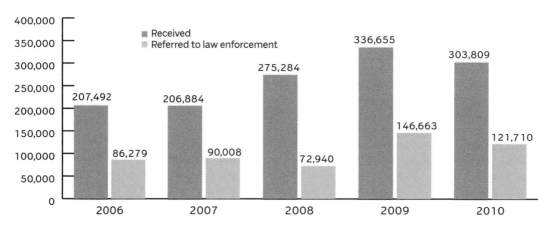

[1]Based on complaints submitted to the Internet Crime Complaint Center.
Source: Internet Crime Complaint Center.

TOP TEN CYBER CRIME REFERRALS, 2010[1]

Rank	Type	Percent
1	Non-delivery payment/merchandise	21.1%
2	Identity theft	16.6
3	Online auction fraud	10.1
4	Credit card fraud	9.3
5	Miscellaneous fraud[2]	7.7
6	Computer crimes	6.1
7	Advance fee fraud	4.1
8	Spam	4.0
9	Overpayment fraud	3.6
10	FBI-related scams[3]	3.4

[1]Based on crimes referred by the Internet Crime Complaint Center to federal, state or local law enforcement agencies.
[2]Includes work at home scams, fake sweepstakes and other schemes meant to defraud the public.
[3]Scam in which a criminal poses as the FBI to defraud victims.

Source: Internet Crime Complaint Center.

TOP TEN STATES FOR CYBER CRIME, 2010

Rank	State	Complaints per 100,000 population
1	Alaska	566.6
2	Colorado	135.0
3	District of Columbia	129.3
4	New Jersey	122.9
5	Nevada	119.2
6	Maryland	117.3
7	Washington	108.1
8	Florida	105.7
9	Arizona	104.3
10	Virginia	93.8

[1]Based on complaints submitted to the Internet Crime Complaint Center via its website.

Source: Internet Crime Complaint Center.

Consumer Fraud and Identity Theft

The Consumer Sentinel Network, maintained by the Federal Trade Commission (FTC), tracks consumer fraud and identity theft complaints that have been filed with federal, state and local law enforcement agencies and private organizations. Of 1.3 million complaints received in 2010, 54 percent were related to fraud, 19 percent were related to identity theft and 27 percent were for other consumer complaints. The FTC identifies 30 types of complaints. In 2010, for the 11th year in a row, identity theft was the number one type of complaint among the 30 categories, accounting for 250.9 thousand complaints; followed by debt collection with about 144.2 thousand complaints; and Internet services, with about 65.6 thousand complaints.

IDENTITY THEFT AND FRAUD COMPLAINTS, 2008-2010[1]

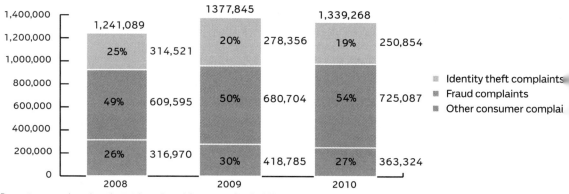

[1]Percentages are based on the total number of Consumer Sentinel Network complaints by calendar year. These figures exclude "Do Not Call" registry complaints. Source: Federal Trade Commission.

HOW VICTIMS' INFORMATION IS MISUSED, 2010[1]

Type of identity theft fraud	Percent
Government documents or benefits fraud	19%
Credit card fraud	15
Phone or utilities fraud	14
Employment-related fraud	11
Bank fraud[2]	10
Attempted identity theft	7
Loan fraud	4
Other identity theft	22

[1]Percentages are based on the total number of complaints in the Federal Trade Commission's Consumer Sentinel Network (250,854 in 2010). Percentages total to more than 100 because some victims reported experiencing more than one type of identity theft (12% in 2010). [2]Includes fraud involving checking and savings accounts and electronic fund transfers.

Source: Federal Trade Commission.

IDENTITY THEFT BY STATE, 2010

State	Complaints per 100,000 population[1]	Number of complaints	Rank[2]	State	Complaints per 100,000 population[1]	Number of complaints	Rank[2]
Alabama	69.9	3,339	15	Montana	39.6	392	44
Alaska	48.2	342	37	Nebraska	47.1	860	38
Arizona	102.5	6,549	2	Nevada	89.7	2,423	6
Arkansas	57.2	1,667	31	New Hampshire	38.2	503	46
California	102.4	38,148	3	New Jersey	77.4	6,807	12
Colorado	78.8	3,961	11	New Mexico	86.1	1,773	7
Connecticut	65.2	2,330	21	New York	85.1	16,494	8
Delaware	73.9	664	13	North Carolina	62.8	5,986	24
Florida	114.8	21,581	1	North Dakota	29.6	199	49
Georgia	97.1	9,404	4	Ohio	59.3	6,844	28
Hawaii	43.3	589	41	Oklahoma	59.6	2,234	27
Idaho	46.5	729	39	Oregon	58.9	2,256	30
Illinois	80.6	10,345	10	Pennsylvania	71.0	9,025	14
Indiana	54.9	3,560	33	Rhode Island	55.0	579	32
Iowa	36.5	1,111	47	South Carolina	58.9	2,726	29
Kansas	60.2	1,717	26	South Dakota	24.6	200	50
Kentucky	42.6	1,847	42	Tennessee	65.8	4,175	19
Louisiana	63.9	2,896	22	Texas	96.1	24,158	5
Maine	32.0	425	48	Utah	53.8	1,488	34
Maryland	82.9	4,784	9	Vermont	39.2	245	45
Massachusetts	61.8	4,044	25	Virginia	63.3	5,065	23
Michigan	69.6	6,880	16	Washington	69.1	4,646	17
Minnesota	49.2	2,612	36	West Virginia	40.5	750	43
Mississippi	67.1	1,992	18	Wisconsin	44.9	2,553	40
Missouri	65.5	3,920	20	Wyoming	51.5	290	35

[1]Population figues are based on the 2010 U.S. Census population estimates.
[2]Ranked per complaints per 100,000 population. The District of Columbia had 153.4 complaints per 100,000 population and 923 victims.

Source: Federal Trade Commission.

Overview

The rankings that follow are extracted from Fortune magazine's analysis of the world's largest corporations based on 2010 revenues, as featured in its annual Global 500. Fortune groups the companies in broad industry categories. Each company is assigned one category, even though some are involved in several industries. For example, some of the leading property/casualty insurance companies also write life insurance.

Financial Services

TOP TEN GLOBAL FINANCIAL SERVICES FIRMS BY REVENUES, 2010[1]
($ millions)

Financial services industry rank	Company	Global 500 rank (all industries)	Revenues	Profits	Country	Industry
1	Japan Post Holdings	9	$203,958	$4,891	Japan	Life/health insurance
2	AXA	14	162,236	3,641	France	Life/health insurance
3	Fannie Mae	15	153,825	-14,014	U.S.	Diversified financial
4	General Electric	16	151,628	11,644	U.S.	Diversified financial
5	ING Group	17	147,052	3,678	Netherlands	Banking
6	Berkshire Hathaway	19	136,185	12,967	U.S.	Property/casualty insurance
7	Bank of America Corp.	21	134,194	-2,238	U.S.	Banking
8	BNP Paribas	26	128,726	10,388	France	Banking
9	Allianz	27	127,379	6,693	Germany	Property/casualty insurance
10	Assicurazioni Generali	33	120,234	2,254	Italy	Life/health insurance

[1]Based on an analysis of companies in the Global Fortune 500.

Source: Fortune.

TOP TEN COUNTRIES BY LIFE AND NONLIFE DIRECT PREMIUMS WRITTEN, 2010[1]
($ millions)

Rank	Country	Life premiums	Nonlife premiums[2]	Total premiums		
				Amount	Precent change from prior year	Percent of total world premiums
1	United States[3,4]	$506,228	$659,915	$1,166,142	1.4%	26.88%
2	Japan[4,5]	440,950	116,489	557,439	6.8	12.85
3	United Kingdom[6]	213,831	96,191	310,022	-0.7	7.15
4	France[6]	192,428	87,654	280,082	-1.4	6.46
5	Germany[6]	114,868	124,949	239,817	-0.1	5.53
6	China[4]	142,999	71,628	214,626	31.6	4.95
7	Italy[6]	122,063	52,285	174,347	2.9	4.02
8	Canada[6,7]	51,574	63,947	115,521	16.1	2.66
9	South Korea[4,5]	71,131	43,291	114,422	16.3	2.64
10	Netherlands[6]	25,102	71,954	97,057	-6.1	2.24

[1]Before reinsurance transactions. [2]Includes accident and health insurance. Does not correspond to grouping of U.S. data shown elsewhere in this book. [3]Life premiums include an estimate of group pension business; nonlife premiums include state funds. [4]Provisional. [5]April 1, 2010-March 31, 2011. [6]Estimated. [7]Life premiums are net premiums.

Source: Swiss Re, *sigma*, No. 2/2011.

TOP TEN GLOBAL INSURANCE COMPANIES BY REVENUES, 2010[1]
($ millions)

Rank	Company	Revenues[2]	Country	Industry
1	Japan Post Holdings	$203,958	Japan	Life/health
2	AXA	162,236	France	Life/health
3	Berkshire Hathaway	136,185	U.S.	Property/casualty
4	Allianz	127,379	Germany	Property/casualty
5	Assicurazioni Generali	120,234	Italy	Life/health
6	American International Group	104,417	U.S.	Property/casualty
7	Aviva	90,211	U.K.	Life/health
8	Nippon Life Insurance	78,571	Japan	Life/health
9	Munich Re Group	76,220	Germany	Property/casualty
10	Prudential	73,598	U.K.	Life/health

[1]Based on an analysis of companies in the Global Fortune 500. Includes stock and mutual companies. [2]Revenues include premium and annuity income, investment income and capital gains or losses, but excludes deposits; includes consolidated subsidiaries, excludes excise taxes.

Source: Fortune.

TOP TEN GLOBAL PROPERTY/CASUALTY INSURANCE COMPANIES BY REVENUES, 2010[1]
($ millions)

Rank	Company	Revenues[2]	Country
1	Berkshire Hathaway	$136,185	U.S.
2	Allianz	127,379	Germany
3	American International Group	104,417	U.S.
4	Munich Re Group	76,220	Germany
5	Zurich Financial Services	67,850	Switzerland
6	State Farm Insurance Cos.	63,177	U.S.
7	MS&AD Insurance Group Holdings	39,754	Japan
8	Tokio Marine Holdings	38,396	Japan
9	Liberty Mutual Insurance Group	33,193	U.S.
10	People's Insurance Co. of China	32,579	China

[1]Based on an analysis of companies in the Global Fortune 500. Includes stock and mutual companies.
[2]Revenues include premium and annuity income, investment income and capital gains or losses, but excludes deposits; includes consolidated subsidiaries, excludes excise taxes.

Source: Fortune.

TOP TEN GLOBAL LIFE/HEALTH INSURANCE COMPANIES BY REVENUES, 2010[1]
($ millions)

Rank	Company	Revenues[2]	Country
1	Japan Post Holdings	$203,958	Japan
2	AXA	162,236	France
3	Assicurazioni Generali	120,234	Italy
4	Aviva	90,211	U.K.
5	Nippon Life Insurance	78,571	Japan
6	Prudential	73,598	U.K.
7	Aegon	65,136	Netherlands
8	China Life Insurance	64,635	China
9	Legal & General Group	59,377	U.K.
10	CNP Assurances	59,320	France

[1]Based on an analysis of companies in the Global Fortune 500. Includes stock and mutual companies.
[2]Revenues include premium and annuity income, investment income and capital gains or losses, but excludes deposits; includes consolidated subsidiaries, excludes excise taxes.

Source: Fortune.

TOP TEN GLOBAL REINSURERS BY NET REINSURANCE PREMIUMS WRITTEN, 2010[1]
($ millions)

- Net reinsurance premiums written by the top 10 global reinsurers fell from $112.2 billion in 2009 to $110.3 billion in 2010, according to Business Insurance.

Rank	Company	Net reinsurance premiums written	Country
1	Munich Re	$29,149.9[2]	Germany
2	Swiss Re Group	19,433.0	Switzerland
3	Berkshire Hathaway Reinsurance Group/ General Re Corp.	14,669.0	U.S.
4	Hanover Re	14,034.1[2]	Germany
5	Lloyd's of London	9,728.6	U.K.
6	SCOR S.E.	8,146.2	France
7	PartnerRe Ltd.	4,705.1	Bermuda
8	Everest Re Group Ltd.	3,945.6	Bermuda
9	Transatlantic Holdings, Inc.	3,881.7	U.S.
10	Korean Re	2,653.8[3]	South Korea

[1]Excludes reinsurers which only underwrite life insurance.
[2]Business Insurance estimate.
[3]Fiscal year ending March 31.

Source: Business Insurance, September 26, 2011.

TOP TEN GLOBAL INSURANCE BROKERS BY REVENUES, 2010[1]
($ millions)

- Commercial retail business accounted for 52.0 percent of the largest brokers' revenues in 2010. The next largest segments were employee benefits (17.9 percent) and services (7.7 percent).

Rank	Company	Brokerage revenues	Country
1	Aon Corp.	$10,606	U.S.
2	Marsh & McLennan Cos. Inc.	10,596	U.S.
3	Willis Group Holdings P.L.C.	3,300	U.K.
4	Arthur J. Gallagher & Co.	1,790	U.S.
5	Wells Fargo Insurance Services USA Inc.	1,650	U.S.
6	Jardine Lloyd Thompson Group P.L.C.[2]	1,138	U.K.
7	BB&T Insurance Services Inc.	1,079	U.S.
8	Brown & Brown Inc.	967	U.S.
9	Lockton Cos. L.L.C.[3]	827	U.S.
10	Hub International Ltd.	762	U.S.

[1]Gross revenues generated by insurance brokerage, consulting and related services.
[2]Fiscal year ending December 31.
[3]Fiscal year ending April 30.

Source: Business Insurance, July 18, 2011.

TOP TEN GLOBAL REINSURANCE BROKERS BY REINSURANCE GROSS REVENUES, 2010[1]
($000)

Rank	Company	Reinsurance gross revenues	Country
1	Aon Benfield	$1,444,000	U.S.
2	Guy Carpenter & Co. L.L.C.[2]	975,000	U.S.
3	Willis Re	664,000	U.K.
4	JLT Reinsurance Brokers Ltd.	198,713	U.K.
5	Towers Watson & Co.	172,289	U.S.
6	Cooper Gay Swett & Crawford Ltd.	120,400	U.K.
7	BMS Group	77,569	U.K.
8	Miller Insurance Services Ltd.[3]	68,158	U.K.
9	UIB Holdings Ltd.	49,446	U.K.
10	Lockton Cos. International Ltd.[3]	35,556	U.K.

[1]Includes all reinsurance revenue reported through holding and/or subsidary companies.
[2]Includes aviation reinsurance business placed by Marsh Inc.
[3]Fiscal year ending April 30.
Source: Business Insurance, October 24, 2011.

Banks

**TOP TEN GLOBAL COMMERCIAL AND SAVINGS
BANKS BY REVENUES, 2010[1]**
($ millions)

Rank	Company	Revenues	Country
1	ING Group	$147,052	Netherlands
2	Bank of America Corp.	134,194	U.S.
3	BNP Paribas	128,726	France
4	J.P. Morgan Chase & Co.	115,475	U.S.
5	Citigroup	111,055	U.S.
6	Crédit Agricole	105,003	France
7	HSBC Holdings	102,680	U.K.
8	Banco Santander	100,350	Spain
9	Lloyds Banking Group	95,682	U.K.
10	Wells Fargo	93,249	U.S.

[1]Based on an analysis of companies in the Global Fortune 500.
Source: Fortune.

TOP SIX GLOBAL DIVERSIFIED FINANCIAL COMPANIES BY REVENUES, 2010[1]
($ millions)

Rank	Company	Revenues	Country
1	Fannie Mae	$153,825	U.S.
2	General Electric	151,628	U.S.
3	Freddie Mac	98,368	U.S.
4	INTL FCStone	46,940	U.S.
5	CITIC Group	38,985	China
6	Cie Nationale à Portefeuille	20,373	Belgium

[1]Based on an analysis of companies in the Global Fortune 500.

Source: Fortune.

Overview

There were 308.7 million people in the United States in 2010, up 9.7 percent from 281.4 million in 2000, according to the 2010 U.S. Census. Since 1900 only the 1930s experienced lower growth than the past decade. Further data from the 2010 U.S. Census are available on the Web at http://2010.census.gov/2010census/. Updates to the U.S. Census Bureau's American Community Survey are posted at http://www.census.gov/acs/.

Geographic Mobility

The percentage of the U.S. population that moved rose from 11.9 percent in 2008, the lowest rate since the U.S. Census Bureau began tracking these data in 1948, to 12.5 percent in both 2009 and 2010. In 2010, 37.5 million people 1 year old and older had changed residences in the U.S. within the past year, up from 37.1 million in 2009.

GENERAL MOBILITY, 2004-2010
(millions)

Mobility period	Total population[1]	Total movers	Moving rate (percent)
2004-2005	287	40	13.9%
2005-2006	290	40	13.7
2006-2007	293	39	13.2
2007-2008	295	35	11.9
2008-2009	297	37	12.5
2009-2010	300	38	12.5

[1]People age 1 year old and older.

Source: U.S. Census Bureau.

■ More than four out of 10 movers did so for housing-related reasons, such as the desire to live in a new or better home or apartment, according to the U.S. Census Bureau. Other reasons were family concerns (30.3 percent), employment needs (16.4 percent) and other factors (9.5 percent).

MOBILITY BY REGION, 2008-2010
(millions)

Region	2009-2010		Moving rate (percent)		Percent of U.S. movers
	Total population[1]	Movers	2008-2009	2009-2010	2009-2010
Northeast	53,976	4,492	8.1%	8.3%	12.0%
South	110,699	15,028	13.7	13.6	40.0
Midwest	65,271	7,729	11.6	11.8	20.6
West	70,129	10,293	14.8	14.7	27.4
Total	**300,075**	**37,542**	**11.9%**	**12.5%**	**100.0%**

[1]People age 1 year old and older.

Source: U.S. Census Bureau.

PERCENT OF PEOPLE WHO LIVED IN A DIFFERENT STATE ONE YEAR AGO, 2010[1]

State	Percent	Rank[2]	State	Percent	Rank[2]
Alabama	2.3%	35	Montana	3.6%	8
Alaska	5.2	2	Nebraska	2.8	25
Arizona	3.5	13	Nevada	3.9	6
Arkansas	2.7	28	New Hampshire	3.0	20
California	1.2	50	New Jersey	1.5	47
Colorado	3.8	7	New Mexico	3.6	8
Connecticut	2.2	36	New York	1.4	49
Delaware	3.6	8	North Carolina	2.8	25
D.C.	8.6	1	North Dakota	4.5	4
Florida	2.7	28	Ohio	1.5	47
Georgia	2.6	30	Oklahoma	2.9	21
Hawaii	4.0	5	Oregon	3.1	18
Idaho	3.6	8	Pennsylvania	1.9	43
Illinois	1.6	46	Rhode Island	3.1	18
Indiana	2.0	41	South Carolina	3.3	15
Iowa	2.4	34	South Dakota	3.2	17
Kansas	3.4	14	Tennessee	2.5	31
Kentucky	2.8	25	Texas	2.0	41
Louisiana	2.2	36	Utah	2.9	21
Maine	2.1	40	Vermont	3.6	8
Maryland	2.9	21	Virginia	3.3	15
Massachusetts	2.2	36	Washington	2.9	21
Michigan	1.2	50	West Virginia	2.2	36
Minnesota	1.7	44	Wisconsin	1.7	44
Mississippi	2.5	31	Wyoming	5.0	3
Missouri	2.5	31	**United States**	**2.2%**	

[1]People age 1 year old and older.
[2]States with the same percentages receive the same rank.

Source: U.S. Census Bureau, American Community Survey.

U.S. MIGRATION, BY PLACE OF ORIGIN, 2010

State	Percent of U.S. population who are foreign born		Percent of foreign born population who were born in			
	Percent	Rank[1]	Latin America	Asia	Europe	Other
Alabama	3.5%	43	58.0%	26.3%	9.9%	5.8%
Alaska	6.9	25	19.2	52.3	17.0	11.5
Arizona	13.4	13	66.8	17.0	9.2	7.0
Arkansas	4.5	36	66.5	19.4	7.4	6.7
California	27.2	1	54.0	35.9	6.6	3.5
Colorado	9.8	18	55.3	21.3	13.8	9.6
Connecticut	13.6	11	42.1	22.0	28.5	7.4
Delaware	8.0	21	47.2	30.9	12.8	9.1
D.C.	13.5	12	44.1	18.6	17.5	19.8
Florida	19.4	4	75.2	9.7	10.6	4.5
Georgia	9.7	20	54.7	26.1	9.4	9.8
Hawaii	18.2	6	5.1	76.8	5.1	13.0
Idaho	5.5	30	62.4	11.8	16.4	9.4
Illinois	13.7	10	47.9	26.5	22.1	3.5
Indiana	4.6	34	47.6	29.4	14.1	8.9
Iowa	4.6	34	42.7	29.7	15.8	11.8
Kansas	6.5	26	56.8	27.1	8.9	7.2
Kentucky	3.2	45	42.7	30.9	18.0	8.4
Louisiana	3.8	42	53.7	31.5	9.1	5.7
Maine	3.4	44	9.2	26.8	23.9	40.1
Maryland	13.9	9	38.8	33.1	10.8	17.3
Massachusetts	15.0	8	36.2	29.1	23.5	11.2
Michigan	6.0	28	20.1	46.0	22.6	11.3
Minnesota	7.1	24	27.4	37.2	11.1	24.3
Mississippi	2.1	49	51.9	33.6	10.8	3.7
Missouri	3.9	41	30.8	35.4	22.0	11.8
Montana	2.0	50	11.2	23.8	37.1	27.9
Nebraska	6.1	27	54.7	24.6	9.9	10.8
Nevada	18.8	5	57.2	29.8	8.5	4.5

- In 2010, 12.9 percent of the U.S. population was born outside the United States, with more than half of those immigrants born in Latin America.

- The percentage of the population that speaks Spanish at home ranges from 13 percent nationally to almost 30 percent in Texas, California and New Mexico.

(table continues)

U.S. MIGRATION, BY PLACE OF ORIGIN, 2010 (Cont'd)

- The Hispanic population increased by 15.2 million between 2000 and 2010, accounting for more than half of the total U.S. population increase of 27.3 million. Between 2000 and 2010 the Hispanic population grew by 43 percent, or four times the nation's 9.7 percent growth rate.

- Sixteen percent of the population were of Hispanic or Latino origin in 2010, up from 13 percent in 2000.

State	Percent of U.S. population who are foreign born		Percent of foreign born population who were born in			
	Percent	Rank[1]	Latin America	Asia	Europe	Other
New Hampshire	5.3%	32	20.3%	33.0%	23.9%	22.8%
New Jersey	21.0	3	46.2	30.8	17.2	5.8
New Mexico	9.9	17	79.7	10.1	7.8	2.4
New York	22.2	2	50.1	26.8	17.8	5.3
North Carolina	7.5	23	57.6	22.7	10.5	9.2
North Dakota	2.5	48	7.2	37.7	21.2	33.9
Ohio	4.1	40	21.4	37.7	26.4	14.5
Oklahoma	5.5	30	58.8	26.1	7.4	7.7
Oregon	9.8	18	46.5	29.1	15.4	9.0
Pennsylvania	5.8	29	29.9	37.7	22.3	10.1
Rhode Island	12.8	15	44.3	18.6	22.3	14.8
South Carolina	4.7	33	54.8	20.4	16.9	7.9
South Dakota	2.7	47	25.8	29.4	19.0	25.8
Tennessee	4.5	36	49.4	26.8	11.3	12.5
Texas	16.4	7	72.8	18.6	4.2	4.4
Utah	8.0	21	62.3	16.8	11.1	9.8
Vermont	4.4	39	10.1	28.1	30.5	31.3
Virginia	11.4	16	37.1	39.7	11.3	11.9
Washington	13.1	14	31.3	40.2	16.8	11.7
West Virginia	1.2	51	23.6	43.8	19.0	13.6
Wisconsin	4.5	36	43.3	32.7	18.2	5.8
Wyoming	2.8	46	56.9	18.4	16.0	8.7
United States	**12.9%**		**53.1%**	**28.2%**	**12.1%**	**6.6%**

[1]States with the same percentages receive the same rank.

Source: U.S. Census Bureau, American Community Survey.

FASTEST GROWING METROPOLITAN STATISTICAL AREAS, 2000-2010

Rank	Metropolitan statistical area	Population growth	Rank	Metropolitan statistical area	Population growth
1	Las Vegas-Paradise, NV	575,504	6	Myrtle Beach-North Myrtle Beach-Conway, SC	72,662
2	Austin-Round Rock-San Marcos, TX	466,526	7	Greeley, CO	71,899
3	Raleigh-Cary, NC	333,419	8	St. George, UT	47,761
4	Cape Coral-Fort Myers, FL	177,866	9	Palm Coast, FL	45,864
5	Provo-Orem, UT	150,036	10	Bend, OR	42,366

Source: U.S. Census Bureau.

Income and Expenses

The percentage of Americans living in poverty rose from 14.3 percent in 2009 to 15.1 percent in 2010, the third consecutive annual increase in the poverty rate, according to a 2011 U.S. Census report. Median income (adjusted for inflation) was $49,445 in 2010, down 2.3 percent from the 2009 median. The number of people living in poverty increased for the fourth consecutive year, rising from 43.6 million in 2009 to 46.2 million in 2010. 2010 marked the largest number of people at the poverty level in the 52 years for which such estimates have been published.

INCOME BY REGION, 2009-2010

	2009		2010		Percentage change in median income
	Number of households (000)	Median income[1]	Number of households (000)	Median income[1]	
All households	**117,538**	**$50,599**	**118,682**	**$49,445**	**-2.3%**
By region					
Northeast	21,479	53,949	21,597	53,283	-1.2
Midwest	26,390	49,684	26,669	48,445	-2.5
South	43,611	46,368	44,161	45,492	-1.9
West	26,058	54,722	26,254	53,142	-2.9

[1]Income before deductions for taxes and other expenses; does not include lump sum payments or capital gains. Expressed in 2010 dollars.

Source: U.S. Census Bureau.

- In 2010 household incomes were highest in Maryland, followed by New Jersey and Alaska.

- Mississippi had the lowest median household income, followed by West Virginia and Arkansas.

HOUSEHOLD INCOME BY STATE, 2010[1]

State	Median income	Rank	State	Median income	Rank
Alabama	$40,474	47	Montana	$42,666	41
Alaska	64,576	3	Nebraska	48,408	26
Arizona	46,789	29	Nevada	51,001	20
Arkansas	38,307	49	New Hampshire	61,042	7
California	57,708	10	New Jersey	67,681	2
Colorado	54,046	16	New Mexico	42,090	43
Connecticut	64,032	4	New York	54,148	15
D.C.	60,903	8	North Carolina	43,326	40
Delaware	55,847	11	North Dakota	48,670	24
Florida	44,409	37	Ohio	45,090	35
Georgia	46,430	31	Oklahoma	42,072	44
Hawaii	63,030	5	Oregon	46,560	30
Idaho	43,490	39	Pennsylvania	49,288	22
Illinois	52,972	18	Rhode Island	52,254	19
Indiana	44,613	36	South Carolina	42,018	45
Iowa	47,961	28	South Dakota	45,904	32
Kansas	48,257	27	Tennessee	41,461	46
Kentucky	40,062	48	Texas	48,615	25
Louisiana	42,505	42	Utah	54,744	14
Maine	45,815	33	Vermont	49,406	21
Maryland	68,854	1	Virginia	60,674	9
Massachusetts	62,072	6	Washington	55,631	12
Michigan	45,413	34	West Virginia	38,218	50
Minnesota	55,459	13	Wisconsin	49,001	23
Mississippi	36,851	51	Wyoming	53,512	17
Missouri	44,301	38	**United States**	**$50,046**	

[1]In 2010 inflation-adjusted dollars.

Source: U.S. Census Bureau, American Community Survey.

HOUSEHOLD INCOME SPENT ON HOME OWNERSHIP COSTS, 2010

State	Percent[1]	Rank[2]	State	Percent[1]	Rank[2]
Alabama	32.5%	35	Montana	35.9%	22
Alaska	32.1	37	Nebraska	25.9	47
Arizona	40.9	10	Nevada	44.7	5
Arkansas	27.4	44	New Hampshire	40.0	12
California	50.9	1	New Jersey	46.5	4
Colorado	37.3	18	New Mexico	35.9	22
Connecticut	41.3	8	New York	41.2	9
Delaware	37.1	19	North Carolina	34.3	28
D.C.	35.5	24	North Dakota	19.0	51
Florida	48.3	3	Ohio	31.8	38
Georgia	37.9	17	Oklahoma	28.7	42
Hawaii	50.0	2	Oregon	42.6	7
Idaho	36.6	20	Pennsylvania	33.1	33
Illinois	39.7	13	Rhode Island	43.5	6
Indiana	27.4	44	South Carolina	33.8	31
Iowa	24.7	50	South Dakota	25.4	49
Kansas	26.4	46	Tennessee	33.1	33
Kentucky	30.1	39	Texas	32.5	35
Louisiana	30.1	39	Utah	35.4	25
Maine	33.9	30	Vermont	38.6	15
Maryland	38.0	16	Virginia	35.0	27
Massachusetts	39.0	14	Washington	40.7	11
Michigan	36.2	21	West Virginia	25.5	48
Minnesota	33.3	32	Wisconsin	34.2	29
Mississippi	35.2	26	Wyoming	28.0	43
Missouri	30.1	39	**United States**	**37.8%**	

- In 2010 California, Hawaii and Florida had the highest homeownership costs, based on the percentage of homes in which owners spent 30 percent or more of their income on homeowner ownership expenses.

- North Dakota, Iowa and South Dakota had the lowest costs, based on the percentage of homes in which owners spent 30 percent of more of their income on homeowner ownership expenses.

[1]Percent of mortgaged owner-occupied housing units spending 30 percent or more of household income on selected owner costs such as all mortgage payments (first mortgage, home equity loans, etc.), real estate taxes, property insurance, utilities, fuel and condominium fees if applicable.

[2]States with the same percentages receive the same rank.

Source: U.S. Census Bureau, American Community Survey.

Demographics

Income and Expenses

MEDIAN HOUSING VALUE BY STATE, 2010[1]

- In 2010 median housing values were highest in Hawaii, followed by the District of Columbia and California.

- Median housing values were lowest in West Virginia, followed by Mississippi and Arkansas.

State	Median value	Rank[2]	State	Median value	Rank[2]
Alabama	$123,900	42	Montana	$181,200	21
Alaska	241,400	15	Nebraska	127,600	40
Arizona	168,800	26	Nevada	174,800	24
Arkansas	106,300	49	New Hampshire	243,000	14
California	370,900	3	New Jersey	339,200	4
Colorado	236,600	16	New Mexico	161,200	30
Connecticut	288,800	8	New York	296,500	7
Delaware	243,600	13	North Carolina	154,200	32
D.C.	426,900	2	North Dakota	123,000	46
Florida	164,200	29	Ohio	134,400	37
Georgia	156,200	31	Oklahoma	111,400	48
Hawaii	525,400	1	Oregon	244,500	12
Idaho	165,100	28	Pennsylvania	165,500	27
Illinois	191,800	20	Rhode Island	254,500	10
Indiana	123,300	44	South Carolina	138,100	35
Iowa	123,400	43	South Dakota	129,700	38
Kansas	127,300	41	Tennessee	139,000	33
Kentucky	121,600	47	Texas	128,100	39
Louisiana	137,500	36	Utah	217,200	17
Maine	179,100	23	Vermont	216,800	18
Maryland	301,400	6	Virginia	249,100	11
Massachusetts	334,100	5	Washington	271,800	9
Michigan	123,300	44	West Virginia	95,100	51
Minnesota	194,300	19	Wisconsin	169,400	25
Mississippi	100,100	50	Wyoming	180,100	22
Missouri	139,000	33	**United States**	**$179,900**	

[1]Owner-occupied housing units.
[2]States with the same percentages receive the same rank.
Source: U.S. Census Bureau, American Community Survey.

PERCENT OF OCCUPIED HOUSING UNITS THAT ARE OWNER OCCUPIED, 2010

State	Percent	Rank[1]	State	Percent	Rank[1]
Alabama	70.1%	10	Montana	69.7%	14
Alaska	63.9	41	Nebraska	67.4	32
Arizona	65.2	40	Nevada	57.2	48
Arkansas	67.4	32	New Hampshire	71.7	7
California	55.6	49	New Jersey	66.4	37
Colorado	65.9	39	New Mexico	67.9	27
Connecticut	68.0	25	New York	54.3	50
Delaware	73.0	2	North Carolina	67.2	34
D.C.	42.5	51	North Dakota	66.9	36
Florida	68.1	22	Ohio	68.4	21
Georgia	66.2	38	Oklahoma	67.8	28
Hawaii	58.0	47	Oregon	62.5	44
Idaho	69.6	16	Pennsylvania	70.1	10
Illinois	67.7	29	Rhode Island	60.8	46
Indiana	70.3	9	South Carolina	68.7	18
Iowa	72.4	6	South Dakota	68.0	25
Kansas	68.1	22	Tennessee	68.1	22
Kentucky	68.6	20	Texas	63.6	42
Louisiana	67.6	31	Utah	69.9	12
Maine	72.7	5	Vermont	70.4	8
Maryland	67.0	35	Virginia	67.7	29
Massachusetts	62.2	45	Washington	63.1	43
Michigan	72.8	4	West Virginia	74.6	1
Minnesota	73.0	2	Wisconsin	68.7	18
Mississippi	69.8	13	Wyoming	69.7	14
Missouri	69.0	17	**United States**	**65.4%**	

[1]States with the same percentages receive the same rank.

Source: U.S. Census Bureau, American Community Survey.

- In 2010 West Virginia, Delaware and Minnesota had the highest percentage of owner-occupied housing units.

- The District of Columbia had the lowest percentage of owner-occupied units, followed by New York, California, Nevada and Hawaii.

- Nationwide, 48.9 percent of renters spent at least 30 percent of their household income on rent and utilities in 2010.

- In 2010 Wyoming, North Dakota, South Dakota, Montana and West Virginia had the lowest percentage of rental units in which occupants spent 30 percent or more of their income on rent. Florida, California, New Jersey, Hawaii had the highest percentage.

HOUSEHOLD INCOME SPENT ON RENT AND UTILITIES, 2010

State	Percent[1]	Rank[2]	State	Percent[1]	Rank[2]
Alabama	46.7%	28	Montana	39.9%	48
Alaska	41.5	45	Nebraska	41.0	46
Arizona	49.1	12	Nevada	50.3	9
Arkansas	43.3	40	New Hampshire	47.7	21
California	54.4	2	New Jersey	51.5	3
Colorado	49.0	13	New Mexico	42.4	41
Connecticut	50.5	8	New York	50.2	10
Delaware	50.9	7	North Carolina	47.2	24
D.C.	47.5	22	North Dakota	36.2	50
Florida	55.6	1	Ohio	47.9	19
Georgia	49.0	13	Oklahoma	41.8	43
Hawaii	51.3	4	Oregon	51.2	5
Idaho	46.9	27	Pennsylvania	46.3	34
Illinois	48.8	15	Rhode Island	48.1	18
Indiana	46.7	28	South Carolina	47.2	24
Iowa	42.3	42	South Dakota	37.2	49
Kansas	41.8	43	Tennessee	46.7	28
Kentucky	43.7	39	Texas	46.3	34
Louisiana	46.4	33	Utah	45.8	36
Maine	45.1	38	Vermont	49.9	11
Maryland	48.7	16	Virginia	46.6	31
Massachusetts	47.8	20	Washington	48.4	17
Michigan	51.2	5	West Virginia	40.2	47
Minnesota	47.5	22	Wisconsin	46.5	32
Mississippi	47.0	26	Wyoming	34.3	51
Missouri	45.8	36	**United States**	**48.9%**	

[1]Percent of renter-occupied units spending 30 percent or more on rent and utilities such as electric, gas, water and sewer, and fuel (oil, coal, etc.) if paid by the renter.
[2]States with the same percentages receive the same rank.

Source: U.S. Census Bureau, American Community Survey.

PERCENT OF PEOPLE WITHOUT HEALTH INSURANCE BY STATE, 2010[1]

State	Percent	Rank[2]	State	Percent	Rank[2]
Alabama	14.6%	23	Montana	17.3%	14
Alaska	19.9	4	Nebraska	11.5	37
Arizona	16.9	16	Nevada	22.6	2
Arkansas	17.5	12	New Hampshire	11.1	39
California	18.5	8	New Jersey	13.2	29
Colorado	15.9	18	New Mexico	19.6	6
Connecticut	9.1	46	New York	11.9	36
Delaware	9.7	43	North Carolina	16.8	17
D.C.	7.6	50	North Dakota	9.8	42
Florida	21.3	3	Ohio	12.3	34
Georgia	19.7	5	Oklahoma	18.9	7
Hawaii	7.9	49	Oregon	17.1	15
Idaho	17.7	11	Pennsylvania	10.2	40
Illinois	13.8	28	Rhode Island	12.2	35
Indiana	14.8	22	South Carolina	17.5	12
Iowa	9.3	45	South Dakota	12.4	32
Kansas	13.9	27	Tennessee	14.4	25
Kentucky	15.3	19	Texas	23.7	1
Louisiana	17.8	10	Utah	15.3	19
Maine	10.1	41	Vermont	8.0	48
Maryland	11.3	38	Virginia	13.1	31
Massachusetts	4.4	51	Washington	14.2	26
Michigan	12.4	32	West Virginia	14.6	23
Minnesota	9.1	46	Wisconsin	9.4	44
Mississippi	18.2	9	Wyoming	14.9	21
Missouri	13.2	29	**United States**	**15.5%**	

- Texas, followed by Nevada and Florida, had the highest percentages of people without health insurance in 2010.

- Massachusetts had the lowest percentage of people without health insurance, followed by the District of Columbia and Hawaii.

[1]Includes private coverage from an employer or purchased by an individual and government coverage including Medicare, Medicaid, military healthcare, the State Children's Health Insurance Program and individual state health plans. People were considered insured if they were covered by any coverage for part or all of the previous calendar year.
[2]States with the same percentages receive the same rank.

Source: U.S. Census Bureau, American Community Survey.

Demographics

Aging

**PERCENT OF HOUSEHOLDS WITH ONE MORE MORE PEOPLE
65 YEARS OLD AND OVER, 2010**

- Florida, followed by Hawaii and West Virginia, had the highest percentage of households with people age 65 or older in 2010.

- Alaska had the lowest percentage of households with people age 65 or older, followed by Utah and Colorado.

State	Percent	Rank[1]	State	Percent	Rank[1]
Alabama	25.8%	14	Montana	26.2%	12
Alaska	15.5	51	Nebraska	23.6	40
Arizona	26.3	10	Nevada	23.8	35
Arkansas	26.3	10	New Hampshire	24.7	28
California	24.3	29	New Jersey	26.7	6
Colorado	20.0	49	New Mexico	25.6	16
Connecticut	26.4	8	New York	26.2	12
Delaware	27.3	5	North Carolina	23.9	32
D.C.	21.0	48	North Dakota	23.9	32
Florida	31.5	1	Ohio	25.4	18
Georgia	21.1	46	Oklahoma	24.9	26
Hawaii	30.1	2	Oregon	25.1	22
Idaho	23.5	41	Pennsylvania	27.9	4
Illinois	23.9	32	Rhode Island	26.4	8
Indiana	23.8	35	South Carolina	25.8	14
Iowa	25.1	22	South Dakota	25.2	21
Kansas	23.7	38	Tennessee	25.0	24
Kentucky	24.3	29	Texas	21.1	46
Louisiana	23.7	38	Utah	19.9	50
Maine	26.7	6	Vermont	24.8	27
Maryland	23.8	35	Virginia	23.4	42
Massachusetts	25.5	17	Washington	22.5	44
Michigan	25.3	19	West Virginia	29.2	3
Minnesota	22.7	43	Wisconsin	24.0	31
Mississippi	25.3	19	Wyoming	22.0	45
Missouri	25.0	24	**United States**	**24.8%**	

[1]States with the same percentages receive the same rank.

Source: U.S. Census Bureau, American Community Survey.

DODD-FRANK WALL STREET REFORM AND CONSUMER PROTECTION ACT: ONE YEAR LATER

On July 21, 2010 President Obama signed into law a sweeping overhaul of how financial services are regulated in the United States. Responding to the events that helped precipitate the country's economic crisis, the legislation calls for systemic risk regulation, giving the federal government authority to seize and dismantle large financial firms that its deems could destabilize the financial system if they became insolvent. The law also creates a separate Consumer Financial Protection Bureau (CFPB) to address some of the practices that are believed to have contributed to the crisis. The law does not dismantle state regulation of insurance, but establishes a Federal Insurance Office (FIO) within the U.S. Treasury Department to report to Congress and the President on the insurance industry. In March 2011 Treasury Secretary Timothy Geithner named former Michael McRaith, Illinois insurance commissioner, to head the FIO. In July the President nominated Richard Cordray, former Ohio attorney general, to head the CFPB, a move that required confirmation by Congress.

A year after its passage, there continued to be uncertainty about how and when the law's provisions would be implemented. As of July 2011 regulators had completed 51, or 13 percent, of the 400 rulemaking requirements in Dodd-Frank, according to a report by Davis Polk. A summary of the law is below.

TITLE I: Financial Stability

Creates the Financial Stability Oversight Council and the Office of Financial Research, imposes heightened federal regulation on large bank holding companies and "systemically risky" nonbank financial companies.

The Financial Stability Oversight Council (FSOC) is charged with identifying threats to the financial stability of the United States, promoting market discipline and responding to emerging risks to the stability of the U.S. financial system. The council brings together federal financial regulators, state regulators and an insurance expert appointed by the President. It consists of 10 voting members and five nonvoting members, who serve in an advisory capacity.

I. Voting Members:

Secretary of the Treasury, who serves as the Chairperson of the Council; Chairman of the Board of Governors of the Federal Reserve System; Comptroller of the Currency; Director of the Bureau of Consumer Financial Protection; Chairman of the Securities and Exchange Commission; Chairperson of the Federal Deposit Insurance Corporation; Chairperson of the Commodity Futures Trading Commission; Director of the Federal Housing Finance Agency; Chairman of the National Credit Union Administration Board; an independent member with insurance expertise who is appointed by the President and confirmed by the Senate for a six-year term.

II. Nonvoting:

Director of the Office of Financial Research; Director of the Federal Insurance Office; A state insurance commissioner designated by the state insurance commissioners; A state banking supervisor designated by the state banking supervisors; and a state securities commissioner (or officer performing like functions) designated by the state securities commissioners. (The state insurance commissioner, state banking supervisor, and state securities commissioner serve two-year terms.)

TITLE II: Orderly Liquidation Authority

Establishes a liquidation fund supported by future assessments on large banks and requires submission of "living wills" detailing how to unwind failing nonbank financial companies.

TITLE III: Transfer of Powers to the Office of the Comptroller of the Currency (OCC), the Federal Deposit Insurance Corporation (FDIC) and the Board of Governors of the Federal Reserve.

One year after enactment the Office of Thrift Supervision (OTS) will transfer its functions as follows:
- Savings and loan holding companies: To be regulated by the Federal Reserve Board of Governors.
- Federal savings associations: To be regulated by the OCC.
- State savings associations: To be regulated by the FDIC

TITLE IV: Regulation of Advisors to Hedge Funds and Others

Requires registration and recordkeeping requirements for private advisers, with limited exemptions.

TITLE V: Insurance

Establishes the Federal Insurance Office (while maintaining state regulation of insurance) within the Department of Treasury, headed by a Director appointed by the Secretary of Treasury.

- Office Functions: The office will handle all insurance (with the exception of health insurance) and will have authority to monitor the insurance industry, identify regulatory gaps or systemic risk, deal with international insurance matters and monitor the extent to which underserved communities have access to affordable insurance products (except health insurance).

- Financial Stability Oversight Council (FSOC) Recommendations: May make recommendations to the FSOC on whether an insurer (including reinsurers) poses a systemic risk under Title I and should therefore be placed under the supervision of the Federal Reserve.

- New Authority to Negotiate and Enforce Narrow International Agreements on Insurance: The Office has the authority to jointly enter into agreements, with the U.S. Trade Representative, which cover prudential measures related to the business of insurance and reinsurance. In doing so, the Office has limited preemption authority over state law in cases where it is determined that the state law is inconsistent with a negotiated international agreement and treats a non-U.S. insurer less favorably than a U.S. insurer. The power of preemption is further limited by a savings clause, which states that the Office has no authority to preempt state laws on insurer's rates, premiums, underwriting, sales practices, capital, solvency or state antitrust laws.

- The Federal Insurance Office Reporting: Annual Reports to the President and Senate Banking Committee are expected of the Office.

- Insurance Study: A study must be completed on how to improve insurance regulation in the United States, including state insurance, due no more than 18 months after enactment.

An amendment to the Act stipulates that equity indexed annuities will continue to be regulated by state insurance commissioners.

TITLE VI: Improvement to Regulation of Bank and Savings Association Holding Companies and Depository Institutions

Expands the authority of the Federal Reserve to regulate subsidiaries of bank holding companies, sets a 10 percent concentration limit for bank mergers and creates the "Volcker Rule," prohibiting banks from proprietary trading, with notable exceptions.

TITLE VII: Wall Street Transparency and Accountability

Introduces significant requirements for derivatives, including mandatory clearing of nonexempt OTC derivatives and limitations on bank involvement in derivative activities.

TITLE VIII: Payment, Clearing and Settlement Supervision

Authorizes the Financial Stability Oversight Council to designate financial market utilities or payment, clearing and settlement activities as systemically important.

TITLE IX: Investor Protection and Improvements to the Regulation of Securities

Imposes risk retention requirements, corporate governance standards, executive compensation requirements and a study on broker-dealer fiduciary duties.

TITLE X: Bureau of Consumer Financial Protection

Establishes the Consumer Financial Protection Bureau, with consumer regulatory authorities consolidated from other banking agencies. Also introduces interchange fee restrictions for debit card payments. The bureau is located in, but is autonomous from, the Federal Reserve.

TITLE XI: Federal Reserve System Provisions

Restricts the Federal Reserve's emergency lending powers and debt guarantees while further authorizing a one time Government Accountability Office-conducted audit of the Fed.

TITLE XII: Improving Access to Mainstream Financial Intuitions

Encourages initiatives to provide financial products and services for Americans with low and moderate incomes.

TITLE XIII: Pay it Back Act

Reduces the TARP spending authority, limiting any future purchase of troubled assets to amounts collected through the Pay It Back Act, and further directs that all amounts collected from the subsequent sale of such assets be directed towards deficit reduction.

TITLE XIV: Mortgage Reform and Anti-Predatory Lending Act

Provides consumer protection through reform on mortgage issuance, mortgage related fees and various mortgage practices.

TITLE XV: Miscellaneous Provisions

Addresses bailouts of foreign governments.

Source: The Financial Services Roundtable and the Insurance Information Institute.

I.I.I. Store

The I.I.I. Store is your gateway to a wide array of books and brochures from the Insurance Information Institute.

Print and PDF formats, and quantity discounts are available for most products. Order online at www.iii.org/publications, call 212-346-5500 or email publications@iii.org.

I.I.I. Insurance Fact Book
Thousands of insurance facts, figures, tables and graphs designed for quick and easy reference.

The Financial Services Fact Book
Banking, securities and insurance industry trends and statistics. Published jointly with the Financial Services Roundtable.

Online version available at www.financialservicesfacts.org

Insurance Handbook
A guide to the insurance industry for reporters, public policymakers, students, insurance company employees, regulators and others. Provides concise explanations of auto, home, life, disability and business insurance, as well as issues papers, a glossary and directories.

Online version available at www.iii.org/insurancehandbook

Insuring Your Business: A Small Businessowners' Guide to Insurance
A comprehensive insurance guide for small businessowners. Special discounts available to organizations and agents for bulk orders.

Online version available at www.iii.org/smallbusiness

A Firm Foundation: How Insurance Supports the Economy
Shows the myriad ways in which insurance provides economic support—from offering employment and fueling the capital markets, to providing financial security and income to individuals and businesses. Provides national and state data. Selected state versions are also available.

Online version available at www.iii.org/economics

International Insurance Fact Book
Facts and statistics on the property/casualty and life insurance industries of dozens of countries. No print edition.

Online version available at www.iii.org/international

Commercial Insurance
A comprehensive guide to the commercial insurance market—what it does, how it functions, and its key players. No print edition.

Online version available at www.iii.org/commerciallines

I.I.I. Insurance Daily
Keeps thousands of readers up-to-date on important events, issues and trends in the insurance industry. Transmitted early each business day via email.

Contact: iiidaily@iii.org

Appendices

Know Your Stuff® Home Inventory

Free online home inventory software and mobile app
>   Software available at www.knowyourstuff.org
>   iPhone app available at the Apple App Store
>   Android app available at the Android Market

Consumer Brochures

> **Renters Insurance** — All renters need to know about insurance

> **Your Home Inventory** — Instructions on how to prepare an inventory of possessions to help identify and calculate losses if a disaster strikes

> **Nine Ways to Lower Your Auto Insurance Costs** — Tips on how to lower your auto insurance costs

> **Settling Insurance Claims After a Disaster** — Helps you understand how to file an insurance claim after a disaster

> **Twelve Ways to Lower Your Homeowners Insurance Costs** — Tips on how to lower your homeowners insurance costs

>   ...and many others

I.I.I. on the Web

Visit **www.iii.org** for a wealth of information for individuals and businesses, from consumer brochures to issues papers to white papers to statistics.

> **Insurance Matters** — www.iii-insurancematters.org
>   Information for policymakers.

> **Insuring Florida** — www.insuringflorida.org
>   Improving understanding of insurance in Florida.

- "Like" the I.I.I.'s Facebook page at www.facebook.com/InsuranceInformationInstitute

- Read about the industry in Claire Wilkinson's blog, Terms and Conditions, at www.iii.org/insuranceindustryblog

- Follow the I.I.I. website on Twitter at twitter.com/iiiorg and on its special interest feeds:

  twitter.com/IIIindustryblog — for updates to the Terms and Conditions blog

  twitter.com/III_Research — for updates to I.I.I. papers and studies

  twitter.com/Bob_Hartwig — for the latest from I.I.I. President, Robert Hartwig

  twitter.com/JeanneSalvatore — for commentary from Jeanne Salvatore, I.I.I.'s Senior V.P. of Public Affairs

  twitter.com/LWorters — for communications updates from Loretta Worters

The Financial Services Roundtable's Fast Facts topic briefs provide timely, reliable research about the financial services industry and its role in financing the economy. For inquiries regarding Fast Facts, contact Abby McCloske, the Financial Services Roundtable's Director of Research at **abbey@fsround.org**.

Fast Facts are posted on the Web at **http://www.fsround.org/fsr/publications_and_research/ fast_facts.asp**.
A listing of selected topics is below.

- Economic Outlook
- Bank Balance Sheets
- Basel Reforms
- Brokered Deposits
- Budgetary Impact of Dodd-Frank
- Commercial Lending
- Commercial Lending
- Consumer Credit
- Consumer Financial Protection Bureau
- Credit Cards
- Debit Cards
- Debt Ceiling
- Derivatives & The Dodd Frank Act
- Disability Insurance
- Dodd-Frank Rulemaking
- Election, 2010
- Federal Debt
- Fiduciary Responsibility
- Financial Exploitation of the Elderly
- Financial Literacy
- Financial Reporting
- Financial Stability Oversight Council
- Foreclosure Process

- GSE Reform
- Holiday Electronic Shopping
- Housing Market
- Insurance and the Economy
- Insurance Investments
- IRAs & Fiduciary Duty
- Life Insurance - Retained Asset Accounts
- Malware Risks & Mitigation
- Mark-to-Market Accounting
- Mobile Banking
- Money Market Funds
- Outstanding Trade Agreements
- Proprietary Mortgage Modifications
- Retirement Security
- Small Business Conditions
- Small Business Lending
- Social Media
- Tax Increase
- The End of TARP
- Trade
- Work Place Benefits

FINANCIAL AND INSURANCE ADVISORS' CERTIFICATIONS

Below is a list of major financial and insurance advisors designations compiled by the American College, an accredited nonprofit educational institution specializing in financial education. The College has posted further information on the designations, including educational requirements on the Web. **designationcheck.com/learn-more-about-credentials/details/chfc**

A comprehensive listing of designations is also posted on the Financial Industry Regulatory Authority (FINRA) website. **apps.finra.org/DataDirectory/1/prodesignations.aspx**

AEP® (Accredited Estate Planner®)

The AEP® designation is a graduate-level specialization in estate planning, obtained in addition to already recognized professional credentials within the various disciplines of estate planning who support the team concept of estate planning.

> Issuing Institution: The National Association of Estate Planners & Councils. NAEPC.org

CAP® (Chartered Advisor in Philanthropy®)

The advisor earning the CAP® designation has taken three courses in philanthropy covering various impacts of planning for family wealth, charitable giving and gift planning for nonprofits.

> Issuing Institution: The American College. TheAmericanCollege.edu/CAP

CASL® (Chartered Advisor for Senior Living®)

CASL® is a rigorous credential in the senior and retirement planning space, with curriculum that covers wealth accumulation, income distribution and estate planning strategies for those preparing for or in retirement.

> Issuing Institution: The American College. TheAmericanCollege.edu/CASL

CEBS (Certified Employee Benefits Specialist)

The CEBS program provides education for advisors working in the employee benefits and compensation industry through an eight-course curriculum.

> Issuing Institution: The International Foundation of Employee Benefit Plans and Wharton School of the University of Pennsylvania. IFEBP.org

CFA (Chartered Financial Analyst)

The CFA designation represents rigorous, in-depth education for investment analysts.

> Issuing Institution: CFA Institute. CFAInstitute.org

ChHC (Chartered Healthcare Consultant™)

The ChHC® designation incorporates the information on healthcare reform and other group benefits issues.

> Issuing Institution: The American College. TheAmericanCollege.edu/ChHC

CIMA Certification (Certified Investment Management Analyst)

The CIMA® designation is designed specifically for financial professionals who want to attain a level of competency as an advanced investment consultant.

Issuing Institution: The Investment Management Consultants Association. imca.org

CLF® (Chartered Leadership Fellow®)

The CLF® designation indicates advanced education in leading financial services teams.

Issuing Institution: The American College. TheAmericanCollege.edu/CLF

CLU® (Chartered Life Underwriter®)

The CLU® designation represents a thorough understanding of a broad array of personal risk management and life insurance planning issues and stresses ethics, professionalism and in-depth knowledge in the delivery of financial advice.

Issuing Institution: The American College. TheAmericanCollege.edu/CLU

CPA (Certified Public Accountant)

The CPA is the respected mark of excellence for public accountants. The Board of Accountancy in each state issues CPA licenses to those who have passed all appropriate requirements for use of the mark, and each state has different regulations in this regard.

Issuing Institution: AICPA, The American Institute of Certified Public Accountants (AICPA). AICPA.org

CPCU (Chartered Property Casualty Underwriter)

CPCU designees have completed an extensive program encompassing broad technical knowledge and high ethical standards focused on risk management for individuals and businesses. Granted by "The Institutes," which administers several other programs, including the Associate in Reinsurance (ARe); Accredited Advisor in Insurance (AAI); Associate in Insurance Services (AIS);Associate in Risk Management (ARM); and Associate in Personal Insurance (API).

Issuing Institution: The Institutes, which consists of The American Institute for CPCU and the Insurance Institute of America. aicpcu.org/Programs/PIndex.htm

FSS (Financial Services Specialist)

The FSS designation provides financial advisors with the core knowledge and skills they need to provide essential planning and advisory assistance to consumers and businesses.

Issuing Institution: The American College. TheAmericanCollege.edu/FSS

Insurance Agents Brokers and Adjusters

In order to obtain and maintain professional licenses, agents, adjusters and brokers must pass state-mandated exams. Information on these requirements is available from state insurance departments. The National Association Insurance Commission website provides links to state insurance department websites. naic.org/state_web_map.htm.

LUTCF (Life Underwriter Training Council Fellow)

The LUTCF designation combines essential product knowledge with the skills financial professionals must have to advise individuals and businesses effectively on their insurance and planning needs.

Issuing Institution: The American College confers the LUTCF in conjunction with the National Association of Insurance and Financial Advisors (NAIFA). TheAmericanCollege.edu/LUTCF and NAIFA.org

PFS (Personal Financial Specialist)

The PFS credential is awarded to CPAs who demonstrate extensive tax expertise and a comprehensive knowledge of financial planning.

Issuing Institution: The American institute of Certified Public Accountants (AICPA). AICPA.org

REBC® (Registered Employee Benefits Consultant®)

The REBC® designation is designed for specialists in the complex field of employee benefits. The program covers pensions, retirement plan funding, group medical plans, long-term care, executive compensation, personnel management and other benefit programs.

Issuing Institution: The American College. TheAmericanCollege.edu/REBC

Source: The American College, 270 S. Bryn Mawr Avenue, Bryn Mawr, PA. Phone: 610-526-1000. theamericancollege.edu. Additional information compiled by the Insurance Information Institute.

YEAR	EVENT
1601	First insurance legislation in the U.K. enacted. Modern insurance has its root in this law concerning coverages for merchandise and ships.
1735	Friendly Society, first insurance company in the U.S., established in Charleston, S.C. The mutual insurer went out of business in 1740.
1759	First life insurance company, established in Philadelphia by the Synod of the Presbyterian Church.
1762	Equitable Life Assurance founded. Was the world's oldest mutual insurer until it failed in 2001.
1782	Pennsylvania chartered first bank in the U.S.
1790	The federal government refinanced all federal and state Revolutionary War debt, issuing $80 million in bonds. These became the first major issues of publicly traded securities, marking the birth of the U.S. investment markets.
1791	Secretary of the Treasury, Alexander Hamilton, established First Bank of the United States.
1792	Insurance Company of North America, first stock insurance company, established.
	The Buttonwood Agreement, pact between 24 brokers and merchants to trade securities on a common commission basis, marked the origins of the New York Stock Exchange. Bank of America was first listed stock.
1809	Rhode Island was the scene of first bank failure.
1849	New York passed first general insurance law in the U.S.
1850	Franklin Health Assurance Company of Massachusetts offered first accident and health insurance.
1863	Office of the Comptroller of the Currency established in the U.S. Treasury Department. Authorized to charter banks and issue national currency.
1875	American Express established first pension plan in the U.S.
1880	First corporate surety company established.
1890	First policies providing benefits for disabilities from specific diseases offered.
1898	Travelers Insurance Company issued first automobile insurance policy in the U.S.
1909	St. Mary's Cooperative, first U.S. credit union, formed in New Hampshire.
	Massachusetts passed first state credit union law.
1911	Group life insurance for employees introduced.
1913	Federal Reserve established to replace J.P. Morgan as lender of last resort.
1916	National Bank Act, limiting bank insurance sales, except in small towns, passed.
1920	Financial options introduced.
1924	First mutual funds established in Boston.
1929	Stock market crash. Nearly 10,000 U.S. banks failed.

Appendices

Brief History

YEAR	EVENT
1932	Federal Home Loan Bank Act established Federal Home Loan Bank System to act as central credit system for savings and loans institutions.
1933	Glass-Steagall Act, separating banking and securities industries, passed by Congress.
	Federal Deposit Insurance Corporation, guaranteeing accounts up to $2,500, opened.
	Securities Act of 1933 passed. Regulated registration and offering of new securities, including mutual funds, to the public.
1934	Securities Exchange Act passed. Authorized Securities and Exchange Commission to provide for fair and equitable securities markets.
	Federal Savings and Loan Insurance Corporation established by Congress to insure savings and loans deposits. Replaced by Savings Association Insurance Fund in 1989.
	Federal Credit Union Act of 1934 authorized establishment of federally chartered credit unions in all states.
1936	Revenue Act of 1936 established tax treatment of mutual funds.
1940	Investment Company Act set structure and regulatory framework for modern mutual fund industry.
1944	National Association of Investment Companies, predecessor to the Investment Company Institute, formed and began collecting statistics.
1950	First package policies for homeowners insurance introduced.
1955	First U.S.-based international mutual fund introduced.
1956	Bank Holding Company (BHC) Act, putting multiple bank holding companies under federal supervision, passed. Stipulates that nonbanking activities of BHCs must be "closely related to the business of banking."
1960	Bank Merger Acts of 1960 and 1966 set standards for mergers and placed them under federal authority.
1961	Banking industry introduced fixed-rate certificates of deposit.
1962	Keogh plans, providing savings opportunities for self-employed individuals, introduced under the Self Employed Individuals Tax Retirement Act.
1968	Mortgage insurance introduced.
	Federal flood insurance program established with the passage of the National Flood Insurance Act. It enables property owners in communities that participate in flood reduction plans to purchase insurance against flood losses.
1970	U.S. government introduced mortgage-related securities to increase liquidity.
	National Credit Union Administration created to charter and supervise federal credit unions.
	National Credit Union Share Insurance Fund created by Congress to insure members' deposits in credit unions up to the $100,000 federal limit. Administered by the National Credit Union Administration.

YEAR	EVENT
1971	Municipal bonds insured for first time in arrangement between American Municipal Bond Assurance Corporation (predecessor to Ambac Assurance Corporation) and Borough Medical Arts Building in Alaska.
	NASDAQ, the first electronic stock market, was introduced by NASD, then known as the National Association of Securities Dealers. NASDAQ was spun off in 2000.
1972	Money market mutual funds introduced.
1974	Automated teller machines (ATMs) widely introduced.
	Employee Retirement Income Security Act (ERISA) set minimum standards for pension plans in private industry; established the federal Pension Benefit Guaranty Corporation to protect pension benefits.
1975	SEC deregulated broker commissions by eliminating fixed commissions brokers charged for all securities transactions.
1976	First individual variable life insurance policy issued.
1977	Banking industry introduced variable rate certificates of deposit.
	Community Reinvestment Act passed to encourage banks to meet credit needs of their local communities.
1978	International Banking Act limited the extent to which foreign banks could engage in securities activities in the U.S.
1979	Congress created the Central Liquidity Facility, credit union lender of last resort.
1980	Depository Institutions Deregulation and Monetary Control Act provided universal requirements for all financial institutions, marking first step toward removing restrictions on competition for deposits.
	The Office of the Comptroller of the Currency and the Federal Reserve authorized banks to establish securities subsidiaries to combine the sale of securities with investment advisory services.
1982	Garn-St. Germain Depository Institutions Act authorized money market accounts and expanded thrifts' lending powers.
	Stock market futures contracts introduced.
1983	Federal government introduced collateralized mortgage obligations.
	Bank of America bought discount securities broker, Charles Schwab. Schwab reacquired the discounter in 1987.
1987	Federal Reserve ruling interpreting Section 20 of Glass-Steagall as permitting separately capitalized affiliates of commercial bank holding companies to engage in a variety of securities activities on a limited basis.
1989	Financial Institutions Reform, Recovery and Enforcement Act established, providing government funds to insolvent savings and loan institutions (S&Ls) from the Resolution Trust Corporation and incorporating sweeping changes in the examination and supervision of S&Ls.
	Savings Association Insurance Fund, deposit insurance fund operated by the FDIC, established.
1990	J.P. Morgan permitted to underwrite securities.
1992	European Union's Third Non-Life Insurance Directive became effective, establishing a single European market for insurance.

Appendices

Brief History

YEAR	EVENT
1994	Riegle-Neal Interstate Banking and Branching Efficiency Act allowed bank holding companies to acquire banks in any state and, as of June 1, 1997, to branch across state lines.
1995	U.S. Supreme Court ruled in NationsBank vs. Variable Annuity Life Insurance Company that annuities are not a form of insurance under the National Bank Act, thus allowing national banks to sell annuities without limitation.
	Private Securities Litigation Reform Act of 1995 enacted to reduce the number of frivolous securities fraud lawsuits filed.
1996	Barnett Bank U.S. Supreme Court decision allowed banks to sell insurance nationwide.
1996	Section 20 of Glass-Steagall amended to allow commercial bank affiliates to underwrite up to 25 percent of revenue in previously ineligible securities of corporate equity or debt.
1997	The Financial Services Agreement of the General Agreement on Trade in Services provided framework to reduce or eliminate barriers that prevent financial services from being freely provided across national borders, or that discriminate against foreign-owned firms.
1998	Citibank and Travelers merged to form Citigroup, a firm engaged in all major financial services sectors.
1999	Gramm-Leach-Bliley Financial Services Modernization Act allowed banks, insurance companies and securities firms to affiliate and sell each other's products.
2001	U.S. House of Representatives Banking Committee renamed itself the Financial Services Committee.
2002	JPMorgan Chase introduced an annuity, becoming one of the first banking companies to underwrite an insurance product under the Gramm-Leach-Bliley Act.
	Sarbanes-Oxley Act enacted to increase the accountability of the boards of publicly held companies to their shareholders. Strengthened the oversight of corporations and their accounting firms.
	President Bush signed the Terrorism Risk Insurance Act (TRIA), whereby private insurers and the federal government share the risk of future losses from terrorism for a limited period.
2003	State regulators and the Securities and Exchange Commission (SEC) launched investigations into late trading and market timing in the mutual funds and variable annuities industries.
	Fair and Accurate Credit Transaction Act (FCRA) enacted to provide uniform rules for banks, insurers and others who use credit information, and to provide credit fraud and identity theft protections.
2004	New York Attorney General Eliot Spitzer, the Securities and Exchange Commission, and a number of state regulators launched investigations into insurance industry sales and accounting practices.
2005	Federal Bankruptcy Prevention and Consumer Protection Act was enacted to tighten rules for personal bankruptcy.
	Citigroup sold off its Travelers' life insurance unit, following the spin off of its property/casualty business in 2002. This dissolved the arrangement that led to the passage of the Gramm-Leach-Bliley Act in 1999.

YEAR	EVENT
2006	President Bush signed the Federal Deposit Insurance Reform Conforming Amendments Act of 2005, which merges the Bank Insurance Fund and the Savings Association Insurance Fund into the new Deposit Insurance Fund, increases the deposit insurance limit for certain retirement accounts from $100,000 to $250,000, and indexes that limit to inflation.
	Congress passed landmark pension reform legislation to close funding shortfalls in the nation's defined benefit system. The act also provides tax incentives for workers to enroll in individual retirement accounts, secures the legality of cash balance pension plans and permits automatic enrollment in employer-sponsored defined contribution pension plans such as 401(k)s.
	Massachusetts passed a mandatory universal health insurance law.
	NASD and the New York Stock Exchange formed the Financial Industry Regulatory Authority (FINRA), a self-regulatory organization to serve as the single regulator for all securities firms doing business in the U.S.
2008	Washington Mutual was taken over by JPMorgan Chase after it was shut down by federal regulators, marking the largest failure in banking history.
	The federal government took over Fannie Mae and Freddie Mac and assumed a 80 percent ownership in American International Group, reflecting widespread turmoil in financial markets.
	Securities giant Lehman Brothers failed, marking the largest bankruptcy in U.S. history. Two other major securities firms, Goldman Sachs and Morgan Stanley, got federal approval to convert to bank holding companies.
	The Emergency Economic Stabilization Act, a $700 billion rescue plan for the U.S. financial services industry, was enacted. The act established the Trouble Asset Relief Program (TARP), which authorized the U.S. government to purchase assets and equity from qualifying financial institutions.
2009	American Recovery and Reinvestment Act, a $787 billion stimulus program to shore up the nation's economy was enacted.
	The Financial Stability Plan was implemented by the U.S. Treasury to promote economic recovery.
2010	New federal rules providing consumer protections related to credit cards were enacted.
	President Obama signed the Patient Protection and Affordable Care Act, requiring most U.S. citizens to have health insurance
	Dodd-Frank Wall Street Reform and Consumer Protection Act, landmark regulatory overhaul of the financial services industry, was signed into law.
2011	Standard and Poor's downgraded the long-term U.S. credit rating by one level to AA-plus, the first downgrading of the U.S. economy in history.

A.M. BEST COMPANY INC. • Ambest Road, Oldwick, NJ 08858. Tel. 908-439-2200. www.ambest.com — Rating organization and publisher of reference books and periodicals relating to the insurance industry.

ADVANTAGE GROUP ASSOCIATES, INC. • 215 SE Wildflower Court, Pleasant Hill, IA 50327. Tel. 515-262-2623. www.annuityspecs.com — A third-party market research firm that tracks indexed annuity and indexed life products, carriers and sales.

AMERICA'S HEALTH INSURANCE PLANS (AHIP) • 601 Pennsylvania Avenue, NW, South Building, Suite 500, Washington, DC 20004. Tel. 202-778-3200. Fax. 202-778-8486. www.ahip.org — National trade association representing health insurance plans providing medical, long-term care, disability income, dental supplemental, stop-gap and reinsurance coverage.

AMERICAN BANKERS ASSOCIATION • 1120 Connecticut Avenue, NW, Washington, DC 20036. Tel. 800-BANKERS. Fax. 202-828-4540. www.aba.com — Represents banks of all sizes on issues of national importance for financial institutions and their customers. Brings together all categories of banking institutions, including community, regional and money center banks and holding companies, as well as savings associations, trust companies and savings banks.

AMERICAN BANKERS INSURANCE ASSOCIATION • 1120 Connecticut Avenue, NW, Washington, DC 20036. Tel. 202-663-5163. Fax. 202-828-4546. www.theabia.com — A separately chartered affiliate of the American Bankers Association. A full service association for bank insurance interests dedicated to furthering the policy and business objectives of banks in insurance.

THE AMERICAN COLLEGE • 270 South Bryn Mawr Avenue, Bryn Mawr, PA 19010. Tel. 610-526-1000. Fax. 610-526-1465. www.theamericancollege.edu — An independent, accredited nonprofit institution, originally The American College of Life Underwriters. Provides graduate and professional education in insurance and other financial services.

AMERICAN COUNCIL OF LIFE INSURERS (ACLI) • 101 Constitution Avenue, NW, Suite 700, Washington, DC 20001-2133. Tel. 202-624-2000. www.acli.com — Trade association responsible for the public affairs, government, legislative and research aspects of the life insurance business.

AMERICAN FINANCIAL SERVICES ASSOCIATION • 919 18th St., NW, Suite 300, Washington, DC 20006. Tel. 202-296-5544. www.americanfinsvcs.com — The national trade association for market funded providers of financial services to consumers and small businesses.

AMERICAN INSURANCE ASSOCIATION (AIA) • 1130 Connecticut Ave., Suite 1000, NW, Washington, DC 20036. Tel. 202-828-7100. Fax. 202-293-1219. www.aiadc.org — Trade and service organization for property/casualty insurance companies. Provides a forum for the discussion of problems as well as safety, promotional and legislative services.

ASSOCIATION OF FINANCIAL GUARANTY INSURERS • Mackin & Company, 139 Lancaster Street, Albany, NY 12210. Tel. 518-449-4698. Fax. 518-432-5651. www.afgi.org — Trade association of the insurers and reinsurers of municipal bonds and asset-backed securities.

BANK ADMINISTRATION INSTITUTE • 115 S. LaSalle Street, Suite 3300, Chicago, IL 60603-3801. Tel. 800-224-9889. Fax. 800-375-5543. www.bai.org — A professional organization devoted exclusively to improving the performance of financial services companies through strategic research and information, education and training.

BANK FOR INTERNATIONAL SETTLEMENTS • CH-4002, Centralbahnplatz 2, Basel, Switzerland Tel. 41-61-280-8080. Fax. 41-61-280-9100. www.bis.org — An international organization which fosters cooperation among central banks and other agencies in pursuit of monetary and financial stability.

BANK INSURANCE & SECURITIES ASSOCIATION • 2025 M Street, NW, Suite 800, Washington, DC 20036. Tel. 202-367-1111. Fax. 202-367-2111. www.bisanet.org — Fosters the full integration of securities and insurance businesses with depository institutions' traditional banking businesses. Participants include executives from the securities, insurance, investment advisory, trust, private banking, retail, capital markets and commercial divisions of depository institutions.

BANK INSURANCE MARKET RESEARCH GROUP • 154 East Boston Post Road, Mamaroneck, NY 10543. Tel. 914-381-7475. www.singerpubs.com — Provides market research and investment sales data to the bank and insurance industries based on surveys of depository and insurance entities augmented by analysis of government data.

CERTIFIED FINANCIAL PLANNER BOARD OF STANDARDS, INC. • 1425 K Street, NW, Suite 500, Washington, DC 20005. Tel. 202-379-2200. Fax. 202-379-2299. www.cfp.net — Group whose mission is to create awareness of the importance of financial planning and the value of the financial planning process and to help underserved populations have access to competent and ethical financial planning.

CFA INSTITUTE • 560 Ray C. Hunt Drive, Charlottesville, VA 22903-2981. Tel. 800-247-8132. Fax. 434-951-5262. www.cfainstitute.org — Global membership organization that awards the CFA designation, the institute leads the investment industry by setting standards of ethics and professional excellence and advocating fair and transparent capital markets.

COLLEGE SAVINGS PLANS NETWORK • P.O. Box 11910, Lexington, KY 40578-1910. Tel. 859-244-8175. www.collegesavings.org — The College Savings Plans Network is an affiliate to the National Association of State Treasurers. It is intended to make higher education more attainable. The Network serves as a clearinghouse for information on existing college savings programs.

COMMERCIAL FINANCE ASSOCIATION • 370 7th Ave., Suite 1801, New York, NY 10001. Tel. 212-792-9390. Fax. 212-564-6053. www.cfa.com — The trade group of the asset-based financial services industry, with members throughout the U.S., Canada and around the world.

THE COMMITTEE OF ANNUITY INSURERS • c/o Davis & Harman LLP, 1455 Pennsylvania Avenue NW, Suite 1200, Washington, DC 20004. Tel. 202-347-2230. Fax. 202-393-3310. www.annuity-insurers.org — Group whose goal is to address federal legislative and regulatory issues relevant to the annuity industry and to participate in the development of federal tax and securities policies regarding annuities.

COMMODITY FUTURES TRADING COMMISSION • Three Lafayette Centre, 1155 21st Street, NW, Washington, DC 20581. Tel. 202-418-5000. Fax. 202-418-5521. www.cftc.gov — Independent agency created by Congress to protect market participants against manipulation, abusive trade practices and fraud.

CONFERENCE OF STATE BANK SUPERVISORS • 1129 20th Street, NW, 9th Floor, Washington, DC 20036. Tel. 202-296-2840. Fax. 202-296-1928. www.csbs.org — National organization that advocates on behalf of the nation's state banking system.

CONNING RESEARCH AND CONSULTING, INC. • One Financial Plaza, Hartford, CT 06103-2627. Tel. 860-299-2000. www.conningresearch.com — Research and consulting firm that offers an array of specialty information products, insights and analyses of key issues confronting the insurance industry.

CONSUMER BANKERS ASSOCIATION • 1000 Wilson Boulevard, Suite 2500, Arlington, VA 22209-3912. Tel. 703-276-1750. Fax. 703-528-1290. www.cbanet.org — This group represents retail banking issues in the nation's capital.

DMA FINANCIAL SERVICES COUNCIL • 1120 Avenue of the Americas, New York, NY 10036-6700. Tel. 212-768-7277. Fax. 212-302-6714. www.the-dma.org — Integrates the direct marketing concept with mainstream insurance and financial services marketing to create a strategic business synergism, a division of the Direct Marketing Association.

EASTBRIDGE CONSULTING GROUP, INC. • 50 Avon Meadow Lane, Avon, CT 06001. Tel. 860-676-9633. www.eastbridge.com — Provides consulting, marketing, training and research services to financial services firms, including those involved in worksite marketing and the distribution of individual and employee benefits products.

EMPLOYEE BENEFIT RESEARCH INSTITUTE • 1100 13th Street, NW, Suite 878, Washington, DC 20005-4051. Tel. 202-659-0670. Fax. 202-775-6312. www.ebri.org — The Institute's mission is to advance the public's, the media's and policymakers' knowledge and understanding of employee benefits and their importance to the U.S. economy.

FEDERAL DEPOSIT INSURANCE CORPORATION (FDIC) • 550 17th Street NW, Washington, DC 20429-9990. Tel. 877-275-3342. www.fdic.gov — The FDIC's mission is to maintain the stability of and public confidence in the nation's financial system. The FDIC has insured deposits and promoted safe and sound banking practices since 1933.

FEDERAL FINANCIAL INSTITUTIONS EXAMINATION COUNCIL • 3501 Fairfax Drive, Arlington, VA 22201-2305. Tel. 703-516-5487. Fax. 703-516-5588. www.ffiec.gov — A formal interagency body empowered to prescribe uniform principles, standards, and report forms for the federal examination of financial institutions by the Board of Governors of the Federal Reserve System.

FEDERAL RESERVE • 20th Street and Constitution Avenue, NW, Washington, DC 20551. Tel. 202-452-3000. www.federalreserve.gov — Central bank of the United States was founded by Congress in 1913 to provide the nation with a safer, more flexible and more stable monetary and financial system.

FINANCIAL INDUSTRY REGULATORY AUTHORITY (FINRA) • 1735 K St., NW, Washington, DC 20006. Tel. 301-590-6500. Fax. 240-386-4838. www.finra.org — Largest non-governmental regulator for all securities firms doing business in the United States. Created in July 2007 through the consolidation of NASD and the member regulation, enforcement and arbitration functions of the New York Stock Exchange.

THE FINANCIAL PLANNING ASSOCIATION • 4100 East Mississippi Avenue, Suite 400, Denver, CO 80246-3053. Tel. 800-322-4237. Fax. 303-759-0749. www.fpanet.org — Group whose primary aim is to foster the value of financial planning and advance the financial planning profession.

FINANCIAL SERVICES FORUM • 601 13th Street, NW, Suite 750 South, Washington, DC 20005. Tel. 202-457-8765. Fax. 202-457-8769. www.financialservicesforum.org — An organization of chief executive officers of major U.S. financial services firms dedicated to the execution and coordination of activities designed to promote the development of an open and competitive financial services industry.

THE FINANCIAL SERVICES ROUNDTABLE • 1001 Pennsylvania Avenue, NW, Suite 500 South, Washington, DC 20004. Tel. 202-289-4322. Fax. 202-628-2507. www.fsround.org — A forum for U.S. financial industry leaders working together to determine and influence the most critical public policy concerns related to the integration of the financial services.

FITCH CREDIT RATING COMPANY • One State Street Plaza, New York, NY 10004. Tel. 212-908-0500. Fax. 212-480-4435. www.fitchratings.com — Assigns claims-paying ability ratings to insurance companies.

FUTURES INDUSTRY ASSOCIATION • 2001 Pennsylvania Avenue, NW, Suite 600, Washington, DC 20006. Tel. 202-466-5460. Fax. 202-296-3184. www.futuresindustry.org — Association representative of all organizations that have an interest in the futures market.

GLOBAL ASSOCIATION OF RISK PROFESSIONALS • 111 Town Square Place, Suite 1215, Jersey City, NJ 07310. Tel. 201-719-7210. Fax. 201-222-5022. www.garp.com — International group whose aim is to encourage and enhance communications between risk professionals, practitioners and regulators worldwide.

THE HEDGE FUND ASSOCIATION • 2875 Northeast 191st Street, Suite 900, Aventura, FL 33180. Tel. 202-478-2000. Fax. 202-478-1999. www.thehfa.org — An international not-for-profit association of hedge fund managers, service providers and investors formed to unite the hedge fund industry and add to the awareness of the advantages and opportunities in hedge funds.

HIGHLINE DATA LLC • One Alewife Center, Suite 460, Cambridge, MA 02140. Tel. 877-299-9424. Fax. 617-864-2396. www.highlinedata.com — An information and data services company comprised of two principal product lines: National Underwriter Insurance Data Services and Highline Banking Data Services.

INDEPENDENT INSURANCE AGENTS & BROKERS OF AMERICA, INC. • 127 South Peyton Street, Alexandria, VA 22314. Tel. 800-221-7917. Fax. 703-683-7556. www.iiaba.com — Trade association of independent insurance agents.

INSURANCE INFORMATION INSTITUTE (I.I.I.) • 110 William Street, 24th Floor, New York, NY 10038. Tel. 212-346-5500. Fax. 212-732-1916. www.iii.org — A primary source for information, analysis and reference on insurance subjects.

INSURANCE MARKETPLACE STANDARDS ASSOCIATION • 4550 Montgomery Avenue, Suite 700N, Bethesda, MD 20814. Tel. 240-744-3030. Fax. 240-744-3031. www.imsaethics.org — A nonprofit, independent organization created to strengthen consumer trust and confidence in the marketplace for individually sold life insurance, long-term care insurance and annuities.

INSURED RETIREMENT INSTITUTE • 1101 New York Avenue, NW, Suite 825, Washington, DC 20005. Tel. 202-469-3000. Fax. 202-469-3030. www.irionline.org — Source of knowledge pertaining to annuities, insured retirement products and retirement planning; provides educational and informational resources. Formerly the National Association for Variable Annuities (NAVA).

INTERNATIONAL FINANCIAL RISK INSTITUTE • 2, Cours de Rive, 1204, Geneva, Switzerland Tel. (41) 22-312-5678. Fax. (41) 22-312-5677. www.riskinstitute.ch — Nonprofit foundation created with the objective of promoting global understanding of commodity trading as well as financial futures and options.

INTERNATIONAL SWAPS AND DERIVATIVES ASSOCIATION • 360 Madison Avenue, 16th Floor, New York, NY 10017. Tel. 212-901-6000. Fax. 212-901-6001. www.isda.org — The association's primary purpose is to encourage the prudent and efficient development of the privately negotiated derivatives business.

INVESTMENT COMPANY INSTITUTE • 1401 H Street, NW, Suite 1200, Washington, DC 20005. Tel. 202-326-5800. www.ici.org — The national association of the American investment company industry.

ISO • 545 Washington Boulevard, Jersey City, NJ 07310-1686. Tel. 201-469-2000. Fax. 201-748-1472. www.iso.com — Provider of products and services that help measure, manage and reduce risk. Provides data, analytics and decision-support solutions to professionals in many fields, including insurance, finance, real estate, health services, government and human resources.

KEHRER-LIMRA • 300 Day Hill Road, Windsor, CT 06095-4761. Tel. 978-448-0198. Fax. 860-298-9555. www.kehrerlimra.com — Consultant focusing on the financial services marketplace. Conducts studies of sales penetration, profitability, compensation and compliance.

THE LIFE AND HEALTH INSURANCE FOUNDATION FOR EDUCATION • 1655 North Fort Myer Drive, Suite 610, Arlington, VA 22209. Tel. 888-LIFE-777. Fax. 202-464-5011. lifehappens.org — Nonprofit organization dedicated to addressing the public's growing need for information and education about life, health, disability and long-term care insurance.

LIFE INSURANCE SETTLEMENT ASSOCIATION • 1011 East Colonial Drive, Suite 500, Orlando, FL 32803. Tel. 407-894-3797. Fax. 407-897-1325. www.thevoiceoftheindustry.com — Promotes the development, integrity and reputation of the life settlement industry.

LIMRA INTERNATIONAL • 300 Day Hill Road, Windsor, CT 06095. Tel. 800-235-4672. Fax. 860-285-7792. www.limra.com — Worldwide association providing research, consulting and other services to insurance and financial services companies in more than 60 countries. LIMRA helps its member companies maximize their marketing effectiveness.

LOMA (LIFE OFFICE MANAGEMENT ASSOCIATION) • 2300 Windy Ridge Parkway, Suite 600, Atlanta, GA 30339-8443. Tel. 770-951-1770. Fax. 770-984-0441. www.loma.org — Worldwide association of insurance companies specializing in research and education, with a primary focus on home office management.

MICHAEL WHITE ASSOCIATES • 823 King of Prussia Road, Radnor, PA 19087. Tel. 610-254-0440. Fax. 610-254-5044. www.bankinsurance.com — Consulting firm that helps clients plan, develop and implement bank insurance sales programs. Conducts research on and benchmarks performance of bank insurance and investment fee income activities.

MONEY MANAGEMENT INSTITUTE • 1140 Connecticut Ave., NW, Suite 1040, Washington DC, DC 20036-4001. Tel. 202-822-4949. Fax. 202-822-5188. www.moneyinstitute.com — National organization for the managed account solutions industry, represents portfolio manager firms and sponsors.

MOODY'S INVESTORS SERVICE • 7 World Trade Center at 250 Greenwich Street, New York, NY 10007. Tel. 212-553-1653. Fax. 212-553-0882. www.moodys.com — Global credit analysis and financial information firm.

MORNINGSTAR® ANNUITY RESEARCH CENTER • 22 West Washington Street, Chicago, IL 60602. Tel. 312-696-6000. corporate.morningstar.com — Software technology and research data firm that helps annuity manufacturers, distributors, and financial advisors implement new technology and business practices in the sale and servicing of annuities.

MORTGAGE BANKERS ASSOCIATION OF AMERICA • 1717 Rhode Island Avenue, NW, Suite 400, Washington, DC 20036. Tel. 202-557-2700. www.mbaa.org — Represents the real estate finance industry.

MORTGAGE INSURANCE COMPANIES OF AMERICA (MICA) • 1425 K St., NW, Suite 210, Washington, DC 20005. Tel. 202-682-2683. Fax. 202-842-9252. www.privatemi.com — Represents the private mortgage insurance industry. MICA provides information on related legislative and regulatory issues, and strives to enhance understanding of the role private mortgage insurance plays in housing Americans.

MUSEUM OF AMERICAN FINANCE • 48 Wall Street, New York, NY 10005. Tel. 212-908-4110. Fax. 212-908-4601. www.moaf.org — An affiliate of the Smithsonian Institution, the museum is the nation's only independent public museum dedicated to celebrating the spirit of entrepreneurship and the democratic free market tradition.

NATIONAL ASSOCIATION FOR FIXED ANNUITIES • 2300 East Kensington Boulevard, Milwaukee, WI 53211. Tel. 414-332-9306. Fax. 415-946-3532. www.nafa.us — Promotes the growth, acceptance and understanding of annuity and life products; provides educational and informational resources.

NATIONAL ASSOCIATION OF FEDERAL CREDIT UNIONS • 3138 10th Street North, Arlington, VA 22201-2149. Tel. 800-336-4644. Fax. 703-524-1082. www.nafcunet.org — Trade association that exclusively represents the interests of federal credit unions before the federal government and the public.

NATIONAL ASSOCIATION OF HEALTH UNDERWRITERS • 2000 North 14th Street, Suite 450, Arlington, VA 22201. Tel. 703-276-0220. Fax. 703-841-7797. www.nahu.org — Professional association of people who sell and service disability income, and hospitalization and major medical health insurance companies.

NATIONAL ASSOCIATION OF INSURANCE AND FINANCIAL ADVISORS • 2901 Telestar Court, P.O. Box 12012, Falls Church, VA 22042-1205. Tel. 703-770-8100; 877-866-2432. Fax. 703-770-8224. www.naifa.org — Professional association representing health and life insurance agents.

NATIONAL ASSOCIATION OF INSURANCE COMMISSIONERS • 2301 McGee Street, Suite 800, Kansas City, MO 64108-2662. Tel. 816-842-3600. Fax. 816-783-8175. www.naic.org — Organization of state insurance commissioners to promote uniformity in state supervision of insurance matters and to recommend legislation in state legislatures.

NATIONAL ASSOCIATION OF INVESTMENT PROFESSIONALS • Tel. 952-322-4322. www.naip.com/ — Promotes the interests and the image of its financial professionals members, and encourages and facilitates higher levels of competency in members so that they may better serve the investing public.

NATIONAL ASSOCIATION OF MORTGAGE BROKERS • 2701 West 15th Street, Suite 536, Plano, TX 75075. Tel. 703-342-5900. Fax. 703-342-5905. www.namb.org — National trade association representing the mortgage broker industry; promotes the industry through programs and services such as education, professional certification and government affairs representation.

NATIONAL ASSOCIATION OF MUTUAL INSURANCE COMPANIES (NAMIC) • P.O. Box 68700, 3601 Vincennes Road, Indianapolis, IN 46268. Tel. 317-875-5250. Fax. 317-879-8408. www.namic.org — National property/casualty insurance trade and political advocacy association.

THE NATIONAL ASSOCIATION OF PERSONAL FINANCIAL ADVISORS • 3250 North Arlington Heights Road, Suite 109, Arlington Heights, IL 60004. Tel. 847-483-5400. Fax. 847-483-5415. www.napfa.org — Organization of fee-only financial planning professionals serving individuals and institutions.

NATIONAL ASSOCIATION OF PROFESSIONAL INSURANCE AGENTS • 400 North Washington Street, Alexandria, VA 22314-2353. Tel. 703-836-9340. Fax. 703-836-1279. www.pianet.com — Trade association of independent insurance agents.

NATIONAL CREDIT UNION ADMINISTRATION • 1775 Duke Street, Alexandria, VA 22314-3428. Tel. 703-518-6300. Fax. 703-518-6660. www.ncua.gov — An independent agency in the executive branch of the federal government responsible for chartering, insuring, supervising and examining federal credit unions.

NATIONAL FUTURES ASSOCIATION • 300 South Riverside Plaza, Suite 1800, Chicago, IL 60606-6615. Tel. 312-781-1300. Fax. 312-781-1467. www.nfa.futures.org — Industrywide self-regulatory organization for the commodity futures industry.

NATIONAL REVERSE MORTGAGE LENDERS ASSOCIATION • 1400 16th Street, NW, Suite 420, Washington, DC 20036. Tel. 202-939-1760. Fax. 202-265-4435. www.nrmlaonline.org — The group educates consumers about the opportunity to utilize reverse mortgages and trains lenders to be sensitive to the needs of older Americans.

NCCI HOLDINGS, INC. • 901 Peninsula Corporate Circle, Boca Raton, FL 33487. Tel. 561-893-1000. Fax. 561-893-1191. www.ncci.com — Develops and administers rating plans and systems for workers compensation insurance.

OFFICE OF THE COMPTROLLER OF THE CURRENCY • Administrator of National Banks, Washington, DC 20219. Tel. 202-874-5770. www.occ.treas.gov/index.html — The primary regulator of all federal and many state-chartered thrift institutions, which include savings banks and savings and loan associations.

OPTIONS INDUSTRY COUNCIL • One North Wacker Drive, Suite 500, Chicago, IL 60606. Tel. 800-678-4667. Fax. 312-977-0611. www.optionscentral.com — Nonprofit association created to educate the investing public and brokers about the benefits and risks of exchange-traded options.

PENSION RESEARCH COUNCIL • The Wharton School of the University of Pennsylvania, 3620 Locust Walk, 3000 Steinberg Hall–Dietrich Hall, Philadelphia, PA 19104-6302. Tel. 215-898-7620. Fax. 215-573-3418. www.pensionresearchcouncil.org/about — Organization committed to generating debate on key policy issues affecting pensions and other employee benefits.

PROPERTY CASUALTY INSURERS ASSOCIATION OF AMERICA (PCI) • 2600 South River Road, Des Plaines, IL 60018-3286. Tel. 847-297-7800. Fax. 847-297-5064. www.pciaa.net — Serves as a voice on public policy issues and advocates positions that foster a competitive market place for property/casualty insurers and insurance consumers.

REINSURANCE ASSOCIATION OF AMERICA • 1445 New York Ave, NW, 7th Floor, Washington, DC 20005. Tel. 202-638-3690. Fax. 202-638-0936. www.reinsurance.org — Trade association of property/casualty reinsurers; provides legislative services for members.

RETIREMENT INCOME INDUSTRY ASSOCIATION • 101 Federal Street, Suite 1900, Boston, MA 02110. Tel. 617-342-7390. Fax. 617-342-7080. www.riia-usa.org — Financial services industry association focusing on the financial and public policy issues related to the income needs of retirees. Members include insurance companies, banks, securities firms and others.

SECURITIES AND EXCHANGE COMMISSION • 100 F Street NE, Washington, DC 20549. Tel. 202-942-8088. www.sec.gov — Primary mission is to protect investors and maintain the integrity of the securities markets.

SECURITIES INDUSTRY AND FINANCIAL MARKETS ASSOCIATION (SIFMA) • 120 Broadway, 35th Floor, New York, NY 10271-0080. Tel. 212-313-1200. Fax. 212-313-1301. www.sifma.org — Association bringing together the shared interests of securities firms to accomplish common goals.

SNL FINANCIAL LC • One SNL Plaza, P.O. Box 2124, Charlottesville, VA 22902. Tel. 434-977-1600. Fax. 434-977-4466. www.snl.com — Research firm that collects, standardizes and disseminates all relevant corporate, financial, market and M&A data as well as news and analytics for the industries it covers: banking, specialized financial services, insurance, real estate and energy.

SOCIETY OF FINANCIAL SERVICES PROFESSIONALS • 19 Campus Boulevard, Suite 100, Newtown Square, PA 19073-3230. Tel. 610-526-2500. Fax. 610-527-1499. www.financialpro.org — Advances the professionalism of credentialed members with resources to serve their clients' financial needs.

STANDARD & POOR'S RATING GROUP • 55 Water Street, New York, NY 10041. Tel. 212-438-2000. www.standardandpoors.com — Monitors the credit quality of bonds and other financial instruments of corporations, governments and supranational entities.

SURETY ASSOCIATION OF AMERICA • 1101 Connecticut Avenue, NW, Suite 800, Washington, DC 20036. Tel. 202-463-0600. Fax. 202-463-0606. www.surety.org — Statistical, rating, development and advisory organization for surety companies.

WARD GROUP • 11500 Northlake Drive, Suite 305, Cincinnati, OH 45249-1662. Tel. 513-791-0303. Fax. 513-985-3442. www.wardinc.com — Management consulting firm specializing in the insurance industry.

WEATHER RISK MANAGEMENT ASSOCIATION (WRMA) • 750 National Press Building, 529 14th Street, NW, Washington, DC 20045. Tel. 202-289-3800. Fax. 202-223-9741. www.wrma.org — The goal of the WRMA is to serve the weather risk management industry by providing forums for discussion and interaction with others associated with financial weather products.

Index

401(k) plans, 43
    assets, 49
    participants, 49

A

acquisitions. *See* mergers and acquisitions
annuities
    bank holding companies, 56, 64
    considerations, 50
    deferred, assets, 52
    direct premiums written, top ten, 109
    distribution channels, 51
    fixed, 50
        writers of, top ten, 75
    fixed and variable, bank share, 74
    sales, 52
    variable, 50, 51
        writers of, top ten, 108
asset-backed securities (ABS), 151-152
assets, v
    401(k) plans, 49
    banking, 2, 118, 120, 121-122
    broker/dealers, 144
    by industry, 2
    commercial banks, top 25, 127
    credit unions, 118-119, 136-137
    distribution
        life/health, 103
        property/casualty insurance, 87
    FDCI-insured commercial banks, 121-122
    finance companies, 2, 162
    foreign banking offices, in U.S., 120
    household, 21, 22
    insurance companies, 2, 87, 103
    mutual fund industry, 157-158
    pensions, 2
    personal sector, 19-20
    private pension funds, 39-40
    property/casualty insurance, 89
    retirement funds, 39-50, 53
        government employees, 42
    securities industry, 2, 144
ATMs, 188-189
    bank owners of, top ten, 189
    U.S. bank owners, top ten, 191
auto insurance sales, online, 186
Automated Clearing House (ACH) network, 187-188
automated teller machines. *See also* ATMs

B

bank and thrift deals, top ten, 116
bank failures, 115
bank holding companies, 55, 56-64, 114
    advisory and underwriting income, 56
        top ten, 57

annuity commissions, 64
    top ten, 64
insurance activities, 59-62
insurance brokerage fee income, 60, 68
    top ten, 61
insurance fee income, v, 60, 68
insurance premiums written, top ten, 62
investment fee income, v
    top ten, 58
mutual fund and annuity income, 62
    top ten, 63
securities brokerage income, 58, 68
    top ten, 61
underwriting fee income, 68
    top ten, 61
bank insurance
    distribution channels, 71
banking industry, assets, 2, 118, 120, 121-122
    concentration, 125
    employment, 119
    regulation, 113
    See also banks; commercial banks; savings
        banks; thrifts
banking offices, by type of bank, 120
bankruptcies, by type, 38
Bankruptcy Abuse Prevention and
    Consumer Protection Act of 2005, 38
banks, 113
    annuities, 72-74
    annuity commissions, 72, 73
    federally chartered, top ten, by assets, 116
    in insurance, 68-71
    insurance brokerage fee income, top ten, 69
    insurance fee income, top ten, 70
    investment banking, top ten, 61, 65
    investment fee income, top ten, 66
    mutual fund and annuity income, 72
        top ten, 72
    proprietary mutual fund and annuities assets,
        top ten, 73
    retail mutual fund sales, 67
    securities activities, 65
    securities brokerage income, 67
        top ten, 67
    state-chartered, top ten, by assets, 116
    underwriting fee income, top ten, 69
broker/dealers, 142
    assets and liabilities, 144
brokers, global, top ten, by revenue, 198
business debt, 27
business finance companies, 163
business lending, 26
business loans, 35-36
business receivables at finance companies, 164

industrial banks, nonbank ownership of, 76
    top ten, 77
information technology (IT) spending, 183
insurance
    assets, 2
    auto, information sources, 186
    bank sales of, 70
    brokers, commercial, top ten, 90
    distribution channels, 89-90
    employment in, 84
    life/health, 107-109
    market share trends, 91
    mortgage guaranty, 94-95
    online sales, 185-186
    property/casualty, top twenty, 89
    regulation, 79
insurance agencies, bank purchases of, 71
insurance companies
    domestic, by state, 85
    global, top ten, by revenue, 196
    thrifts owned by, top ten, 74
insurance industry
    income analysis, 88
    property/casualty
    world market, 86
insurance premiums
    bank produced, 62
    life/health, by line, 107
    property/casualty, by line, 91-92, 93
    world, life and nonlife, 86
insurance underwriting
    bank holding companies, top ten, 61
    by bank holding companies, 60
insurers, life sales through banks, leading, 76
interest-only mortgages, 170
internet activities, 184
internet usage, households, by state, 181-182
investment banks, 147
Investment Company Act of 1940, 157

K
Keogh plans, 43

L
Latin America, remittances, 134
liabilities
    broker/dealers, 144
    credit unions, 136-137
    FDCI commercial banks, 121-122
    finance companies, 162
    personal sector, 19-20
    securities industry, 144
life insurance, 107-109
    bank sales of, 70, 71
    distribution channels, 106
    online sales, 185-186
    ownership, 105

premiums, world, 86
    sales through banks, leading insurers, 76
    worksite sales, 102
life/health insurance, 103
    annual rate of return, 74
    asset distribution, 103
    companies
        global, top ten, 197
    companies, U.S., top twenty, 105
    financial results, 103-104
    net income, 104
    premiums, 83
        direct written, 82
        growth in, 83
long-term care insurance, 112

M
McCarran-Ferguson Act, 79
Medicare Modernization Act, 111
mergers and acquisitions, 3-4
    banks, 116
    by sector, 3
        number of, 3
        value of, 3
    cross industry, 4
    financial services companies, v
        acquisitions, top ten, 4
    insurance related, top ten, 81
    securities firms, 141
        top ten, 140
    specialty lenders, top ten, 161
metropolitan areas, fastest growing, 205
migration, state by state, 202-204
mortgage and real estate investment losses, 139
mortgage guaranty insurance. See private mortgage
   insurance (PMI)
mortgage lending, thrift industry, 132
mortgage market, 167
mortgages
    by holder, 168
    originations, 167, 176
    single-family, 169
    total outstanding, 169
municipal bonds, 14
    number and value of, 149
municipal loans, U.S. holdings, 16
municipal securities, U.S. holdings, 16
mutual funds, 157-159
    assets, 2
    bank holding companies, top ten, 63
    bank holding company income, 62
    by holder, 17
    companies, top ten, 159
    net assets, 159
        by number of funds, 157
        by type of funds, 158
    number of, by type, 158, 159

I.I.I. Member Companies

ACE USA

ACUITY

AEGIS Insurance Services Inc.

Allianz of America, Inc.

Allied World Assurance Company

Allstate Insurance Group

Alterra Capital Holdings Group

American Agricultural Insurance Company

American Family Insurance

American Integrity Insurance Company

American Reliable Insurance

Amerisafe

Arthur J. Gallagher

Aspen Re

Auto Club South Insurance Company

Bituminous Insurance Companies

Catholic Mutual Group

Catlin U.S.

Century Surety Company

Chartis

Chubb Group of Insurance Companies

Church Mutual Insurance Company

The Concord Group

COUNTRY Financial

CNA

CUMIS Insurance Society, Inc.

DeSmet Farm Mutual Insurance Company
of South Dakota

Dryden Mutual Insurance Company

EMC Insurance Companies

Employers Insurance Company

Enumclaw Insurance Group

Erie Insurance Group

Farmers Group, Inc.

FM Global

GEICO

Gen Re

Germania Insurance

Grange Insurance Companies

GuideOne Insurance

The Hanover Insurance Group Inc.

The Harford Mutual Insurance Companies

Harleysville Insurance

The Hartford Financial Services Group

The Horace Mann Companies

Ironshore Insurance Ltd.

Kemper Corporation

Liberty Mutual Group

Lloyd's

Lockton Companies

Magna Carta Companies

Marsh Inc.

MetLife Auto & Home

Michigan Millers Mutual Insurance Company

Millville Mutual Insurance Company

Missouri Employers Mutual Insurance

Munich Re

Nationwide

New York Central Mutual Fire Insurance Company

The Norfolk & Dedham Group

Ohio Mutual Insurance Group

OneBeacon Insurance Group

PartnerRe

Pennsylvania Lumbermens Mutual Insurance
Company

Providence Mutual Fire Insurance Company

QBE Regional Insurance

Scor U.S. Corporation

SECURA Insurance Companies

Selective Insurance Group

State Auto Insurance Companies

State Compensation Insurance Fund of California

State Farm Mutual Automobile Insurance Company

The Sullivan Group

Swiss Reinsurance America Corporation

Travelers

USAA

Utica National Insurance Group

Westfield Group

W. R. Berkley Corporation

XL America Group

Zenith National Insurance Corporation

Zurich North America

Associate Members

Deloitte

Farmers Mutual Fire Insurance
of Tennessee

Florida Property and Casualty Association

Mutual Assurance Society
of Virginia

Randolph Mutual Insurance Company

Sompo Japan Research
Institute, Inc.

Transunion Insurance Solutions

The Financial Services Roundtable Member Companies

AEGON USA, LLC.

Affiliated Managers Group, Inc.

Allianz Life Insurance Company of North America

Allstate Corporation, The

Ally Financial Inc.

American Honda Finance Corporation

Ameriprise Financial, Inc.

Ares Capital Corporation

Associated Banc-Corp

Assurant, Inc.

Aviva USA

AXA Financial, Inc.

BancorpSouth, Inc.

BancWest Corporation

Bank of America Corporation

Bank of Hawaii Corporation

Barclays Capital, Inc.

BB&T Corporation

BBVA Compass

BlackRock, Inc.

BMO Financial Corporation

BNY Mellon Corporation

Brown & Brown Insurance

Capital One Financial Corporation

Caterpillar Financial Services Corporation

Charles Schwab Corporation, The

Chubb Corporation, The

CIT Group, Inc.

Citigroup Inc.

City National Corporation

Comerica Incorporated

Commerce Bancshares, Inc.

Discover Financial Services

Edward Jones

E*TRADE Financial Corporation

Fidelity Investments

Fifth Third Bancorp

First Commonwealth Financial Corporation

First Horizon National Corporation

First Niagara Financial Group, Inc.

Ford Motor Credit Company

Fulton Financial Corporation

General Electric Company

Genworth Financial

Hancock Holding Company

Hanover Insurance Group, Inc., The

Hartford Financial Services Group, Inc., The

HSBC North America Holdings, Inc.

Huntington Bancshares Incorporated

ING

John Deere Financial Services, Inc.

John Hancock Financial Services, Inc.

JPMorgan Chase & Co.

KeyCorp

Legg Mason, Inc.

Liberty Mutual Holding Company, Inc.

Lincoln National Corporation

LPL Financial

M&T Bank Corporation

MasterCard Worldwide

Mutual of Omaha Insurance Company

NASDAQ OMX Group, Inc., The

Nationwide

New York Life Insurance Company

Northern Trust Corporation

Northwestern Mutual Life Insurance Company

People's United Bank

PMI Group, Inc., The

PNC Financial Services Group, Inc., The

Popular, Inc.

Principal Financial Group

Private Bank, The

Protective Life Corporation

Prudential Financial, Inc.

Putnam Investments

Raymond James Financial, Inc.

The Financial Services Roundtable Member Companies

RBC Bank, USA

RBS Americas

Regions Financial Corporation

RenaissanceRe Holdings Ltd.

Sallie Mae, Inc.

Sovereign

Springleaf Financial Services

State Farm Insurance Companies

State Street Corporation

SunTrust Banks, Inc.

Swiss Reinsurance America Corporation

Synovus

TD Bank

Toyota Financial Services

Trustmark Corporation

TSYS

UnionBanCal Corporation

United Bankshares, Inc.

Unum

U.S. Bancorp

Visa Inc.

Webster Financial Corporation

Wells Fargo & Company

Western & Southern Financial Group

Zions Bancorporation

Insurance Information Institute
110 William Street
New York, NY 10038
Tel. 212-346-5500. Fax. 212-732-1916. www.iii.org

President – Robert P. Hartwig, Ph.D., CPCU – bobh@iii.org

Executive Vice President – Cary Schneider – carys@iii.org

Senior Vice President – Public Affairs – Jeanne Salvatore – jeannes@iii.org

Senior Vice President and Chief Economist – Steven N. Weisbart, Ph.D., CLU – stevenw@iii.org

Publications

Vice President – Publications and Information Services – Madine Singer – madines@iii.org

Managing Editor – Neil Liebman – neill@iii.org

Research and Production – Mary-Anne Firneno – mary-annef@iii.org

Director – Technology and Web Production – Shorna Lewis – shornal@iii.org

Production Assistant – Katja Charlene Lewis – charlenel@iii.org

Information Specialist – Alba Rosario – albar@iii.org

Special Consultant – Ruth Gastel, CPCU – ruthg@iii.org

Orders – Daphne Gerardi – daphneg@iii.org

Media

New York:

Vice President – Media Relations – Michael Barry – michaelb@iii.org

Vice President – Digital Communications – Andréa C. Basora – andreab@iii.org

Vice President – Communications – Loretta Worters – lorettaw@iii.org

Terms + Conditions blog – Claire Wilkinson – clairew@iii.org

Impact **Magazine** – Diane Portantiere – dianep@iii.org

Web/Media Producer – Justin Shaddix – justins@iii.org

Administrative Assistant – Rita El-Hakim – ritae@iii.org

Administrative Assistant – Lilia Giordano – liliag@iii.org

West Coast:

Insurance Information Network of California:

Executive Director – Candysse Miller – cmiller@iinc.org

Tel. 213-624-4462. Fax. 213-624-4432.

Northern California:

Communications Specialist – Tully Lehman – tlehman@iinc.org

Tel. 925-300-9570. Fax. 925-906-9321.

Representatives

Davis Communications – William J. Davis, Atlanta – billjoe@bellsouth.net
  Tel. 770-321-5150. Fax. 770-321-5150.

Hispanic Press Officer – Elianne González, Miami – elianneg@iii.org
  Tel. 954-389-9517.

Florida Representative – Lynne McChristian, Tampa – lynnem@iii.org
  Tel. 813-480-6446. Fax. 813-915-3463.

The Financial Services Roundtable
1001 Pennsylvania Avenue, NW
Suite 500 South
Washington, DC 20004

Tel. 202-289-4322. Fax. 202-628-2507. www.fsround.org

The Financial Services Roundtable

Steve Bartlett, President & CEO

Richard M. Whiting, Executive Director and General Counsel

Tanya Bailey, Vice President, Meetings and Events

Wattie Bennett, Executive Asst./Office Coordinator

Brenda Bowen, Government Affairs Manager

Elise Brooks, Communications Manager

Judy Chapa, Vice President, Community Services

Sarah Drew, Co-Director, Membership & Information Services

Tatiana Fittipaldi, Director of Meetings and Events

George D. Forsberg, CPA, Chief Financial Officer

Peter Freeman, Vice President for Insurance & Trade

Blake Grimm, Co-Director, Membership & Information Services

Robert Hatch, Counsel for Legal and Regulatory Affairs

Aleksia Ilic, Community Service Project Manager

Abby McCloskey, Director of Research

Carrie M. Neckorcuk, Sr. Vice President of Human Resources and Administration

Cindy G. Nettles, Executive Assistant to the President

Christeen Phelps-Butler, Director of Meetings and Events

Scott E. Talbott, Sr. Vice President of Government Affairs

Brian Tate, Vice President for Banking

Kim Ward, Accounting Assistant

Kim A. Wheelbarger, Senior Executive Assistant to the Executive Director

BITS

Paul Smocer, President

Daniel Schutzer, Chief Technology Officer

Jenny Cleveland, Communications Manager

William Henley, Sr. Vice President, Regulation

Andrew Kennedy, Project Manager, Security

Nicole Muryn, Program Manager, Regulation

Ann Patterson, Vice President, Member Relations

Jim Pitts, Project Manager

Roxane Schneider, Program Administrator, Fraud

Craig Schwartz, General Manager, Registry Services

Ashley Stanojev, Administrative Assistant

Heather Wyson, Vice President, Fraud

FSIC (Financial Stability Industry Council)

Don Truslow, President

HPC (Housing Policy Council)

John Dalton, President of the HPC

Paul M. Leonard, Vice President of Government Affairs, HPC

Joan Gregory, Gov't. Affairs Manager, HPC

Todd Hill, Gov't. Affairs Assistant, HPC

ITAC (Identity Theft Assistance Center)

Anne Wallace, President of ITAC
            Senior Director of Consumer Financial Services

AFC (Agents for Change)

Peter Ludgin, Executive Director

HOPE NOW

Eric Selk, Director of Outreach

Joseph Putney, Operations Manager